# THE SEVEN SIGNS
# THE SEVEN SEALS
## AND
# THE SEVEN VEILS

### REVEALED SO THAT
### MANKIND MAY KNOW THE WAY

## The Prophecy of Christ Revealed

## ROBERT GEORGE CROSBIE

GW00585178

## 4 ELEMENTS PUBLICATIONS

Cover photograph: Denis McGowan

Cover Design & Illustration: Bill Dobson

Edited by: Barbara Dobson

Published by:  4 Elements Publications

P.O. Box 10, Tubbercurry, Sligo, Ireland.

ISBN    0 - 9538206 - 0 - 2

# Index

# Introduction.

There have been several books written recently about the life of Jesus, and the investigations that have been carried out into the mysteries and truths of his life. Men still ask what was it all really about? What was he all about, and did he in fact exist at all? Will he come back to us again as promised, or is it all just one big joke? He did exist, it was not a joke, though it was turned into something else that really isn't very funny. The truth of Joshua Ben Miriam is strange to say the least, far stranger than fiction. As was and is the life of the author of this book. Read it all. To do less means that you will get the wrong idea, and miss the whole point of the book.

The author of this book was born according to the last prophesy of Jesus, which has been known of for two thousand years. He was born according to his prophesy, behind the veil or as it is more commonly known with a Caul. He was born with both hands bleeding, and as prophesied with the mark of the last agony, a mark of birth, and according the prophesy unfakeable, in fact a mark of birth in his right side between the groin and the navel. He has all the marks on his body and in his hands exactly as prophesied. All the numbers given add up exactly as prophesied, far too many for there to be any doubt even in the mind of the most sceptical among us. His life has been strange and eventful to say the least. He has tried alternately to avoid his responsibilities, and come to terms with them. Eventually he has had to follow the path set for him.

This book however, is not the story of Bob Crosbie. It is the story of Joshua Ben Miriam know as Jesus the Christ. It is the story of his last Prophesy as he awaited his exit from the stage as he knew before his historic ride into Jerusalem that his purpose was lost as he said "Man Shall Know No reason". Those who have gone before him have said the same: that, "Man Shall Know No Reason" and we hope that it will not be said by the one he prophesied would follow him in his purpose. The prophesy also says that this Prophesied One is the last to come.The prophesy was given by Jesus to Peter and to John before the crucifiction, and has been faithfully kept by the Lost Brotherhood as they are more usually known these days. Their true name is The Nazarenes, of which Jesus himself was a member.

Bob Crosbie is a member of that same brotherhood who have taken care of him all his life, though he would often disagree, and even before he was born, as they knew of his Sign and were waiting.

His life has followed the prophesy to the letter, till the present day. Again his life like the life of Jesus is far stranger than fiction, punctuated with attempts to kill him, the first being when he was only two years old. Like all those who have gone before. Like Jesus himself. He is feared to the extent that his life is in

4

constant danger. When the Sign of Jesus was seen, all the first born were killed to make sure that he was dead, and like Jesus who was moved out of harms way, so was he. More than once and only just in time on more than one occasion. He does not ask that you believe what he has to say. He has reached the point of despair in his fellow man that he does not even care one way or another.

The prophesy demands that he write it and set it before the eyes of men. From there it is up to you. His purpose is only to set it before you. Yours is to read, and to reason, to look about you at the state of your World.

Look at all that is happening in this World and on this World. Then you can accept it or not. It is your choice. "Many will come and few will be chosen" the Churches tell us. They as usual are only partly right. He is right, in all reason. When people start to accept the reality of The Ending Of Days they will all want to be chosen, but alas far too late. Those who will be chosen will only be chosen because they have the power of reason in advance, and those driven by fear will not be men of reason, and so will die, if Jesus is to be taken seriously. I for one will take him very seriously as so far he has proved never to be wrong, and that is some record.

Have no fear of letting down Jesus or any of those who have gone before. Reflect the countless thousands from Qumran to the present day who have died in the protection of the knowledge handed down for your salvation and the salvation of your species. They have suffered and died violently and often in unbelievable agony at the hands of the Beast in the service of The Beast's own interest. The choice, as always is yours .

This is Sunday the 12th of July 1998. I've just woken up after fifteen hours in bed, and it's a wind-torn, miserable, depressing day. I've had a lot on my mind, as I am being pressed by friends and family to put into writing all that I have been taught since childhood, about the journey of man. Things like where it all started exactly, and most importantly, where is it all going to? What is the point of man's existence on Earth, or is there a point? It's not much to ask, especially if you don't know what you are asking. As far as we have been concerned, that is an easy one on the surface, but again that's only the surface. For instance T.V. today is all about the trouble in the north of Ireland. In Drumcree everyone seems to want to go to war.

I was talking to a man the other night, who seems to think that the World is going to end. Could you blame him for thinking so? However, it concerned me that he should be under some illusion that this is the dogma of the Old Order. The dogma that is preached by the Order. But it isn't. The man isn't listening. Men never do except to what suits them at the time. Men only ever seem to listen to what fits in with what they believe. When facts don't fit belief, get rid of or alter the facts.

I don't speak of the end of the World, only of the end of a species. The species of man, who isn't nearly as important as he likes to think he is to the continuance of the Earth's existence. If he was as important to the survival of the World as he has been in it's destruction, and in particular in his own destruction, then the game would change. When you think of it, Odin, Buddha, Marduk, Moses, and the Christ all had it about right. But as usual men weren't listening. Except to the sound of their own voices, yammering on about being godlike. Made in the image etc. Man was only listening to the sound of his own interest, and is about to suffer the aftermath of his own stupidity, and mindless, wanton greed. The beast rides high, without thought, without reason, or even the slightest sign of that humanity he so often professes.

The World cup dominates the news while people starve, while microbes mutate and become immune to every weapon in our medical arsenals. People are dying of starvation. They say that £2 will help to save a child, while at the same time, on the same news channel, people are paying £2000 for a ticket to watch a game of football. Imagine, 1000 children could be saved for the price of one mindless man watching a meaningless game. Imagine. Men pay large sums of money to have sex with street whores, risking their health and the health of their families while at the same time, religious leaders argue over homosexuality in the churches. Yet they all know the writings of The Bible and how homosexuality is condemned. Just believe and God will provide. So what do they want the £2 for then? Or don't they believe that much, and if not why not? Why do they still preach the dogmas of "believe, have faith and all will be well"? The Lord works in mysterious ways his wonders to perform. Don't look at the facts. Ignore reality, and God will provide.

Brethren, ignore the old prophesies no matter how often they prove themselves right. The more they prove themselves right, the more you are to ignore them. Should they disagree in any way with what we say, then be assured they are the work of the Devil, whom I hasten to add, does not, and never did exist. If belief is contradicted in any way, then raise all the points you can against the contradictions, even if these points are pointless. Don't bother me with facts, my mind is made up. Do you still think that man's days are not numbered? Look around you. Open your ears and listen, and I mean really listen and hear. Odin wasn't just some Nordic god or something vague. Buddha wasn't just a pot-bellied model for rows of porcelain statues etc. Marduk wasn't just a man who is now a planet. Moses wasn't some man who climbed a mountain to bring down laws we already had. Not forgetting Christ of course, who is believed to have wandered more or less aimlessly round the middle east, letting people slap him on both cheeks, and hallucinating all over the place while he wrestled with a Devil who doesn't exist.

Is he not the man that the Pope in Rome says he represents? The man that listens to every word that the Pope speaks, and grants him his requests on your behalf, so that you may go to Heaven when you are dead? The very man of whom one of his predecessors Pope Leo the tenth called a myth? He really did you know. He said, "It has served us well this myth of Christ." And the Papacy claims infallibility, so he should know. The head of the Anglican Catholic Church, the Archbishop of Canterbury makes more or less the same claims as the Papacy. They follow the same lines; even the catechism is the same.

"I believe in God the Father Almighty, maker of heaven and Earth,
and in Jesus Christ his only Son our Lord, who was born of The Virgin Mary,
suffered under Pontius Pilate, was crucified died and was buried.
He descended into Hell. The third day he rose again from the dead,
he ascended into Heaven, and sitteth on the right hand of
God the Father Almighty, from whence He shall come to judge
the quick and the dead. I believe in the Holy Ghost,
the Holy Catholic Church, the communion of saints, the forgiveness of sins,
the resurrection of the body, and the life everlasting, Amen."

Not bad for a non-Christian to remember all that from school, when I had to learn it or else.

This and so many contradictions, leave it hard for us mere mortals to know which one of them isn't being entirely honest with the World, and why men are fighting and killing each other. Each of these men claims precedence over the other in these matters. In the first place we know that the World was not made in seven days. Jesus was not buried. He did not ascend into heaven. The facts are there, but these people preach "Believe my brethren". The Roman Catholics, Anglican Catholics, Turkish, Greek and Russian Orthodox etc. All preach believe and be saved. Believe in the true faith. What true faith I ask you?

If it is true you don't need faith. If you need faith, it can't be true. It's a contradiction in terms. But all these religions are a contradiction.

The Buddhists and Muslims demand belief just the same, and in more or less the same things. With little twists, and variances in story lines, and mythology. In all logic and reason they cannot be right. Give me your money and God will make it right. No matter who that God may be. This just cannot possibly be right. If you know with certainty, if there is some proof of the existence of this old man sitting on his cloud, then let us see it. Then there will be no need for belief, as belief can only be present where knowledge and fact are absent. The facts are before your eyes, they resound in your ears and echo in the chambers of your mind. But sadly, if you have been trained from childhood to just believe, no matter what then you will not be interested in facts as your mind is already made up, and I am about to waste still more of my life, on what is probably the greatest and saddest lost cause ever. That lost cause of trying to get some of the human race to simply look, listen, and use your natural senses to observe the World around you. To see, to be aware of your Mother Earth dying beneath your feet being crushed to death beneath the wheels of the chariots of greed, of false pride, of ego, and every possible negative thought, emotion and deed.

Become aware of the things in life that have been made so important, simply because the engines of power want you to look in a different direction, and so give these things that illusion of importance, in order to divert your gaze and your mind. Because the powers that be cannot stand up to any scrutiny of their actions. Roman Catholics and Anglican Catholics (protesters to the rule of Rome or Protestants as they are known), hate each other and fear each other, because they are taught to do so. The Indians and the Pakistanis, the Croat, the Muslim, the blacks, the whites, the haves, the have nots, your team and my team. We are all at war all the time, and while we watch each other so intently, those in power are screwing all of us, and we lose. Even when we win, we lose. But "Fear not," they tell us. "Have faith in God. He works in mysterious ways, and he is on our side." Whose side? Your side? My side? Somebody else's side? Maybe he is on nobody's side.

Who is this God chap anyway? Has anyone really seen him lately? Perhaps he is among the street children of South America, protecting them. It is said that he loves little children. Ask any Christian priest, either Anglican or Roman. They will tell you with certainty of belief, that God loves little children. Though I hope not in the same way that some of them do. But then again perhaps he is busy in Africa. Everyone is in trouble out there, especially the little children. On the other hand perhaps he is busy with one of the Ayatollahs, or the Pope, or some Archbishop or other. Maybe he is discussing the homosexuality problem in his churches. He could be on the side of the homosexuals. Perhaps he is a homosexual, you just never can tell, unless you watch where the expediency of power resides. I'll bet you any money that that's where he will be, close to the cash. Think about it, and decide what you want to believe, and maybe if you believe strongly enough it will come out all right in the long run. We can always hold on to that comforting thought, that many will come but few will be chosen. Now, who do you believe will be chosen? Maybe you will be chosen. Maybe even a terrible boat rocker like me. Maybe some top rankers in religious orders. Now they are sure to be chosen.

So I'm in. I am the head of The Order Of The Ancient Way. But maybe it doesn't mean just any old religious leaders. Perhaps some kings will be chosen. After all, they have been put over us by no lesser person than God himself. Maybe queens will be chosen, (I mean the royal type). But they are all rich people, and we are taught that it is easier for a camel to pass through the eye of a needle than for a rich man to enter the Kingdom of Heaven. So none of them are going to be saved. So why don't they give their wealth to the little children, or someone else, and clear the way to eternal Paradise for themselves? It all seems a bit fishy to me. I would have thought that they would all be lining up. But maybe they don't believe it, they just want you and I to believe it. Why? As well as all these things, there are those among you who have committed that terrible sin of lust, and those of us who have indulged in, dare I say it, sex. Looking at the population explosion I think some of us out there must even be guilty of the sin of overindulgence in this matter. So we can forget it, we have no chance. If you have ever told lies or cheated, then you can't go. That lets out the bankers and lawyers, the insurance people and above all politicians. If you go through the list according to the teachings and beliefs of the powers that be, then Heaven must be empty, and will stay that way.

Still you must remember that Christ preached forgiveness. Or did he? It appears to be an important and intricate part of organised religions in general, that forgiveness it at hand for all those truly repentant. Is this idea just so that you will forgive all the rulers of this sad World, should you find them out?
All you have to do is support the system, and make a donation of some kind to the people at the top who are already filthy rich, and Bob's your uncle. You're in. All is forgiven. It does not matter what sin you commit on this Earth, all you

have to do is repent, ask forgiveness and you can go and do it all over again. Rape, robbery, murder, it doesn't matter. Isn't it great? It's all a matter of profit and loss. Magic.

I am sure that you have worked out the fact that I am not too impressed by the powers that be. By the World's leaders, and particularly by those who have set themselves up in the name of Jesus Christ, to rule our lives and tell us how they want us to live, and expect us to obey them without question. Nor am I impressed by the seas of "bullshit" that they make us swim through. I know it's supposed to be for our own good, so aren't they thoughtful? Or is it just possible that they have their ability to control us in mind, for their own good and not ours. Maybe I am just being paranoid, or perhaps I am a bit thick and can't understand the intricacies of it all. Perhaps it is because I have my own axe to grind, as I am a follower of the oldest religion in the World. The one that all other religions have been developed from, and sadly seem to have lost their way. Or even more sadly have deliberately ignored their way.

I woke up one morning to find that the head of the Old Order was dead, and I was the "named one." It was on the 28th of September 1997. It was not a position I relished at that time, and I am still struggling with the idea. I have no option or say in the matter, and therefore I have no choice. It has always been the way of things. The old religion up till fairly recent times had no name. It never seemed to need one. It has no dogma. It was a way of life that evolved out of the needs of early mankind, and was a way of life with rules designed for the benefit of man, the Earth and all it contained and still contains, to a sustainable level. These rules or laws were followed religiously and its similarity to modern ideas of religion end there. As well as there being no dogmas, no deities and no system of worship, there is great elasticity, which allows us to change as we learn to improve, and we accept happily that we do not know it all. In fact we know very little, but neither does anyone else. And because we have no gods or systems of worship, we are therefore the only religion that can not be classed as a cult, because a cult requires all these. It may be a shock to many to find that they belong to a cult, but the dictionary describes a cult as, and I quote, "a system of belief and worship; a subject of devoted study." Now as far as devoted study is concerned we are guilty as charged, as the Order is about knowledge, and knowledge requires study, and a lot of devotion to it. The search for that elusive thing called knowledge takes a great deal of devotion indeed, and it is elusive. We have not evolved nearly as far as we should have and could have, because the belief systems of other religions cause us to remain very low profile. Everything to us must be provable, logical, or at least be demonstrable. It must make sense.

Now I have no doubt that a lot of people are sick of me saying these things, as they are a hard concept to come to terms with in the light of the faith and belief systems of the big organised religions. This is one thing I find it difficult to grasp. They say, "You must believe in something." "Why"? If it is the truth you do not need to believe. If it is not true then what's the point? The only outcome of following something that you know is untrue must be catastrophe. Now as far as we have noted over the last two millennia, just about everything Christ, Buddha, Moses, Marduk and Odin said has required interpretation, by men who consider themselves above these chaps, and profess to know what they really meant, better than they did. Then we all fight over which interpretation is the right one.

This has never ceased to amaze me. It defies understanding to say the least, and at worst it blatantly flies in the face of reason and common sense. It shows the pure arrogance and conceit of these people, who claim that God has set them over us. I think you will find a stout army, and a complete lack of humanity and conscience had more to do with it. Who do these people think they are? Talk about pure conceit. Christ knew exactly what he meant, so did the others. They were neither raving mad, nor were they morons, or indeed members of the lunatic fringe. Wouldn't it be nice if you could honestly say the same about those who interpret them? The only reason these interpreters have for their actions is, that every time Christ, Buddha, Odin, Marduk, or Moses said anything that might throw doubt on anything the powers that be wanted us to believe, they would and still do, alter everything to suit their purpose. If they don't alter it, they take it out altogether, as though it was never stated. It does not exist.

Everything in the Christian Bible was put there by committees, who decided whether or not it fitted their ideas. If it did it was in. If it did not then it was out, and after all that they started to disagree over what they had decided on in the first place. They took what Christ had to say, and decided that he didn't really mean that at all. Or he never said that. Suddenly it fits exactly what they want it to mean. What is even more amazing, they do not expect to be questioned. They expect, and will tolerate, no resistance to anything they say in such matters. So secure are they in the power that they wield over the minds and hearts of men, they were even able to crucify St Peter as a heretic, because he dared to object to the things they were teaching in Christ's name. He was the chap who knew what Christ really said or didn't say. St Peter wouldn't toe the expected line, and so important did he consider these matters that he would rather die than bend. Such was his respect and feeling for Jesus and what Jesus stood for. The people with the power just used a trumped up charge of heresy as an excuse to be rid of him. Guess who the real heretics were? Certainly not Peter. They even had the audacity to lead people to believe that he was the first Pope, to help swing peoples minds in the desired direction. They left it a long time, so that no one would still be alive at the time to argue with them on the matter. The same as they did with The Christ. At the time it was just as well if you let your mind believe the desired direction, because they had some not so pleasant ways of making you accept and believe whatever they wanted you to accept and believe.

Sheer unbridled brutality has been the mark of Christianity throughout its history. It has always been the case, that if you do not accept and believe what they want you to believe, you will be put to death by some horrific means or other, as a deterrent against anybody daring to question, ever again. But they did and still do, in spite of the efforts invested in cruelties meted out. They have even professed the power to gain entry for you into Heaven through all this torture, as though pain opened the doors. "Suffering is the way to Paradise they say." I'll bet many a poor wretch was grateful to them for this considera-tion, just as they stretched him on the rack, or lit the fire. They didn't think that spilling blood was right, do you see. It went against the teachings of the Bible, hence the fire. It didn't spill your blood while you burned. I wonder who dreamed up that idea. If they really believe in pain and suffering so much, why don't they indulge in a lot more for themselves? These horrible ways of putting people to death, with which we are all so familiar, were designed as a warning to others not to transgress, and a direct demonstration of their power. Should you think it all wrong, you would keep your council, and follow the rule, their rule. The rule of fear. If you think about it, the same psychology is used even today by those who wish to oppress. If you can get people to either believe enough, or just follow along for their own ends, then reason is blown away on the winds, in a mixture of self interest, fear, and self justification, and it's all done in the name of God, so it's OK.

When you think about it we have not come very far in evolutionary terms, have we? We haven't come very far at all. In our present society there are many ways of destroying, a man, or woman for that matter. The powers that be are not fussy in that regard. Their cruelty knows no bounds, it never did and it looks as if it never will. They profess love and justice while practicing the expe-diency of power and wealth, with cruelty and injustice on all levels as the badge of their dishonour. What saddens me even more, is the fact that all reli-gions were developed out of the Old Religion. The Old Order has been so oppressed as to drive it underground for over 1600 years. Its members hunted, and if caught tortured to make it look as though they worshipped the Devil, who never existed except as a figment of their sick imaginations. They have invented untruths against us, which they have paraded as truths, knowing exactly what they do. They are not even slightly disillusioned or deluded in any way in these matters. They know exactly what we are and what we stand for, and the Old Order can stand the light of day.

We stand only for provable knowledge, for logic, for reason and for the truth of that knowledge and reason. We do not fight in the protection of these things, as the truth needs no protection. The truth just is, and therefore cannot be altered, so the truth protects itself. They talk about "Paganism" as though it really existed and is lurking about somewhere ready to pounce and carry you off to the pits of Hell. Yet another invention. The word *pagan* means "villager", that's all. If you think about it, it fits what we originally were, a sort of tribal, village dwelling race. As there were not too many people about thousands of years ago, it was the most sensible way to survive against the odds of the time. But still the Old Order evolved, and enabled us to live together with not too much upset. They use the word Pagan as some sort of a bogeyman from the past, but again it's just an invention born in the minds of the truly evil ones. These things were conceived in the wild imaginations, in my opinion, of men of doubtful sanity. They were always attributed to "Paganism". They were watered by the waters of conceit and arrogance, warmed by the blazing sun of fear, forged and shaped upon the anvils of hunger for power, and harvested by the sickles of downright stupidity. These people did not just stray from the path, they tore it up. Even today they still practice "sick" rites in our opinion. Things that we would never dream of doing. For example in many ancient cultures being a king had a time limit, and when your time was up you were killed ritually. They all had a party, and you were the menu. They drank your blood and ate your flesh. This was thought to give the consumers your strength and your wisdom.

Now think of the Christian Communion. They drink the blood of Christ the King and eat his flesh, albeit symbolically, but think about its similarities. We never involved ourselves in such barbaric practice, yet they will tell you that the Old Religion with no name was Pagan, and therefore evil. Its amazing how organised religion kept up ancient and evil rituals that had no basis in the Way of the Old Order. They invented it all themselves in order to gain conversions, no matter how barbaric these rituals were. Later in Christian history "Divine Right" was only conferred by the heads of religion on kings, so long as they converted to Christianity, which allowed the most base among us to gain and hold power, under the protection of the various religions. Especially that of the Christian Church. The Roman Church even gave itself power to create kings. Thus was the ultimate power over the hearts and minds of men achieved. All this in spite of the fact that Jesus said, "Render unto God that which is God's, and unto Caesar that which is Caesar's." Meaning religion and politics should be kept on different plains, and apart. This was mainly the reason for getting rid of St. Peter.

Another odd thing that is kept dark, but is coming into the light slowly, is that the very divinity of Jesus was decided by vote at the Council of Nicea, in the year 325 A.D. Oddly, the Church of Rome claimed Constantine as Messiah. Constantine was a worshipper of the sun, and had absolutely nothing to do with Jesus. Instead it was decided by vote at the council, which explains in my mind why those who claim to be Christians are so un-Christian. All that we in the Old Order have known of him has been under constant attack from "Christians" since his death. Because we not only know exactly what he was really about, we also know they have it wrong, as they know they have got it wrong, and why they persist in getting it wrong.

Even the story of the crucifixion is wrong, and they know it.Whatever reasons they may have thought that Jesus was crucified for, are of little consequence. There are so many inconsistencies. His crucifixion according to the gospels should not have been fatal. They know that. The Romans were very exact in all that they did, and after sentencing it would have been usual for the prisoner to be flogged, to weaken him through pain and by the loss of blood. They would then fasten his outstretched arms to a heavy wooden beam, placed across his neck and shoulders and secured by thongs, but sometimes nailed. Carrying the beam, the prisoner would be led to the appointed place of execution. Usually being beaten, scourged and whipped as he went. This helped to weaken him even further. It was not unusual for crowds to gather to enjoy the spectacle. Such is the way of the beast, to take pleasure in the suffering of other beings. On arrival at the appointed place, the prisoner would be hoisted up a pole, or in some cases a tree, by the beam. Hanging from his hands put pressure on his chest thus preventing him breathing, except with great difficulty. If his feet should be tied to the upright pole this would make him live longer, because he could push up with his legs and relieve his breathing. In spite of the pain of nailing, a man with his feet fixed could last a long time. More so should he be a strong fit person. Up to a week was not unusual for a man to last crucified before giving up the ghost. At times mercy would be shown and the executioner would break the legs. Some mercy! This would not allow the prisoner to relieve the pressure on his chest and he would suffocate more quickly.

In the gospels, the executioners of Jesus were just about to break his legs when they were stopped. By none other than Pilate. Why? According to the Bible the feet of Jesus were attached to the pole, but he had a foot rest, and his legs were not broken. This would allow him to live a lot longer, for days at least. He was only on the cross a very few hours when he was declared dead. "I cannot trust my friends," he said. He did put his trust in his enemies and he was not let down by that trust. He took a terrible chance. In St. Mark 15 : 44 it says; "And Pilate marvelled if he were already dead: and calling unto him the centurion, he asked him whether he had been any while dead." It goes on to say that they fetched fine linen and wrapped the body in it, and they laid him

14

in a sepulchre and rolled a large stone into the doorway to seal it. Again why? They would not go to this trouble ordinarily. So why did they on this occasion? Why was this poor penniless carpenter not buried like all the other poor victims?

It goes on to say that Mary Magdalene and Mary the mother of Jesus saw where he was laid. What was Mary Magdalene doing there if she was not "family"? Again, unusual. It would not have been seemly, if it were even allowed. Jesus was not dead because of the crucifixion, nor of the spear in his side. Remember, the Roman soldier was a well experienced man with a spear, and would have known exactly what kind of wound to inflict. This added credence that he was dead but would not cause any lasting damage. None of the things that they did to him would have been fatal, certainly not so quickly.

Remember too that Pilate was sympathetic to Jesus. He knew him to be a "High Caulbearer" and would not want the repercussions of killing him. Neither would the centurion. The only people who wanted him dead took no part, for the same reason. They did not mind someone else carrying the can for them but would not get their own hands dirty, especially in the matter of a "Caulbearer." The preventing of the breaking of his legs happened just in time. If his legs had been broken it would not have been convenient to say the least. It is more or less an accepted fact that Jesus modelled his life on the Prophesies, and by arranging all this he could fulfil them, such as the riding on the ass into Jerusalem. There is a lot of evidence to say that he actually planned the whole thing. Using his enemies as he has said, to enable him to survive. He could then go on to live his life, and leave the Prophecy fulfilled in as far as his part was concerned. The Romans, thinking him dead would not go looking for him. He was thought to be a dead man.

Jesus Christ, as you have been told of him was in fact a very different kind of man. To say that he was intelligent and wise, courageous and strong is to say little. No matter what you say or think of him, no matter how great you think he was, you are wrong. He outshines even that by miles. His greatness was way beyond the imagination of men, and that is saying a lot.

And they say that I follow this act. That I, am the answer to his Prophecy. And that it is to me he speaks, across the span of 2000 years, on the opening of his Seal Which was entrusted to The Brotherhood to be kept alive, for my mind, and my eyes alone. They say that I must fulfil his Prophecy and his will. I ask them "How?" For I don't know how. I don't know how anyone could possibly stand in that shadow. Least of all me. And I do not speak out of false humility. I really can't see it at this time, or at any time.

The Old Religion developed mainly by trial and error, when man was young and knew no guile. We learned that there is a lot that cannot be

15

explained in palatable ways, but if it made good sense, we learned that we could accept it as a theory. At the same time we learned that it is folly to accept theory as fact, until it is proven one way or another. We do not believe in anything that is not provable beyond question, or doubt.

Imagine what it must have been like when Adam Edam first stood upright and walked upon the Earth and gained reason, as it is said in the Old Order. Hence was the beginning of the first man. Imagine all that time ago if you can. Imagine what it must have been like. Science has more or less taught us the way it was. Strange beasts. Humanoids evolving. Living wild. They stand up on their hind legs, and then reason dawns in their minds. Can you imagine the difference that reason must have made to the beast that was later to be called man?

It did not happen all at once. Slowly natural selection started to sort out the men from the beasts, but never managed to sort out the beast from the men, yet. Imagine natural selection making improvements, the reasoning ones overcoming the unreasoning ones. They started to work things out, to think and to experiment. Imagine how early reasoning man must have looked up into the skies, seeing the sun, the clouds, the stars, the moon. You can almost see old Adam sitting there, starting to realise that there is a pattern to it all. An apparent purpose to it all. Imagine him sitting on a rock or a fallen tree, perhaps drawing what he saw on the ground with a stick, a tool. See him in your mind taking notice of how the moon came up in different places each evening, and sometimes not being able to see it at all. You can easily imagine him making marks or driving sticks upright into the ground, to line up with the sunrise and moonrise. He studies and learns as he puts up more sticks each morning and evening. Then changing the sticks for rocks that are more permanent, more stable, more reliable. Then you can see him marking the rocks, perhaps with grooves, or notches to make it a more exact thing, more scientific. Adam begins to learn, to expand his knowledge, his outlook and his World, and still learning marvels at the stars and their movements. He can now forecast happenings in his World, such as the lunar changes, her 28 day cycle. He sees, but probably doesn't quite understand for generations. Then he slowly starts to associate the cycles of the moon with other things in his World, and starts to form the idea that the moon plays a part in his everyday life. He learns to number the days. His science expands. He watches the birds, the animals and the plants of his World that he depends on. Things start to add up in his mind slowly.

Adam's interest is sparked and becomes a driving force, a driving thirst to know more and more about his little World. He grows and realises the benefit of what he has learned. Because of knowledge and reason Adam's little tribe thrives a little better than other tribes. He can now judge the time of the year exactly. He now can judge exactly when the fish will run, and which phases of the moon will be best for catching them. He knows when he can find ripe berries and fruits in the various parts of the plains, forests, or mountains.

He can now plot the longest day of the year and the shortest day of the year and how many days in between. He now knows when the days get shorter. When the spring will come with its bounty of eggs. Easter is born. He knows when the young things will be born. He can now get ready for winter and hard times. He learns to store for this time so that his tribe can survive more easily.

On the shortest day of the year people have too much of one thing and not enough of another. Adam holds gatherings of tribes to share these things out. Meeting places were arranged for the purpose. They give away that which they can not sustain through the winter, and receive from others that which they need. Solstice giving is born. Later the idea is stolen by the Christians, and from this Christmas is born.

At the longest day of the year when everything is plentiful another gathering is organised. Young men and women from one tribe meet young men and women from other tribes and marriages are arranged. Because by now Adam has learned many things, and one of the most important is that close breeding is not a good idea. A law is made forbidding such dubious practice. He has learned that children born of marriages performed and consummated at the summer solstice will not start to be born till the end of February. Food will be more plentiful, and the summer months of warmth and plenty will be a good start for the young. Men still have no idea of property or ownership either of goods or people. This comes later, with guile, and the greed that is the mark of the beast that still lives within men.

Later the Christians grab onto the idea of Winter Solstice and say it is the birthday of Christ. They know it is not, but who is there to argue and survive? And as they set the date just a few days after Solstice, it will bungle up the celebrations of the hard-nosed members of the Old Order, and it also appeared that those who converted to Christianity would not lose out on the gift giving. Clever! Today, we still give gifts to the women of our families on the Solstices, we call them, "appreciations." To show a little gratitude on the part of us males for all that women do for us throughout our lives. At winter it is a gift of white, and summer it is a gift of yellow. A funny little tradition that is thousands of years old, but we like it. It was almost to be idyllic, and it should have been, but the beast was strong in man. Or perhaps I have it wrong and man is weak within the beast. Those with little, or in fact no knowledge began to fear those with this power they could not understand. I have the same problem myself today, so nothing changes. Men still destroy for the most base of reasons.

Some would come to respect the learned ones, while some grew jealous and hated them, and feared them and plotted to kill them. Have I heard this story somewhere recently? Funny how nothing really changes, is it not? Fear of knowledge created trouble from those who did understand it, or didn't. They wanted to kill all the Adams of their World. After all they were getting the best of everything by evil means. The idea of magic is born, white and black. All this meant that the less mentally agile couldn't understand. The wise ones got the best, and most women, because they could provide the most food and skins for clothing, and because of their knowledge, led a better and easier life. Because it was easier they had time to learn even more, to study the World about them, and to teach it to their offspring. The lesser types only knew and understood force. But early men were learning something far more important. During these times the lesser ones started to improve a little, and realised that they too could benefit from the ways of the learned ones. Even if they didn't have the minds to understand what the learned ones were about, they soon worked it out. The learned ones were useful to give guidance in all matters, and in return the learned ones would get protection from them. So they started to protect the wise ones and their kind and give them food. So the learned ones could learn even more, in a kind of mutual benefit society. They started to listen to him and to follow his lead. They did not feel so inferior any more, as the learned ones relied on them, and they relied on the learned ones. So a primitive society and a new age came kicking and no doubt screaming into being. The age of co-operation  for the good of all was born. None would be considered lesser or greater, as they all had their place in the scheme of things, sadly this was not to last.

The endless battle for survival was made a little easier. Men learned to work in a tribal fashion, (villagers) and as knowledge increased within each tribe and group of tribes so mans lot improved. Each group of tribes started to serve its own interest, and the interests of all the tribes within range. Leading to further and further advancements like the ripples left by a stone thrown into a still pond. All following the lead of the knowing ones, and so the idea of the teacher, the priest came into being, and entered into the lives and minds of man. The idea of nationhood was also born from the same seed. The learned ones became the guides to them all, and the protectors of their very lives with their knowledge. The first, really great wonder of the World

Imagine, man had learned to reason. Even the most backward could reason. He could work out what was in his best interest and what was not. However some were cleverer than others. So it began, as one door opened another closed. The game began. The game of one "upmanship" or one "downman-ship." Some would rule while others slaved. Some started to abuse their positions, and the power of fear was soon to be understood. Together with it, came all the other negative attributes of man. Not the least of these was the idea of ownership.

One little tribe cleared the land and started to farm. While another more warlike watched till the crops were ready, and war was born. At first to steal, to gain that which was needed at the expense of another. Then for the protection of that which one had managed to gain. As time went by it became necessary for groups of men to journey further and further away from his fellow men, so that he could hunt, and grow, and build without fear of attack. But it was not to be. Wives and husbands of different blood were still needed to keep the little tribe strong. The question was how to achieve their needs, without letting others know exactly where they were, for fear that they would be followed and again attacked.

The wise ones were expected to come up with all these answers, and they did. At first it seemed simple. Sally forth and attack, take what you needed and run for it, back to your own neck of the woods. Setting up ambushes as you went to discourage anyone who would dare to follow. It probably wasn't all that good an idea as no doubt they would be followed, and then they would be attacked, and on and on it went, attack and counter attack. Too much fighting, and not enough time for learning and farming. So a better idea came into their minds - a great idea! Steal more women and put them to work, while the warriors did nothing but fight to get more women and goods. It was a great idea for the few, not so good though, as you couldn't kill all the workers lest the few would starve. Or horror of horrors, the warriors would have to do menial work themselves. Men working like women. It was simply unthinkable.

Early man came up with all sorts of ideas most of them did not work satisfactorily, as indeed they do not even today, but the same mentality still exists. Eventually men started to notice differences in men, more than who was the tallest, or the best fighter or whatever. There were other subtle differences. Some men and women had particular gifts that could not be easily explained. Again they turned to the learned ones to try to find out why. They found that the learned ones were themselves, mostly, but not all, gifted ones. Why only some and not all?

The heavens were consulted as usual and they started to be able to tell character from the stars. Astrology came into being. They started to notice that certain groups of stars formed patterns of character. Certain physical attributes seemed to run through people born during the same phases. They began to note that there were differences between people born under the same astrological Signs, and they learned how to tell the difference between those of negative character and those of positive character. They then started to be aware that people were sometimes born with oddities which were of particular interest.

Then as their knowledge grew they noted one particular very peculiar type of person was born when certain movements were seen in the heavens, and they became able to predict the birth of a "Caulbearer," or as it is sometimes known someone "born behind the veil."

"Caulbearers" are reputed to have all sorts of what would have been seen as magical powers, so long ago, and even today. Because of all these oddities they were soon deemed to have been sent from some sort of power in the heavens, due to the predictive patterns of the stars. All this was beyond the understanding of men. The "Caulbearers" were soon to be considered great leaders among men. It was noticed that they often prophesied events in the future, and were right in these matters, They proved themselves great healers. They watched, studied and observed the "Caulbearers." They taught them all they knew to advance them further in the ancient arts.

And so those "born behind the veil" became the first Priest Kings by right, and were still considered so, right up to the time of Christ, and even today.

Hence the slaughter that occurs every time a "High Caulbearer" is to be born. He must be killed at all costs as far as the powers that be are concerned. Lest he takes their power from them, by showing men a better way. Men may also prefer the leadership of a "Caulbearer" than the leadership of a tyrannical king, who rules only by fear.

Now for some reason, we do not know why, the Signs in the heavens are different for the seven "High Caulbearers" than for other "Caulbearers." No doubt the reason was either never known for sure or it has been lost in time. So the idea and the title of "Lord Of The Veil" came into being and "High Lord Of The Veil" for those born under the Sign of the Seven.

As a "Caulbearer" I was brought up in the Old Way as we call it. And I was taught all manner of things. By all sorts of "uncles and aunts" mostly. I don't think I had much idea of what was going on. Even now, late in life I still can't come to terms with the enormity of it all, never mind the meaning of it all. I will explain later on, what it is all about.

It causes me to think from time to time that The Prophesy speaks of someone else, as I simply find it very difficult to place myself in the shoes of someone so unfortunate as to have the salvation of man on his back. I ask the question "Why me?" every ten minutes as I write and go through the Seals. Every time I approach a member of the High Temple I question. I always to get the same answer "If not you then who else?"

I am told that I fit the Prophesy far too closely for coincidence. Every single point fits, and there are so many of them. There are times when I am convinced and quite sure that it is me, only to doubt again. I look at my veil or "caul," still. Yet I heal things that are impossible.

I know the trouble everyone has gone to all down the centuries to protect the Prophesy of Christ and his instructions. I know of the Nazarenes, who are better known as the "Brotherhood Of Light". The name was changed at the time of Constantine to the "Brotherhood Of The Flame", of which I am a member, Christ was a member, and all the five before him were members.

It is said that Odin so loved knowledge that he formed the Brotherhood to protect all knowledge. He even lost his eye in pursuit of knowledge. He knew, as we know, that knowledge is all. It is the only thing that will save man from the end that is to come, and sustain him in the poisoned world that he has developed, and so destroyed all that his children will inherit. They restricted the Brotherhood to "Caulbearers," the "High Caulbearers" leaving and adding something to the Prophesy, which is then protected for future use, when the time is right. It is handed down from Brother to Brother hypnotically. As Jesus said "You shall not forget for you will not remember." That is the way of hypnotic information. We have always known that to write these things down is dangerous as it can then be proved against you, and the writings then destroyed. So much knowledge was lost. However a great deal has survived through the Brotherhood. They were very particular that the last Prophesy of The Christ would survive until it could be written and set before all men. And so, as a ten year-old child I had more information imprinted, or if you like implanted in my mind than any ten men would acquire in a lifetime. It just takes triggers and out it comes. It is a pity they did not include the use of modern computers in there as well, and come to think of it a lot of other things that would help me.

There was a lot I think I should have been taught, and wasn't. However they assure me that what they didn't teach me was all for my own good, and for the good of the Prophesy. So the secret of the money tree escaped me, but I can see why now. As I open the Seals and see the Prophesy unfold, I start to understand a little. It's still mind-boggling though. Imagine you were me. As the Irish man said, "Sitting in my shoes." Imagine what I feel like. I am just an ordinary chap, perhaps a bit different, but we are all different. I am usually broke, have the usual problems and mess up quite a bit, just like anyone else. Yet even the messing up seems to have a direction, a sort of a purpose. I have failed more times than you can shake a stick at. I started farming seriously when I was eleven. I failed. Yet later on I went to an agricultural college. I really know my farming. I should do, I was also brought up to it.

My stay in the medical profession wasn't so very clever either. People just seem to take exception to my funny little ways. I live in a Christian World, and Christians find it hard to understand how a non-Christian can heal the way I do. They believe it is solely their prerogative.

I have recently found the need to call in the Irish police to take shotguns away from my neighbour. He thinks that I am the devil incarnate, because there were a couple of articles in a newspaper and a magazine about me getting a chap with spinal cord severance, walking, having been wheelchair bound for ten years. Therefore, because I am not Christian I must give him the keys to my home and get out of the area, or I will be killed. Now there's reason for you. Sometimes these things are sheer bad luck, yet it always seems to lead to somewhere else, and each time I learn something more as the Prophecy unfolds. As the High Templars keep saying, "It all appears to follow a purpose." I haven't failed at a thing really. I have gained a great deal of experience and knowledge, and I use every piece of knowledge or information I can get, every day of my life. I couldn't manage without a single bit of it, and as the membership of the Old Order increases with all its responsibilities, I need it more than ever.

I am a "High Caulbearer" not just an ordinary one. No not I. I had to be unfortunate enough to born be a "High" one, with all the problems that go with it. When you are a "Caulbearer" life is hard enough, but as a "High Caulbearer," one of the Seven, you are on your own. You can't talk to anybody. There's no one to understand. How could they?

Then there's the problem of trust. You must be very careful, as believers don't reason and often take offence or feel threatened. So you can't talk to anyone, just in case. But I am starting to let caution go to the wind, and am making up for it now. I still can't allow myself to get too close to anyone. I doubt if I ever can, just in case I cause them harm. Or they may be used by the unsavoury ones, simply to get at me. I can't stay in the one place or in the one job, because people start to wonder what it's all about, and someone might find out. I have always had to keep passing out what is so nicely called "misinformation," about myself, where I have been etc. Again just in case.

I have been in some funny places, and I have done some funny things, just to stay alive. I have to try to keep moving. I must never relax. The purpose has always been far too important to allow anything normal to enter into my life. Well now I am the Supreme High Priest Internationally, and I can do as I like. At least that is what I thought. Little did I know, but I know now. I am even more restricted than ever. The danger is more acute, to both myself and to my family. Threatening phone calls which promise death to us all. Irate neighbours going to petrol bomb my home. Who is there to listen? Even more important who is there to help? The police are Christian, and I am not. Which side will they take? The side they are told to take of course. Now I understand better. I know exactly what it is all about. That makes it easier for me, as I realise there is little or no point to it at all. The only point is that men are facing the ending of days, and some of us can avoid the inevitable. I have been given the key, the flame to follow, and the instructions to follow it, so that a future for the species may be attained and maybe even assured.

I have the weight of the Seven Veils and the Seven Seals on my shoulders, and they weigh very heavy. But I now have the fulcrum, the lever of understanding to help to carry them. I have the strength of all those who have gone before me in that cause. I hear the words of the greatest man who ever lived, in my mind speaking across two thousand years, and suddenly I know. I have not become schizophrenic, or gone mad.

I know. I hear. Deep in my psyche the words run. I see the marks of the Prophesy on my body, and in my numbers, and suddenly I know. I know without doubt that the end of days is at hand. Anyone who has a mind must see it coming, unless they turn and look the other way. It will not be as depicted by the scruffy little men with placards, but the real ending of days. I know that you can all see it coming, that even those of you who are blind, bothered and stupid can see it coming.

Read the Prophesy and know that it means what it says, and that I and my followers will carry it out to the bitter end, and it will be bitter. I will carry it out to the last drop of blood in my veins. I cannot do otherwise. I have not been left any option in the matter. Christ himself has said in the Prophesy that I will be sickened unto death if I do not do all that is possible. I will follow this man and all the other men of the "Veil" who have gone before me, to their last word in that Prophesy. Even those words that I have been commanded not to speak of. So you who will come with me, be ready, as the road will be long and the task wearying to the body and to the mind, but the rewards will be great. The reward of life is always great, there is none greater than that, and to be permitted to spend your life in the service of your fellows, is an even greater gift than life. You shall have both.

Let me tell you more of the "Caulbearers" that have gone before me as far as I can at this time.

# THE "HIGH CAULBEARERS"

## THE FIRST

It is said that one such "Caulbearer" was born about fifteen thousand years ago, This person, we are not sure if it was a man or a woman, is reputed to be the first of the Seven Signs that everyone has been talking about for so long. Some believing it to be seven events or seven angels bearing veils, coming down from heaven on a cloud, or some such thing. While in fact the Seven Signs are seven people. All born behind the "Veil". Each contributing to the Prophesy in his own way, and coming as it were in times of great danger to men. Warning them of things to come and sadly no one hearing them. So it looks bad for me.

When they first appeared we are not sure what problems were facing man, as he or she was not clear on this point and seems to feel that he or she was just there to prophesy the coming of the other six. To warn man of his folly, then and in the future, and to pass on the Seal, in what so far has proved a waste of life, and of time. The bringing of reason into the minds and lives of men, is not a simple task by any stretching of the imagination. The Seal being a key to each Prophecy, and to the main Prophecy which would be opened at the ending of days. Which will be, if by then man has gained no reason, and he certainly has not. If he carries on in his usual blind and destructive way the fears of the first comer are not unfounded. The ending of days approaches.

The second of the "Caulbearers" was Odin. All the points are in his direction, he is the only one who could possibly fit the description in the Prophecy. There are not many people who in the past have lost an eye in the search of knowledge, and who went about with two ravens and a wolf as constant companions. It is said that Odin was not pleased with the way that men were starting to treat their World, and the animals that lived in that World. So he trained the ravens, because at that time they were despised as creatures of all ills and dangers, as was the wolf.

Again men used belief instead of knowledge, and as a result men hunted them out of stupidity, and often just for fun. They were considered nothing less than moving targets, with no thought for their pain or their suffering. Odin was of the opinion, as we still are, that if men should treat the wild things so, then soon they would start to differentiate between men in like manner. Of course as history has unfolded we have seen this on a great scale, with all the torture and mayhem caused by those in power over others, and the diabolical methods employed over the unfortunate.

We see as I write, the Chilean slaughter and the attempt of Spain to extradite the man responsible, so that he might be tried for these crimes. There are the recent massacres in Bosnia. All wanton, unnecessary brutality and pointless cruelty. One religion against the other, and going against the teachings of both. It seems that the mind of the beast knows no limits in this matter. Sadly we see it every day in the news all over the World. Even more sadly it is increasing, as men appear to have no respect for anything outside themselves, and very little for themselves.

I know a lot of lip service is employed to the contrary, but it is only lip service. No one actually does much, and those who do are considered slightly mad or worse, are quickly dealt with should they upset the Status Quo. As it is said, "As long as God is in his heaven all is well with the World" That's what many seem to believe. It is a sort of thinking that allows reality to be ignored and unreality to reign in its stead. Dangerous stuff! This kind of unreality is precisely what messed things up in the setting up of the Christian religion, and made it not of the The Christ, and mostly against his teaching.

Christ was set aside for Constantine who was hailed as a Messiah. For three hundred years the Christians had defied the might of the Roman Empire, though they had been martyred and abused. They found solace in their belief of heaven and life after death. Suddenly they recognised the Imperial power of Rome that had crucified Jesus three centuries before. Why? They must have become tired of being outcasts and grabbed the opportunity for acceptance.

The opportunity to prosper, even though it meant giving up a lot of the things that they stood for. Christianity was dead on its feet at this point. The dirty word "compromise" raised its ugly head, and The Christ was once again sacrificed. This time on the cross of convenience, and the fish, the symbol of Christians, was cast aside. Later the cross was to be born as the new symbol. It was not until the fourth century A.D. that the Romans started to use the cross as a method of execution. Until then they used a tree or a pole for the purpose, so even the cross is a lie.

The Roman Church was content to give to the Emperor Constantine that which was due to Jesus, he had succeeded where Jesus was thought to have failed. By denying The Christ his rightful position as a King, effected a shield against the children of Jesus from asserting their true claim. Thus any lineal decent from the family of Jesus could not lay any claim to its rightful place in the hierarchy of the church, nor as a monarchy. This left the church in the hands of the papacy. The bloody hands of the papacy! Unchallenged, free to carry on their doctrines that defy all reason, and just believe. Ignore facts, and history, even the most basic common sense, and believe.

Odin is seen as a man who many believe did not really exist, that existence being confined to myth alone. This of course is not true. He was very real. A "High Caulbearer" - a "High Lord Of The Veil." A man like Christ, lost in the myth that has been built up around him. Odin and what we know of his life, some of which is enshrined in the mythology that surrounds him, fits the description of the second comer right down to a "T". Odin was also named by the third comer, before he was about to be murdered with his whole family. He had over stepped himself, as did The Christ. He thought that the people who he served were worth him taking the risk of speaking out against false deity, and a king who used belief of this deity as a control mechanism over his people. For his own benefit not for theirs. The king used that same method as did Herod in the time of Jesus, and the Pharaoh in the time of Moses. They used murder as they always have and still do, right up to the massacre of the Jews by Hitler on the instigation of the Pope. For the very same reasons of protecting some religious or royal dynasty. It was also designed to "get" the "Caulbearer"

The thing that first stands out in the life of Odin is that of the invention of the runes, which is laid firmly at his door. He is said to have first seen the symbols in a pool of his own blood, as he hung crucified upside down for nine days, and like Jesus he survived.

Odin laid great value on knowledge. It is said that he lost his right eye in the search of it. He came, as do all the Signs, in a time of danger to mankind, and as have all the Signs he failed in his mission. But, he left something behind to mark his coming, something of importance and assistance to man. The runes as I am sure you will know are still around today, and from the runes Tarot cards were developed. The Old Rune Masters became the Guild Of Tarot Masters we know today.

Odin was also directly responsible for the founding of The Brotherhood Of Light which I have already explained. It is now the Brotherhood Of The Flame, the so called lost Brotherhood. He formed this to not only gather knowledge, but to protect it from those who would destroy it, or use it for base reason.

He was a warrior, probably because he had no choice. In those days it was either that or die. Odin was concerned with the well-being of man, and the direction man was taking. Cruelty knew no bounds. Not just to each other but to our fellow beings. Odin tamed and trained two ravens to show that they were not just targets to be slaughtered for fun. He did this in the hope that men would learn. He trained a wolf which was his constant companion. He must have been some sight dressed in black, with a patch over his eye, two ravens on his shoulders and a wolf at his side.

After his death, as was Jesus, he was worshipped as a god, and is said to rule in Valhalla over twelve lesser Lords. Again he is described as "The High Lord," which of course he was in reality if you can see the man through the myth, as he really was. A tough man, who could stand a great deal of pain and suffering. He must have been something to have stood up to crucifixion for nine days and live. Although I am told that nine days is the usual length of time for a strong man to last, nailed to a tree or cross, before death. But he was crucified upside down, which makes it an even greater feat. St Peter chose to be crucified upside down, as he knew that the heart floods rapidly, so death and the end of suffering comes more quickly. The heart tires quickly when it has to push the blood up to the legs, as it is designed to work the other way.

To say that Odin was a great and intelligent man is a gross understatement. He was far more than just that. He was courageous as well as strong in body, and mind. He was a poet, and an inventor of stories and songs. He painted pictures in the minds of his people. He gave them a sense of pride in themselves and so developed a new type of thinking, caring society. This was again altered after his death, by those who wished to control the masses, and harness them for their own benefit without consideration for the needs of those they harnessed. And so the myths were built up, later to be torn down by the Christian Church, as they became the new taskmasters.

## MARDUK.

Marduk was born in similar circumstance to all the six. As usual his Sign was seen and the powers that be wanted him found and killed. His mother is said to have gone to hide in the mountains, guided by two wise men. There she gave birth to him, and the mountain upon which he was born was afterwards considered holy.

He was born early in the year under the Sign of the ram, with "Caul" in place. He was moved from place to place, and hidden together with his mother for some time by the wise men, and their helpers. After a time people came to know that he was the "High Lord" who was due to be born, so they turned to him and the kings that feared his coming and wanted him dead had to stand back, as the people would kill anyone who they thought threatened him. A plot was hatched by his brother and the kings that wanted him dead in the first place, to kill him, and so remove the threat to their power. By now they were very afraid for their positions, as he grew stronger everyday. They did not want to kill him themselves as they were also afraid of the curse that befalls anyone who harms a "Caulbearer," and as a "High Caulbearer" they were doubly afraid. Better to get someone to do it for you, or so they thought.

After Marduk killed his brother, his sister-in-law went on the rampage, fighting wars all over the place. When it came to going against Marduk in the final battle as it were, she would not raise a hand against him. A man called Ninurta did, and lost as a consequence.

Marduk was a scholar and a seeker of knowledge as well as a warrior. He went against all the religious teachings of his time, which upset the priesthood of those religions. No believer wants to be asked to prove his belief, for if it was provable he would not have to "believe" in the first place. And as is the way, arguing with established belief systems, as in the lives of any "Caulbearers" who have followed this line, eventually cost him his life, and the lives of his family.

Marduk was well aware of the meaning of his "Caul," and as no attempts had been made on his life for some time, he became careless. His skill as an astrologer, was renowned. He was a man of many other talents as well. He reintroduced Odin's calendar of twenty-eight day months and thirteen-month years. He travelled widely, some say as far a Stonehenge but we are not too sure of this. He did however have a hand, and no doubt a pen it the construction of other astrological sites. He did nothing without consulting the stars. He warned of the folly of irrigation to excess, and warned of the dangers of continuous cropping. He was later to be proved right. He was against sacrifice of either man or beast, which did not sit well with the religious leaders of that time.

It was a legal obligation for all women to present themselves at the temple for the purpose of ritual prostitution, no matter how high or lowborn they might be. The temple gained considerable wealth from this practice. A man had to stay faithful to his wife where all women were concerned, but he could go the temple prostitutes whenever he liked, and it did not count.

Marduk was a "High Caulbearer." He was a King by right, and he used his position well. He altered many things and argued with others on the rights and wrongs. He tried to bring about changes that would benefit all, as he was aware that prosperity could only come about if all the people enjoy it at the same time. There can be no prosperity for the few at the expense of the many, which remains sustainable. Homosexuality was rampant, to the point where it was almost obligatory. He set out to "clean up" his own Kingdom. He used the natural laws wherever possible, and in doing so gained the love and loyalty of his own people. He and his people prospered.

People from other kingdoms saw what was happening. All the old religions and religious beliefs together with their deities were cast down. Knowledge and reason reigned. His people were happier and healthier than those in surrounding lands. So something had to be done. There were murmurs and rattling among various leaders both religious and royal, who feared the loss of their kingdoms, and their power, to this man. Their people no longer turned to them in times of trouble but to Marduk, the astrologer, healer and prophet. He was a man of wisdom and justice. Virgins were not sacrificed, nor wives prostituted under his rule. Homosexuality and all unnatural behaviours were outlawed. Disease was reduced, and stability reigned. It is said that his sword of wisdom shone in the sunlight, brighter than swords of steel.

He made a fatal mistake. He started to educate his people in the temple, instead of it being used for religious ritual. This scared everyone in power at that time, and a plot was hatched to dispose of him. The very idea of an educated populace was as abhorrent to them as it was to the Christian Churches in recent times. But unlike the Christian Churches, who decided to give in and do the teaching themselves, thus controlling what you could and could not know. Instead of fighting it any further, knowing that they could no longer hope to win, their thoughts turned again to murder.

It was a simple plot. As it is said he was a man without guile, despite his astrological knowledge, and experience in battle. He fell for it hook, line and sinker against all advice. He thought that to show distrust to his fellow rulers at this time, would cause insult at least, or show cowardice at worst. They invited him to a "council of kings," All friends of course, so there was no need for armies, or even large escorts. It was reputed to be more or less a trade meeting. So off set old Marduk with his sons and a few men, bearing gifts for those he thought were his friends, but who had other ideas. He was quickly set upon by carefully chosen men, as they would have had some difficulty getting anyone willing to harm him considering the consequences. His sons were stripped before his eyes. Tied to wagon tongues and systematically raped by the soldiers of his "friends", they were then dragged to death as he watched helplessly. They killed his whole company, in as cruel and bloodthirsty a way as they could, disembowelling, and dismembering them all.

They put out Marduk's eyes, after stripping him naked. He was disembowelled, by dogs. They had a nasty little way of cutting a hole in the abdomen just big enough to pull a piece of small intestine through. Then they would get the dogs, who had been starved just long enough, to pull the rest of the bowels out, eating them before your eyes. It was believed that to spill the blood of a "Caulbearer" would bring down the wrath of the gods so they burned him alive to avoid spilling blood. The Christians did the same thing for the same reasons some three and a half thousands years later. A soldier, who felt sorry for him as he had heard of his goodness, killed him with an arrow to end his pain. He paid for his act of compassion with his own life as a warning to all. The power of the brute was once again returned to the hands of the brute.

They were so overjoyed at their easy victory over Marduk and his handful of followers, they forgot about his horses and his chariot. The horses bolted in fear and ran off at great speed back to the city. As they ran through the streets driver-less, they killed people under the wheels, and caused mayhem in their panic. They smashed a pathway through the streets. They dragged the chariot along the sacred road. They dragged it across the city at breakneck speed. His golden chariot slewed all over the place. Eventually the horses stopped outside the temple, where they often stood. His people knew that something was terribly wrong, but were not sure exactly what. Behind the chariot walked a single woman, a priestess. She was crying for the loss of her Priest King, who was also her husband. She was also shamed before the people and brutally murdered.

It is said that fear was struck into every heart that terrible day. Some set out to search for Marduk, as he was their protector and there was none else like him who could follow in his footsteps.

The King, their mentor and saviour was dead. Thus ending the life of yet another "High Lord Of the Veil." Thus once again, a Lamb had died at the hands of the beasts.

It was springtime in Babylon. The die had been cast and neither the kings of that land, or the land itself would survive. It's people scattered to the four winds. This green and fertile land was cursed and turned to desert, forever.

He who was sent to walk amongst them was no more. The kings who plotted his demise hid in their cities, they were so afraid of what they had done. Abandoned by their priests, who also hid in mortal fear of the consequences of which they knew well, and had previously thought they could escape, knowing they could not, in spite of the priests earlier bravado and assurances.

In time the priests gained control once more. The people had experienced a taste of knowledge, but sadly only a taste, which they soon forgot. Marduk's Kingdom and his City was again turned into a place of blood sacrifice, a place of abomination, and of false gods. Once again man knew no reason, as was prophesied. The dynasties perished, and the land succumbed to the desert. Even the soil was blown away. As the prophesies say, only the culverts are now visible, all that remains of a land of great promise brought to ruin by stupidity, greed and above all the following of false belief, without logic or reason.

Marduk was exalted to the position of a "High God," once again after he was long dead. He like all the others was used after his death, by lesser men, to control the people for the benefit of the few. The prophecy of the coming of Marduk is complete.

The same prophecy says that all the land that is now Iraq will turn to base ways. It will destroy itself with wars and with the lies that will come from the mouths of its leaders. It states, that which is untrue will be valued beyond that which is true, as it will be used in bargaining, and all the people of that place will be known throughout the World as men without honour, though they will make much noise of honour.

This reminds me of The Christ's own prophecy, where he talks of the things that will rise from the desert, to destroy one third of the land and one third of the seas. Marduk the man, like The Christ and like Odin is lost in the myth that surrounded him. He is said to be the god Jupiter, seen watching over his Kingdom from the night sky, together with one of his sons Mercury. The other son seems to have just disappeared altogether.

Jupiter, with the exception of the sun, is the largest planet known to man. Astrologically Jupiter rules Mercury and ironically justice and morality. The things that Marduk was renowned for, and received little of. On its darker side its abuses range from hypocrisy, to tyranny and excesses. The very things that Marduk spent his life trying to remove from his Kingdom, from the minds of men, and from the World. Little changes.

# MOSES.

The story of Moses is very well known, but there is so much of it that is just myth, and again mostly written after his demise. Much has been changed in the Bible, especially anything to do with "Caulbearers." We have the same effect on those who rule as we always did. I hope this time that things may be different as it really is the last chance, and there is much evidence of this.

The story of Moses has of course also been changed. It is written that the Pharaohs were worried about the numbers of the Jews and were afraid that they might join with their enemies in the event of battle, against them. It is written that they set taskmasters over them to work them so hard that they would no longer multiply. Yet from all these writings the same old routine shines through.

Out of the blue the king of Egypt instructs the midwives of the Jews to kill all the sons as they are born. It is said that the midwives feared God and wanted no part of it. And the Jews multiplied. Again the Pharaoh was not happy, and instructed that all the male children should be cast into the river, and drowned.

Now a woman from the house of Levi bore a son, and when she saw him he was a goodly child, so she manages to hide him for three months. And when she could no longer hide him she wove a basket out of bulrushes, and sealed it with slime and pitch so that it would float, and not leak. She then put the child in the basket along with his "Caul", and set it among the flags at the side of the river, hoping he would not be found. She got his sister and set her to watch over the basket from a distance, to see what would happen to him. The daughter of the Pharaoh came down to the river to bathe. She and her servants walked along the bank of the river, and of course she saw the basket and sent one of her maids to fetch it. She looked into the basket and when she saw the child, the child cried and she felt sorry for him. Moses sister was soon down to the Pharaoh's daughter, and offered to fetch a wet nurse for him, and of course she brought his own mother as his wet nurse. The Pharaoh's daughter gave her the child and ordered her to care for him, she even gave her wages so it worked out well for all. The boy grew and his mother had to take him to the Pharaoh's daughter to be as it is written, her son. She called him Moses as she had drawn him from the bulrushes. This is the reason that a "Caul" is considered a talisman against drowning, even today.

Now what is not in The Bible is that the "Caul" was in the basket with him when he was found, and this was the reason that the Pharaoh's daughter kept him, as she was aware of the "Caul" and its meaning. She may or may not have been aware that he was a "High Caulbearer," but the king would have been more than aware of this.

Again he would have been sought out by The Brotherhood who were very active in those parts at the time, for obvious reasons. There is not much said about him till later on when he killed the Egyptian for beating a Hebrew. His education would have been well on the way. He was aware that although he was considered a son of Pharaoh's daughter, he was in fact a Hebrew himself. He went out on the following day and seeing two Hebrews fighting, tried to stop them, pointing out that it was wrong for them to fight. They asked him who he thought he was. Was he not the chap who killed the Egyptian and buried his body in the sand the day before? So, the cat was out of the bag. The Pharaoh wanted to kill him for the deed, and he had to run. Again the old pattern emerges. His life in danger, and he was alone. He had to hide himself away. Fate was at the controls.

As he rested by a well the seven daughters of a Priest who lived nearby, came to draw water. The shepherds tried to chase them away but Moses helped them to water their flock. He was then given one of the priest's daughters, who had a son by him.

Eventually the Pharaoh died, and it was time for Moses to return and deliver his people from slavery. It is written that he took his flock by the backside of the desert, where he came to the mountain of God. The story of the burning bush is well known. Again the pattern emerges of "enlightenment'. Unusual twists and turns in the life, fate seeming to always lead somewhere. He was the lawgiver of his people, their leader.

Why did they accept him so easily, as Marduk was accepted and Odin? If you look at the lives of these men the pattern is more or less consistent. All are seekers of Knowledge. All are men with the ability to fight and win. All are unusual. All came at a time of great trouble. All are shrouded in myths that are used to underpin religious belief that would otherwise be unacceptable to any reasoning mind.

Imagine Moses now an old man going up into the mountain all alone to bring down the ten commandments chiselled in stone. Meant to last. The golden calf. A false god. The mystical Ark Of The Covenant. Why ten commandments? Especially as they were already well known in the form of the twelve laws of the Old Religion. One might ask why were the Jews only chosen? Or were they? We think not.

Now I know that this is a controversial thing to say, but when you think about it, they preach all men as equal under God. So why should they be more equal than anyone else? Don't get me wrong I have great respect for the Jews, I admire their fight for their homeland, and their even bigger fight to keep it. When they took over Israel it was a desert, and look at what they have done. It is now a fruitful productive place, this you have to give credit for.

All religions are more or less based on the same psychological formula. You do not tell people that they are beasts as we do, if you wish to get them to accept what you say. Instead you tell them that they are made in the image of God, or that they are somehow superior and so are chosen above all others. Conceit does the rest. Imagine God looking like some of the people you know, what a "deitical" turn off. Yet these same people will insist on this particular belief. Now it follows that if they believe one thing they will accept another and then another and so religious dogma is born. You lose and the puppet masters win, and you deserve to lose if your mind can go no further than your own self-indulgent conceit.

Moses was a great man, a "High Lord Of The Veil", and his portrayal does him no justice. He was a great leader of men. He changed the thinking of his time. He taught, sadly what he taught was forgotten or readjusted to suit base purpose as it seems to always be. He never saw the result of his life's labour, and probably just as well as it was made waste in the long run.

Moses had the traditional job of saving mankind from himself, and in his time, and after his time, sadly, "man knew no reason".

Buddha was high born. He was the son of the head of the Sakya warrior caste. His private name was Siddhartha, he was also known later in life as Sakyamuni, meaning "sage of the Sakyas." The name Buddha means "enlightened one". He came, again at a time of great crisis in the World, a time of unnecessary violence and war.

The accounts of Buddha's life were mainly written many years after his death and like all the other "High Lords," he too was lost in the myth. There is, if fact is as I see things, little difference between the myth and the mist, both hide, conceal, and cause shadow. And men get lost in both. That which is written of him, as with the rest, was written by idolising followers who wished to revere him, and also by those of a more base intent. As a result of this it is difficult to piece the true picture of his life together. A certain amount is known by the Brotherhood, as we know a certain amount for sure about all the six that have past. Buddha followed in his father's footsteps but not from personal choice, and a little under protest. To him it was a duty, it was in those days unquestioned for someone of his caste. Being a warrior did not suit him, as it would obviously go hard against his "Caulbearer" nature.

It is a funny thing, that violence goes against the "Caulbearer" nature, yet we all have experience, and have all been instructed in the arts of war as a part of our general training. As with all "Caulbearers" he would be confused by the conflicts of his mind. Life, duty and manhood demand, but the inner self, the inner being, cannot and will not be denied.

So Buddha went against his father, because he would in fact have no option, and he became a religious philosopher, a thinker, and a seeker of knowledge. Earlier he had yielded to his fathers wishes and married at an early age, finding court life shallow, boring, pointless and unrewarding. His "Caulbearer" mind screamed for something else. He left home and family and wandered in search of knowledge, trying to fill the void of his existence.

In 533 BC he had his first experience of the real meaning of the World and life in general. He met a monk whose serenity and purpose effected him deeply. He had come into contact with The Brotherhood, and thus he entered into the life of the "Caulbearers." His education was about to begin. He became determined to forsake his old way of life, including family, and all the wealth and power that went with it, according to the Buddhist tradition, and what we know, ourselves. He was about twenty-nine years old at the time. No longer a boy, experienced, yet with little experience that would make his decision more relevant. It is said that he wandered around India as a mendicant monk. This is only nearly the real truth of him.

He was at this time under the care and tuition of The Brotherhood. The Brotherhood would teach him about all the known religions, because it is important that we understand what they are about, and it also helps us to avoid their wrath, and avoid them. They always prefer us dead.

Firstly he investigated Hinduism, and received instruction. He however found the Hindu caste system a bit much, and despised it, as it is far too rigid and makes no sense. As far as we are concerned, and as far as he was concerned, it is futile in its purpose. His education continued, and he was introduced to like minded people who became his companions. As he travelled, still finding it difficult to accept his meaning, and what he really was. Weighed down by the weight of his purpose and all that goes with it, he travelled on. According to tradition he gained enlightenment beneath a Bo tree, where he met another old man, again a member of The Brotherhood. It is said he came across a corpse and a beggar and from all this he gained his enlightenment. The old man was however the main player on the field and it was from the teachings of The Brother and The Brotherhood that he started to learn.

He became a diligent and valued member of that following of brothers that sought knowledge, and retained and protected it. Buddha is said however, never to have been able to accept his importance in the scheme of things. His modesty got in the way of his reason, or perhaps the idea was outside the plane of his reason. His being a "High Caulbearer" never sank in. He never accepted fully who and what he was. He knew but had great difficulty in realising, but he served his purpose none the less to the best of his ability, which was considerable. He carried on to speak and to teach as well as he could. He gathered a following of disciples much the same as did Jesus, Odin, Moses, and Marduk.

The pattern follows from one to another like a fingerprint. He gained Divine status after his death, as has happened to all the six "High Caulbearers." No wonder I am a bit reclusive. Like all his counterparts he too was lost in the myths, told and written of him some three hundred years after his death. He too gave up all he loved, stood ridiculed by lesser men, and bore the teeth marks of ill intentioned parasites, who tried to raise themselves up through him, without even possessing enough humanity that might enable them to just begin to understand what it was, and is all about.

The Prophesy of life has never been put into writing before in complete form. Parts have been written by some who have managed to piece bits of it together as far as they could.

I am a member of the Brotherhood Of The Flame, which was known up to the time of Constantine as the Brotherhood Of Light. It was changed at that time because he was a sun-worshipper, and as the sun is to do with light, it was no longer thought fitting to maintain the word 'light' as we did not wish to give reason for misunderstanding. At that time and indeed until now we oppose such beliefs, as they obviously have no foundation. Until this time we have held the Prophecies secret, partly because those who laid out the groundwork knew what they were doing, and made it impossible after Christ for them to be understood till the coming of the last Sign and his Seal.

So we have held the Prophesy till the time is considered right, or till it no longer matters, for reasons that will become obvious.

The reasons are simple. Man has come to the end of his time on Earth, but there is still some hope for a few. There is still some hope that some will learn and be saved. The Christian idea of being saved came in part from the old order, but was, and is as usual completely misunderstood and bastardised to suit the purpose of the furtherance of belief.

Those of you who will be saved will not reside in a heavenly paradise, only your genetic information will survive, through your children. Your sole purpose in life is to survive, reproduce your kind, and to learn and pass on that which you are, and that which you have learned. Thus making this World a better place and showing improvement with each generation. Such is your purpose. And if you who should survive and learn, and do according to this purpose, then the World will surely become Paradise.

Mans everlasting life is a very old idea, but we never meant men to misconstrue the idea. You only live on in the blood, as we have always said. In other words you only live on, in, and through your children. The idea was taken up by those who sought and still seek mastery of all mankind, and they have made it seem as if, when you die, you go to this paradise for eternity. If you do not live as they command, paying both material things, as well as homage to the ones who claim the ears and favour of some deity or other, you will go to Hell or its equivalent. Where the Devil who was invented for the purpose of creating fear among those who would believe them, is waiting as it were, to give you hell and damnation for your misdemeanours.

The idea of the Devil came from a bastardisation of the Old Order's idea that you are just a beast, and all things that crawl on the face of the Earth are just beasts. But the order also says that there is a varying degree of humanity in all beasts. Beware the beast, or as it was meant your base nature and mine. And from this very simple and accurate observation Old Nick was invented. His sole purpose to burn your soul and torment you for all eternity. It makes no sense at all, but it has worked since the beginning of Judaism till now, and hopefully it will stop here. But I know that many people will hold on to this idea out of that even worse invention called 'belief' for some time to come, but reason, hopefully will reign.

The Prophesy is in seven parts. The first to Prophesy in his Sign and his Seal says, "One part will be revealed and unfold with the coming of each of the prophesied ones, for each one will be that Sign. Each of the High Lords Of The Veil is a Sign unto himself, and each one will reveal many more lesser Signs." You who know the meaning of the number 7 and the nature of it and will understand its significance. It is the number of change.

Each High Lord in his time will show men the way and the need of change in that time. With the coming of each of the High Lords man will be shown the Way. But it is prophesied that he will learn not reason till his end is near. And his end is now upon him.

### The First to come said..............

The Seventh will be the final comer to offer change to the minds of men. It is said, "The Seventh will gather to him his own. He will gather those less than he for he will be great." Such will be the way of the Lords sent to walk among men for their own sake.

If he should be prevented, and it will go hard for him as many will fear him and hold him to ridicule. If no other Lords in his time follow him, and if no sufficient change shall come about, man and all his kind will perish from the face of the Earth and shall be doomed, and the Earth will empty itself of him.

And the Mother shall die and her breasts will no longer feed him, and all that is of him shall perish and he shall be no more.

Man in his mindless ways shall eventually destroy the World almost to its death, and to the death of his own kind.

And at the end of man he shall be given his final chance and so shall be born the last of the Seven Signs. And if he shall fail there shall be no more to be the saviour of man. He shall be the last High Lord Of The Veil. He is the end of prophecy. The last.

And he shall gather men unto him, and they shall be men of reason and pure in their purpose, and they shall build the Paradise that man has brought to death and ruin.

His strength shall be knowledge, and his weakness his fellow man, his message reason. Many will fear and hate him, and those who will hate him will do so because they will know him, and be afraid. But they will not deter his purpose except at the cost of their lives, and their children's, and the lives of all of their blood to the last drop of that blood.

Seven High Lords Of The Veil will come in all, to different peoples to show the Way.

I am the first, and will be lost in time and no one shall know my name but it matters not.

My purpose is only to speak The Prophecy as I see it will be.
In my time man is young, and will not be deterred from the way of the beast. But I have found those of good faith in matters that will carry my prophecy forward and let it and my purpose not be lost.

Each of the Seven High Lords will add to the prophecy as he sees. Each shall add more knowledge than the last and so shall it be.

A High Lord will be born after me of a warrior and barbaric race, and great barbarity shall be rife in that time. He shall hang impaled on a tree for nine days. The meaning of nine is of perfection and concord for it unites into one all others.

Nine days shall he suffer, and he shall see in a pool of his own blood, signs, and he shall speak and reveal the secret meaning of those signs so that men can use them in the prophesying of the future. And he shall tell of others to come after him.

He shall bind men in brotherhood and the search for knowledge.

He shall befriend the raven and the wolf so that men shall know better of them. And he shall put high value on knowledge, on thought, and on memory.

He shall be worshipped after his death as a High God, until the coming of the last of the Signs to walk among men.

He shall be set up by those who want to gain power over his followers, but they will not find the brotherhood or gain knowledge of it.

God-likeness will not be his purpose nor shall it be his want in this thing.

Men will set up all the High Lords as godlike after they die, in order to gain power over the hearts and minds of other men, so that they may rule them to their own advantage.

They will be revered as gods in death, yet hated, feared and tormented in life by those who will use them and their names. Such will be the wickedness of men.

And the Sixth will be the most revered of all the High Lords until the coming of the Seventh.
As each comes his duty will be greater.

The Sixth shall he repeat the Prophesies of all that have gone before him to his closest friends as the hour of his testing comes close.

And the Seventh shall be prophesied by him before his final hours, as he shall know that he cannot change the ways of men at that time, and it must be placed upon the shoulders of the Seventh to complete the task or turn his back upon man.

He shall prophesy, and his number will be ten, and he shall be the first and the last to come after the Sixth.

One shall be born in a place of thirteen cities, which will be turned to dust by the time of the coming of the Seventh Sign. And all the cities will be laid waste as the punishment for this evil against the High Lord. And by his murder shall he fail in his purpose.

For he will do great things, and the Kings of that place of thirteen cities shall fear him, and hate him for his goodness. And they shall plot and shall kill him and his wife, and all that is of his blood, lest they claim their kingdom by right, from those who hold it only by might, and by trickery, and by lies. As will be the way at the coming of the fifth and the Sixth.

And after his murder men shall pay the price for the harming of this "High Caulbearer" and all will die and be cast down. The thirteen cities will be laid to dust.

And men in that time will mount one upon another, and women will mount one upon another. And the vileness of men at that time will not be surpassed till the coming of the Seventh. And this vileness will cause the same evils to come upon man, for man shall not learn.

41

One will be born among a race of slaves, and there will be much killing at that time to rid the King of that place of the fear of him. But the "Caulbearer" shall be King and lead his people away from that place. And his trials shall be great.

His people shall turn away from his teaching. His every word will go unheard, and men will hear only that which suits them.

When his Sign shall be seen the Kings of that time will have small knowledge of it, yet shall know of it's meaning, and they will do great and shameful slaughter. But the child will be cast afloat. And because of this the veil shall be known as a talisman against drowning in the times up to the coming of the last High Lord. Its real purpose hidden by design, that men shall forget the purpose of the veil, and the High Lords that bear it and of the Lords that bear it.

And the power of the beast shall remain in the hands of the beast. Namely those who know no humanity and seek to rule over their fellows by trickery, and by fear and by force. And it shall be the mark of man the beast that he shall only learn that which suits his purpose and his exaltation, and like the beasts of the forests he shall know not when his belly be full.

And though this High Lord shall prove himself many times, and shall show his greatness, men shall still twist his teaching in greed and in wickedness to their own ends.

The freer of slaves shall give men laws to live by, and they again shall be altered to suit a lower purpose, and that purpose shall be vile, and man shall know no reason.

Another shall be born in a land of great forests and great beasts. Again his words will be misunderstood, as he shall be above other men. He shall try to teach men to reason and study in contemplation so that he might grow to understand. He will show men the path to their inner beings. He shall show men to care for their World and all that which lives upon and shares the Earth with man.

Great statues shall be raised up to him, which he would tear down in life, and he shall be worshipped and this shall cause him to become devoid of his purpose.

He shall be a modest man as will all the High Lords Of The Veil. And so shall his coming be marked for all men to know and to follow. But they will raise statues and idols to him in his image, and they shall be made of wood and of stone, and men will in their ignorance worship them as givers of life, and thus defeat him in his purpose.

They shall raise up priests in his name, and in their madness and they shall make men fear them and him, though the statues and the idols and the priests will be devoid of substance except in their own eyes. And man shall show no reason.

A man shall be born of the Veil but he shall not be a High Lord of the Seven. He shall have a great impact within his land. And he shall say that he has come to prepare the Way for the coming of the Sixth High Lord, and shall declare him to be the greatest of all the High Lords. For he is the Sixth, and his task and his trials shall be great, and he will be great indeed.

And the Signs of the coming of the High Lord Of The Veil shall be seen in the skies and calculated upon their time.

He shall show great vision and little sense, and he shall give of his best, as he shall be a good man. But he shall show jealousy and jealousy will be the end of him, and it will cause his murder.

And it shall come to pass that the Sign of the bearer of the caul shall be seen to grow. But this time men will know of the greatness of this Sign and of its meaning. They shall see his Sign and they shall come from distant places to witness his coming.

They will be learned men in these matters, and because of this their King will send them so that he will know when the child shall be born so that he may kill him.

In his life he will be hailed as a great king, which he will be, and he will be scorned to keep him from this rightful position. And his life shall have great meaning.

And as the end of man draws near each High Lord will be revered more than the last, as it is the way of the things, that men shall learn and follow at all costs. As the end of men upon the Earth, and the end of his life is his final cost and thus cannot be measured in material things, as in which manner man measures all things.

And the death of the Sixth comer shall be at the hands and of the minds of the beasts that call themselves men. And as his hour closes he shall repeat this

Prophecy, as will all the High Lords, and it shall thus be passed on one from another in a great sleep so that it shall not be forgot.

And he shall repeat it to another who shall die, and one who will not die. And the one who shall live will make the Prophecy live until the coming of the Seventh Veil, the Seventh Sign. And he, the Seventh High Lord shall break it with his Seal and spread it for all mankind to look upon, so that they might not die, and the Earth might not die.

And men of that time will not want it to be known that they are not great, and will not have his shadow cast over them.

And he shall say that one will follow, and bear his mark between the navel and the groin.

And the mark shall be recognised, as it shall be the mark of his last agony at the end of his ministry. The mark of the final insult. And it shall be set upon him, as he is believed dead, and to make it look so. And men will believe it so.

But he shall live on, in his seed and in the hearts of all just men who shall protect his word.

Men that shall be as beasts shall gain power over all the Earth by the use of his name, and shall choose to ignore the final utterances of his Prophecy, as they shall believe that cunning and murder shall save them from the loss of their power.

And they shall try to destroy that Prophecy though they know it to be true, and because they know it to be true. And they shall say that they know it not. Yet shall they strive to destroy it for two thousand years, and make false claims against it, so that they may possess it and the power that they shall desire of it. Their dishonesty and their evil shall be so great that they will believe even that which they know to be untrue.

Such shall be the folly of man in his final hour. Even though they know that they die and that the Earth beneath their feet dies, still they shall gain no reason.

Near to the ending of days, there shall rise up great priests and great kings in the name of the Sixth claiming dominion over all things and all men. And king shall turn against king, even against their own blood. And murder shall be done in the shadow of his name.

44

And Queens shall be as harlots, and use their baseness in their greed for power and for dominion over the Earth.

And a great priest who shall hide knowledge from men, and in its stead shall he teach men to believe even in that which is madness and cannot be. This same priest shall painful kill all those who will not believe his evil.

And he shall create an army of priests skilled in tortures and in debasement, and he shall send such men that are less than beasts, to kill and to do murder in the name of he who will be crucified. And thus shall spit upon the name and upon the honour of the Sixth. And he shall do him that which is evil and unjust, and even offer his place to a warmonger (Hitler) in his lust for power.

People will cry in pain and they shall submit, but many will not submit.

Wars will be fought, and those who are misguided will believe that they do well by the Sixth. For they shall believe and know not what they do, for devious ways shall be used upon them which have been learned by the priests from the crucified one in his goodness, and twisted by them to do evil. And so shall they use the twisting of words in the minds of men.

And men will discover new lands and be in awe of them. But again they will destroy as the beasts without thought and without reason, and shall lay to waste. And they will take that which is below the Earth which they will use to dubious purpose. It shall be used to destroy that which is above the Earth and that which is below the Earth. As man will only know how to serve his greed in that time, and in his haste he shall destroy that which is meant to be an awakening in the discovery of other worlds.

And in that discovery men will lay waste all they do not understand, they shall rape and murder. Countless will be slaughtered and all will be laid waste. And cruelty, even to his own kind will be his shameful mark. And it shall be done in the name of a false god, and in the name of the Sixth to come. And such shall be the evil of that great priest and his followers.

Men shall live in belief alone, and reason will be dead as if it were not born, beneath the weight of belief, in that which has no reason, and cannot be sustained under reasons light.

But they shall claim dominion over all, down to the smallest thing, as though the followers of false belief alone, and only they, have any purpose, and all else shall be considered unworthy of existence in that time.

And so shall the Earth be laid to waste. Her goodness will not be harvested in sustaining manner.

This will be man's greatest time, but he will see it not and his greatest moment will pass him by and be lost to him. And he shall show no reason.

Then will come a time when men can no longer be made to believe, and this time will be the time of the final comer. And he shall bid men reason. Some will listen to him but their belief will still render them deaf to his words and blind to his Sign.

And so shall he be put to his test, and he will go in despair to a high mountain. And often shall he despair of man to ten times in all. And he will turn away from men. The tenth time that he despairs shall be the last, and should he stay turned, man will perish to the last man and woman, and to the last child.

He shall ask of you, "Follow me", three times only. And if the answer still not be "Yes", then he shall write your name in The Book Of The Damned and shall ask you no more.

And should you come to him later when you see the way of things and are afraid, then he shall not suffer you to come unto him, and will turn from you, for you be lost.

And it shall be forbidden for him to speak to any man for the fourth time.

And his number shall be ten.

He shall be commanded to show men reason for the last time. And many will perish of abuses, and of disease, and of stupidity, and of greed. And greed knows not reason.

And his number shall be ten, as he shall be the first and the last to come during the final throes of mans existence.

He will come among men to give unto them their last chance, and to show him the Way and to teach him so that he may not die. He will ask little of man, as man will have taught him to beware of man. And he shall know well of the beast and of the base nature of the beast. And it will be strong in his time.

It will be a time of false greatness, of greed and of abomination upon the Earth.

Men will show only the nature of the beast, and no humanity or reason which is meant to be the mark of men.

Man will oppress in that time in his pursuit of gain without consideration. The Seventh will be born in the first half of a century whose number will be ten. All there is of him will be ten as shall be told unto you. His birth will be noted twice, and he shall be the last to explain the Way. And death will be the reward of those who take no note of him, or of his sayings. Their ignorance will not save them from the wrath to come. Their blood shall no longer enjoy the fruits of life, or of the Earth, or of that which is beyond the Earth.

The final Sign shall be obvious to even the most stupid of men, that the time is over for him, and for his stupidity.

The very Earth shall rage. Even the skies shall show strange lights and colours. There will be torrents of rain and great floods, and fires will light up the World.

Starvation will be rife and crops will fail.

The World will erupt with many wars and terrors brought about by the baseness of the beast.

It will be that man shall couple with man, and woman with woman in their abomination.

And that which is an abomination, and those who commit abomination will be honoured in that time by those who know better, and choose the path of gain against the path of that which is right.

At this time those who sing songs will be rewarded above the rewards of kings and honoured above their proportion.

And a woman shall rise up among the rulers of a fallen nation, and in her wickedness she will befriend such abominations and help bring them to greatness, by her patronage. She shall know of what she does, and even though she be great in her own eyes and in the eyes of men she shall know no peace. And so shall she die, in darkness as she has lived. Let this be another Sign unto you.

At this time the Seventh shall gather unto himself those who will be chosen, that they will enjoy everlasting life. And it shall be bought at a high price, for the beast will try to take that which is yours from you in that time.

He will show you the Way, and you will rule your domain as he instructs you to do. So you will be saved.

All others shall die, and no sign of them will be seen upon the Earth, except that which will warn of the folly of base ways. And you that will be saved will mend the Earth and it will be good.

The end of man will be the result of his own greed and depravity, and he will cause disease that will kill him. He will lay waste the World, and still expect that the Mother will succour him. Such will be his conceit.

He will follow false doctrine even though he know it to be false.

He shall worship false gods, killing men in support of them. And his killing will be in the justification of the wrong the he knows that he commits.

He shall render the seas unfit for the fishes to live in, and it shall be poisoned by him and destroyed by him.

The rivers and the waters shall putrefy, and both man and beast will thirst for clean water. And its value shall be above all things.

This together with his unwillingness to follow reason, and instead follow that which is base, will be the end of his flourishing upon the Earth for two hundred and fifty years. And it shall come to pass.

And at this time of men's madness they will believe themselves as gods, and the most stupid of them will consider his opinion of great import to the way of things. Even though he knows of nothing, he shall be satisfied with his beliefs though they have no foundation. He shall forget that he is beast, and no longer follow his purpose.

At that time he will claim ownership over all things, even though his own body is not his and is but dust.

The mad will be believed blessed with knowledge, and men will even look as mad so that they can be seen as great among their fellows.

That which is ugly will be considered more beautiful than the flowers of spring, which will be seen flourishing on midwinter's day outside the window of the house of the Seventh Lord Of The Veil. Their flowering at such a time, shall be a Sign to that Lord, that the end of man is now about to begin, and he must now do as he is commanded to do, ( This appeared midwinter's day 1997 as predicted), and that man is too late for his salvation.

And now he shall know is the time for the gathering of the few, and of their beasts, and seeds, and of the time of seeking clean waters. This is the sign for men to turn away from their path.

And at the final reckoning many will come to advantage themselves of the efforts of the few, and will have nought to give except excuse, and will expect to receive from you as you are goodly men. But in their hearts they will carry their false belief which will confound reason, and within their bodies disease.

At this time will also be witnessed in the South East from this Lord's house, two stars and they will appear to mount one upon another, as men will mount one upon another, and so the judgement begins.

And that Lord will prepare, and many hands will be against him and many will not help but shall wait so they can profit best from waiting, and shall do nothing. Cursed be they above all.

Even those who profess loyalty shall deny him to others to save face, and in fear of their own beliefs. And they will show no reason.

Some shall be turned by their spouses, and by their parents, and one shall be divided from another.

But the greatness of his purpose shall be great and he shall triumph. Even in death he shall triumph.

Beware you who turn against his purpose, even by doing no thing shall you be cursed. Even unto death.
Beware those who show no reason, and those who profess to show reason. Good intent will not save, nor will ignorance excuse. And it shall be so.
And it is written in the minds of the Seven that they the Seven Signs of man, and the Seven Seals of prophesy, and the Seven spirits of man. Each representing in his own time the salvation of his kind.

And unto the Seventh shall be charged the care of his kind in his time.

And at the ending of days when man has learned not reason, the last to come is charged to offer again to men the knowledge of reason, so that the ending of days shall not come about.

One shall come after the Prince of all the Kings of the Earth, who shall be the Sixth Sign and the Seventh shall come after him, and his number shall be ten.

And he shall be the last sign of the forgiveness of man, and man shall no longer be forgiven for his vileness.

And the Seventh that shall come after him shall be King in his own right, and his blood shall be King after him over the salvation of man.

To all those who follow him in his word, and he shall wash away their foolishness, and cast out the abominations. He shall heal the sick in his own blood as a sign to all. And behold he shall raise smoke from clear water and the water will show blood at this time, and he shall not die from it.

And the kindred spirit of the beast that is man shall cry tears of joy at the mention of his name for as long as man lives. And his number shall be ten. For he will be the first and the last to come after the Sixth Sign. He shall be the Alpha and the Omega, the new beginning and the end to all evil that has past. He shall be the beginning of that which is to come, and the avoidance of the end of days of man.

And I the prophesier whose name will be lost, by my prophesy shall I be with you to the end of days.

And he whose number will be ten, the Seventh of the Signs will give you of his spirit, and you will hear the wisdom of his voice before that day. So prepare ye, for he shall be the first and the last. And you will see what he says written down, and what he says will be born of the wisdom of all the Seven Signs.

And he shall light Seven lights and set them before you, and seven great plumes of smoke shall rise from the Earth in that time, as great forests shall burn, which men will not quench; as only the rains of the heavens can cool such fires.

The seven plumes will be the Sign of the beginning of his reign of reason. He shall be dressed in black, and on his head shall be the white hairs of his years. His voice will be pleasant and bring peace to those who are troubled. In his right hand will be written Signs, and these Signs will be the Signs used in prophesy, and in the seeing into the future. And they will first be seen by he who has come after me as he hangs sorely wounded. And he shall see the signs written in his own blood and in his agony shall be blessed with the knowledge that he has wished for, that he shall have given his right eye for.

And he shall know of the meanings of such signs in nine days of agony and shall be hailed as a God, and honoured even until the time of the coming of the Seventh Sign. And his Signs shall be written and men will use them to prophesy in that time.

And he who is the Seventh and the last shall lay hands upon you saying, "Have no fear, I am the first and the last. I am he that lives though I was dead for a short time." And it will be so. (Heart attacks)

And he shall hold in his mind and in his being the key to the salvation of men. And he shall be charged to tell of the things of which you have seen in writing so all men shall know of the coming, and of the things which are real, and of the things that will be hereafter. And the mystery of the Seven Signs which men know of, and the mystery of the Seven Signs in his hands, written there only by the power of the worlds in that wonder.

And of the seven plumes of smoke that have risen into the heavens all over the Earth, shall he tell unto you of the wrath of the power of the Earth against the beast that is man. For man knows no reason, and shows unto the Earth and to his fellow man no reason but that of the beast, without the goodness of a man that is above the mind of the beast. And it shall be so.

Seven will come unto you, and each will try to show you the Way. But six will fail through the fault of the beast that is man, who will not show reason to his brothers or even to that which his life depends upon. Such is the evil and the stupidity of man, and knows no bounds.

The Sixth will be of great importance to men so far as he shall be sorely abused, as shall all those who come for man's sake. And their very sayings will be altered to suit the purpose of the few, and so shall man be damned in the eyes of the power of the universe and that beyond the universe.

The Seventh Sign will be the most important of all the Signs as he shall be the last, and many men will not want to follow him for they shall believe him not as they look only upon the outward signs of him in their baseness. And if he is not followed in his word then men shall die and be no more. For he shall be the last chance that will come unto man, and man shall deserve not that, as he will abuse even that which will save him. Even the righteous ones will cling to false Gods, knowing their falseness yet still cling to them for salvation. Such will be the follies of men.

And the Sixth shall prophesy from the prophecies of those who have gone before him, and he shall prophesy the coming of he who shall come after him. And it shall be hid from the eyes of men till his coming and his making is complete at the ending of days.

Listen carefully to the Sixth, and if you hear him not then listen to the Seventh, and if you hear him not then the almighty power of the World will not hear you in your agony. And you shall see proof of it.

And I know that most of you will still close your minds and your hearts, and still not hear. And lay waste the life of the last High Lord Of The veil, even unto you who shall hate him for what you believe he is, and not for what you shall know in your hearts that he is.

Many of you will show him no reason. I know this and he shall know this, and all the High Lords each in his own time will know this and suffer at the hands of you who they are come to save from damnation. Cursed shall you be, for you shall know better yet still do this evil unto them, so that they shall look lowly before thine eyes, and the eyes of all men. And this shall make you feel great, and exalted above them, for you are only the lowliest of beasts, and thus take your importance and your pleasure by the destruction of that which is above you.

I am the first of the Seven, and even my name shall be lost as I am of little importance in this matter, and of little point to the Seven, and unto what is to come. But not my words, as they are of import, and they shall be carried in the minds of goodly men even until the ending of man's days. And my words shall be heard as an echo among high mountains, and the six who shall come after me will know of me and know of me, and my purpose shall be complete.

**Ending of the Prophecy of the First to come.**

*And Jesus said.........*

These words have been given to me as I have wandered in the wilderness for many years, so that I may learn the wisdom of the Nazarene's, the Brotherhood Of Light.

Words that have been spoken one to another for many thousand years, and passed down to me, and to you, and to he who comes after me. And to those who come before me in The Brotherhood, so that I might know my purpose and the purpose of men upon the Earth, and so that I might know the minds of men.

And I shall pass on the prophecy and I shall prophesy unto you so you might hear me, and he who comes after me.

And I, Joshua Ben Miriam, who is known and will be known, as Jesus Christ the anointed one, sayeth unto Peter and unto John, in the deepness of their sleep that I have brought upon them. "Write these words that I speak into your minds, before the eyes of man where he will not be able to see them, and will be hidden from man lest he shall make abuse of them in his final time of testing. Give to him that comes after me, whose number will be ten, the six keys and six Seals as I have instructed thee."

Only he that comes after me shall possess the Seventh key and the Seventh Seal for he shall be the Seventh Sign to come among you. He whose number according to that Prophecy and my Prophecy will be ten.

And he shall bear the mark of my last agony in his right side, and his Sign will be seen in the sky as was mine and that of Moses, and of those who have gone before me in this purpose. For he shall be wise and be ready close to the end of days, for he shall be the Seventh Sign and the last to come before men.

And unto he who is the Seventh Sign these things shall be commanded of him. At the opening of his Seal, Seven crosses shall there be in his hands to remind him if his duty to man, and to remind him of his obligation to me, and to those who have suffered and gone before at the hands of men.

And he shall be schooled in the meaning of the seven obligations.

And I know of the labour and the work that he must commit to his purpose, and of the patience he must possess to bear the pain and the shame that man will pour upon his head. For he will cause threat to those who say that they are my apostles and faithful followers of my word, and are not. And he will make men know that they be liars, and they will question all that he says and twist what he says and make little of him.

And he will be told that he must not weaken in his purpose ten times. Even those who have fallen and repented will attack him in their fear, and shall bear false witness against him even to his own blood.

He shall be seen to abandon his first love. And all he has held dear shall he abandon six times. And he shall sicken, and he shall sacrifice all he holds dear in his service unto man.

And all of you who shall heed him and follow in his purpose, must first change your way and put aside all malice and evil thought. For you to do less is to snuff out the light of all the seven lights, liken unto blowing out the candles of their purpose.

Let all you who have ears listen, and all you who have mouths spread his word as it is spoken unto you. For all you who visit upon him will be saved in the paradise he will found for the chosen, to build and keep as he instructs forever, and the end of their days shall never come upon the Earth or beyond the Earth.

These things must be done by all men of all races and differences, as their differences must be put aside as they are without meaning, on the word of the first and the last to come after me. Man must make sacrifice in order to gain Paradise.

And be you prepared to suffer slight from those who will bear false witness against you in the protection of their stations. These evil ones will find you guilty as they will find him, but the judgements will be false and the pain of them none the less for their falseness.

And the hypocrites will mock and scourge you and make you all to look like fools. They will defame you and he who comes in order to make men look away from him and those who follow him, lest they be shown in their own light to be false and unworthy of their position.

He who has an ear listen unto him and overcome, lest the end of days shall come again to you for the last time and you are lost. Listen unto his words, as his tongue will be as if it has two edges, and men will make play of his every word and yet hear him not. For they will show no reason. But his tongue will speak words that are sharper than the sharpest sword to the minds of those who are of good will.

I know the workings of your minds. Beware you of evil intent, you will not prevail over him of this. I promise and do swear. Beware how you be.

I know the beasts that you are and you will reap the harvest of your wickedness, even though you will say that your evil be done in my name. And only he will keep good faith with me. And should he be slain among you, you will all perish. Harm not this lamb, as he is the last to come, and you will stand condemned by your own actions and there will be no forgiveness.

I have many things against you and upon the attempt of men to slay me. I will forgive you of them, though I know that you will not repent nor will you change your evil ways, and I will live beyond that slaying.

And because you learn not, this I will hold against you. For you will make idols of those who abominate the meanings of life in their fornications. And those who honour them near the end of days though they be kings and rulers of men shall be destroyed, and all their blood shall be destroyed from the face of the Earth, and their very names shall be cursed. For man shall not lie with man nor shall woman lie with woman, but near the end of days men shall be less than the beasts of the field, and they shall spread disease in their perversion, and you will surely die.

Turn your backs upon such as they, no matter how exalted they be, or the end of days will be quickened. He who comes after me shall fight them with his mouth and they will hate him for he speaks the truth and they shall know it. Listen all you who will be saved, hear him with your hearts and minds, for he shall feed your needs.

At the ending of days many shall come unto him but few will he take unto himself. He will shine among you for a million generations and more. Like a white stone in the darkness of night. And in his heart shall be written that which no man knoweth save he who comes after me. Who shall receive it from me, and from the brotherhood, who shall survive in secret because of the sacrifice of those who keep faith with me, and with those who have gone before me.

Spread you this word throughout the Earth and beyond the Earth, so that the very air shall carry it to all mankind in every tongue. I know the workings of your minds. I know of your charity and your lack of it. I know of your good faith and of your lack of it. I know of your patience and your fear.

Be assured the last will be more than the first, for man will see the coming of the end of his days and his fear shall make cause for him to reason, though many will not till the time is gone for his salvation. I shall hold it against you that you will follow false prophets who seduce you to follow wrongful ways. To fornicate one with another and not know of each other. To take into yourselves things which will confuse your minds and abominate your bodies. And I curse all those who encourage you in these evil ways.

Cursed shall be all publicans, as they shall know what they do. Double shall I curse such men who also claim my name, and seek my assistance in their purpose.

I have given you time by my coming to change your ways, but you will not till death breathes upon you. And you will listen to false priests who will tell you to repent and all will be forgiven, but they lie and it will not be so. And I curse them above all for they know more.

You will all be killed unto death for your evil ways. For I am he who searches your hearts, and he who cometh will search your minds. And unto each will be given that which is earned.

And those who follow he who shall come in good faith, even those who have known the depths of their own natures and answered the will of the beast, I shall consider you cleansed and place no other burden upon you, so long as you hold yourself in the goodness of that faith and follow in the light of his wisdom which is delivered upon him for all time.

And to he who shall overcome, shall be given the power over the nations of the Earth and beyond the Earth. And man will rule himself with a rod of iron for his own sake, for he must not wander from the path of life for beyond it lies only death. And he shall wear the star as his symbol, and a circle so that he shall be reminded of his burdens.

He that has ears listen unto me for thine own sake, and for the sake of your children to come.

And I ask of he that is to follow after me, to look unto he who sits among the seven hills. For he shall know that you are the Seventh Sign, and the Seventh spirit of the Way of man. And command him to cease. For I know his works, and I know that he will have a name for which he lives, though he be as if dead. For there shall be blood upon his hands.

Be thou watchful of him, and bid him again cease, for I take offence at that which he carries out for his own glory sake. And he shall ask of you proof. Give none unto him. For he seeks only clever argument by which he shall hope to overcome you and overcome me in his wickedness. For he is the king only of cunning and of hypocrisy.

Be mindful that you have been told of my word, which I command of Peter and of John, that whichever of them shall live shall hide these things before the altars of men, before their eyes where they cannot see it. As I instruct them so I instruct thee, to hold fast.

Tell he that sits among the seven hills that he knows not when death shall come upon him, as he shall be damned by his own utterances. And I twice damn him for the evil that he says and does as he shall know better of it, as he and those of his kind who have gone before have always done.

After I shall go into Jerusalem to lay claim unto my kingdom, I shall be betrayed. And my betrayer shall know of the consequences of that which he does but will not accept that they be so, and will hang himself out of his fear when he shall know of the truth of it.

No man shall live who shall offend against a "Caulbearer". And he who shall offend against a "High Caulbearer" shall he be damned to the last of his blood.

And those who shall sit among the seven hills shall raise themselves up a false prophet, and claim him Messiah in my stead, as he will be a man of war and much feared.

They who sit among the seven hills will deny me. And later they will draw me in lots, for power over the kingdom that is mine and yours, so be watchful as that which they have done unto me shall they attempt unto you.

Their mark until your time shall be a mark of lies and evil that is even beyond the bounds of all beasts. And power at all price, their only goal. They shall proclaim goodness as they do the utmost evil and all that they are, is, and for ever shall be evil. Cursed be they for they will do much in my name and know what they do.

I shall defeat the design of those who would destroy me and I shall live in a far land that has been designed to my ending, and know peace there and knowledge. And I shall be beyond the eyes of those who hate me and would kill me.

Oh Lamb, I pity thee, for thy road is long and full of sorrows, for they will also try to kill thee from thy purpose.

Cursed are all that shall sit among the seven hills, as their evil knows no bounds. They have no honour nor have they any kindness in their beings. They shall create many trees of shame for men, behind which they will hide their own shame so that men will not see it. He who sits among the seven hills, and others of his design through the World shall know no shame as they shall only know of their power over the World and care not of else.

In the time of you the last to come one such shall rise by even the foulest of means. He shall plot with others who profess his righteousness and do murder. They shall kill a goodly man and steal from him even unto his name. And the murderer shall be named after him. Cursed be they. For they know the evil they do cannot be to good purpose, nor can such a thing be forgiven.

And he who will live after me and write my words, shall write it down so all men can know of it, and dare to accuse he who sits among the seven hills. For he and those who go before him be steeped in murder and in the blood of the innocent. Flames shall not cleanse, nor shall water purify.

He who shall come after me shall name some names of those that have not spoiled the purpose, nor spread their filth upon the air. These goodly ones shall obey his every word and advise him in matters, and be worthy of him and of me.

He that cometh shall clothe himself in black as he will be instructed as a boy. And his priests shall clothe in black, and show white in honour of the purity of the Seven Signs. And they will blot out the names of those who have ruled over the spirit of men for their own benefit, and for their own glory. All their names and the names of those who shall have given their lives in their cause shall have their names removed from the Book of Life.

He that hath an ear let him hear my words as I speak them, and listen to the words of the Sixth Sign, and of the words of those who have gone before me, and he who shall come after me for thine own sake.

And he that hath an ear, hear what shall be told unto you for as you hear the changing of ways, the coming of paradise is close at hand. And serve he that is true, as he shall hold the final key to open thine eyes. And henceforth let no man shutteth his fellow man into darkness, and let only he that comes after me, alone open your darkness for you.

Oh man, I know your ways, and before you is set an open door, and no man shall shut it except at his own peril. And for you who have kept my word, and have not strength, fear not, as he who comes after me shall be that strength and they shall not be denied their right.

And the word I give you shall be kept. And to he who shall come after me I say, that those who worship the beast and the ways of the beast, shall bend their knee to you and I shall make them honour you. And they and all man shall know that I shall love thee all the days of your life.

And I say unto him that comes after me, I know you and the workings of your mind, and I know that men will have caused you to fear by the time of the beginning of the ending of days has come upon you. As the beast only knows of fear, and does not understand love for he possess it not.

Because you will keep good faith with me through many trials, and times of great pain that you must suffer, my words will come quickly unto you and no man shall take from you your crown. For we of the Seven Signs are Kings above all Kings by the very right of our birth. And we that are the Seven Signs are the High Lords Of The Veil, and all who are born behind the veil are Lords Of The Veil.

And they whose coming is written in the stars shall come before you, to meet of your blessing upon them. For they shall be of your advisors and of your elders.
I shall keep you close to my spirit as the final temptation draws nigh, which shall come upon the World. Be strong and know of me, for I shall write upon thee my name which shall cometh down to you from the heavens.

And let he that has an ear, hear you who are the Seventh High Lord, in their darkness and come unto you. I know your works, your temperament be neither hot nor be it cold. Better for you if it be hot, as men will spew thee from their mouths.

Men shall say unto you that they be rich and have boundless goods and need for nothing, and have no need of what you say or of you. They shall know not that they be wretched, miserable, poor, and naked before thee and before me, and above all things, blind.

You who shall come after me shall council these wretches, and give unto them gold of the spirit that they may be rich of mind. Teach unto them wisdom, that they may clothe their minds with good things. Open up their eyes with deeds that will make them look upon you for their sake. *Be they zealous in their work.*

Stand you fearless at the door, and knock boldly. He who shall hear you shall open it unto you, and you will go into him, and he shall follow you to his salvation. Grant him to sit by your side and share the glory of the throne of the new beginning. Let him serve you and all mankind each to the best of his way, and gain reason as commanded.

And should you do this, a door will be opened to you, and pictures shall talk in your hands, and by these signs shall the Way be shown. And as your blood flows men shall be healed in my name. And you will lead the way to Paradise which you will teach men to foul not, as they have always done in their stupidity. Take those who will follow through this door and show them the things that must be thereafter.

And you will be viewed as a King upon a golden throne by some, and a charlatan by the many who shall believe all, and know of nothing.

Around your throne shall you place four and twenty seats, and upon these seats shall you sit four and twenty elders whose lives will they pledge unto you in your service. And should they be not of good faith unto you then kill them. For the purpose is great, and must be protected against all who will do ill.

And they who be with you shall wear of the circle and the star as a reminder unto them of their burdens, and of the weight of their commitment to you and to me. Even the symbol that I say unto you shall be cast as evil by he who sits among the seven hills, so that men will turn from you and from that which I was and am, and hear you not.

You will instruct all men who will follow you in good faith, in the ways of the beast. And they in their turn will instruct after you have gone from them. Others there shall be who will instruct in the ways of the beast and its four natures.

Seven golden lamps of fire shall burn about the throne, and the priests will come naked before you both of men and of women, as children before a loving father, as they were born asking nothing for themselves and hiding nothing from thy sight.

And the priests will teach to all that which is gone and must never be forgotten, as it will be a lesson and a guide for the betterment of the future. They will teach of that which is to come and men must not take their eyes off it. They will teach of that which is, so that the future may be adjusted and all may be in harmony both with that which is above the Earth, that which is below the Earth and that which is upon the Earth, so that it will be good.

And the twenty and four priests will sit beside the and honour thee. They shall give glory unto thee. For they shall have created for them Paradise and have charged them to keep faithful unto their purpose.

And I shall command of you to write in a book. And the first Seal will be given unto you in your youth. You will be sent into a deep sleep, and you will see visions, and in these visions will be given unto you the Seventh Seal, and you will understand it not for your protection, and none other will understand it.

And as age comes upon you, you will be exalted to high position, which will also be at the ending of days. And it shall be proclaimed with loud voices that you are the one worthy to write.

And twelve followers of high position and born behind the veil will each give you six more keys, and you shall unlock my sayings and write them for all men. You shall speak them to all who have ears to listen, but you alone shall look upon these things and no other will know the Seven Seals.

And I shall weep for thee. For all men will be against the, even numbers of those that were born behind the veil and should be your strength. For you have been dead, and be risen from that state and know it well. Fear not they will change of their thoughts of you and change of their fear of you, and they will come unto you and be your support in matters.

But should you despair and go to live upon a high mountain and turn your back upon man in despair, you will see signs. And about that time you will be exalted to high position. You will be worthy of the Seven Seals and the knowledge they shall bring unto you.

And any man who shall raise hand or voice against he who is born behind the veil will perish to the last drop of his blood upon the Earth. Even to his brother, his cousin, and the children thereof, and their children's children till they are no more upon the Earth. Such shall be your protection against wrong-doers.

Fear not as thousands of elders and priests who are beasts without reason, yea tens of thousands gather about you to bring about your destruction. Say unto them, "Worthy is this Lamb who you would slay." For with the wisdom of the Seven Seals shall you overcome and you will be strong and covered in glory, and the beast will hate you, for you will answer his question and his taunts with silence.

Be of mind that every creature that is upon the Earth, in the waters and the air, and that which is above the Earth shall they depend upon you as they depend upon the Seven Signs and the Seven Seals that you possess. And the almighty force that created you from the Earth shall be strong within you, and shall strike down your enemies though they try to kill or destroy you. Face you their noise with silence.

And upon the opening of the Seals the beasts will gather round you, as they will want to see that which is therein. And kings will wish to gain the Seals to use for the damnation of their own kind, for they are but beasts and know no reason.

And the first Seal, will tell of wars that will come in your time, and the second will tell of a king of a great land who has the power to give peace to the nations and pretendeth to do so, but instead causes war for the honour of his position. And the third Seal will deal with the balance of things, and you will know of that balance and its meaning to men. And the fourth Seal will tell of disease, of starvation and of death, which need not be. But the beasts rule. It shall also advise of the new beginning, as one must know darkness to know light. And the fifth Seal shall warn of your own burdens, of which you will preach only Seven as no other will know of the rest as they will not be of mind. And men shall cry unto you asking, "Why me, I have done nothing", and you will answer "That is your crime. You have done nothing and nothing therefore shall you deserve".

Before one year, as the closing of the time of the opening of the Sixth Seal draws close unto you, there shall be as a sign, seven plumes of smoke rising to the skies from the Earth. Floods and great winds, even great earthquakes will there be, and death of men in their thousands. So you be sure of the Sixth Seal. Let these be a sign unto you so that you will not weaken in your task. There shall be mighty winds and disease as you open the Sixth Seal, and few will listen, saying all is well the wind has blown not about my house.

Stars shall be seen to the south west of the house in which you dwell, before one year to the beginning of your task. And above a tree shall appear two stars, and they will look as if to mount one on the other, as man shall mount man and woman shall mount woman in their perversion. This will be shown unto you for six nights. And the flowers of spring as they will be named, in that place of the house where you shall abide, will bloom on midwinter's day before the window of you who will come after me, so you may be sure that you are the chosen one. As your doubt will be strong, and you will despair ten times.

And the things that I prophesy unto you shall come about. And you shall lead your people to a desolate place and make the Earth fertile, and you shall have clean waters as they will be short in that time as all will be poison. And you shall have strong beasts of all manner.

You shall build houses of stone so that they will stand for generations and waste not your labour, and all that you have shall be made in such fashion. And waste not labour for your lives will be precious unto you. And you shall have dogs of war set about your perimeters, and all your followers shall abide within the protection of his brethren.

And the rich men will hide themselves to avoid the disease, and the death and the hunger, and these things will come unto them.

And these things will not be visited upon the goodly men who have followed your word, and built themselves barns, and dug wells.

And those who do not follow in the Way shall come unto you saying, "Give unto us that which you have, if you be good men and let us not die." But give them not, as they will cause your destruction, as they are only beasts, and less than beasts, and know no reason.

And the twenty four elders and their followers shall fall down and worship you and the goodness of your word, for their blood shall live forever and forever because of you. And you will bid them give only thanks for their deliverance.

And the rich men and the kings shall say unto the mountains, "Hide us from the wrath of the Lamb who was born in his place at the time of the birthing of lambs. And was marked after he that has gone before and was ill used."

In my time and your time even my words will be ill used, and the dread of what will come after my end is more to me than that of the dread of my end. As men shall twist all of me to his own ends, and spit upon my name in the doing of it for their own sake, and their prides sake, and for their powers sake.

And should they kill you and twist you because you will follow this lamb they shall surely die, and their children shall die and they shall be no more upon the Earth, or above the Earth or of the Earth. For even the Earth will cast them out from it.

And they shall fear the Lamb, as he shall be as a great eye watching them, and knowing of their evil.

And should you turn away from the Lamb, the end of days will come upon the Earth and man shall no longer exist. And the World shall belong to the lowly things of the Earth and it shall be as if man did not live. Everything that is of man and everything that was of man and everything that will be of man shall disappear. As it shall be that man did not live upon the Earth, and all sign of him shall be gone from the face of the Earth and from below the Earth and from above the Earth.

And the almighty force of the Earth shall turn away from his memory, and the four forces of the Earth that are at the four corners of the Earth shall come over the Earth and over the seas. The winds will blow strong across the seas and across the lands, and the fires will burn up the lands. The very Earth shall shake in its anger and it shall split, and the very air that you breathe to give you life will turn, fouled by your own filth. And disease shall come upon men so that they will perish. And lightening shall plough furrows in the cities of man.

But if men should show reason, they that shout reason and turn away from false gods and follow the words of he who is sent after me shall live on in his word, for ever and ever. And there will be no end of him that follows the Lamb, and the almighty power shall smile upon you, and it will be good.

And the seven nations that will be created under his word, shall be each of the Seven Seals that he shall be. And of those Seals that have gone before him and abused by men there shall be, one nation for each Seal. And all the nations under the Seventh Seal and under his blood for ever and ever, so that man will not stray away from the path and shall always know reason and give honour to the bearers of the Seals.

And of that purpose, and to those who have kept faith with me in the protection of my words and his words, and of the Seals that are the Seven Signs, for which men shall wait for two thousand years.

And his number shall be ten and he will bear the mark of my last agony in his right side, in his groin, and it shall be half way between the groin and the navel, and it will be a mark that many will try to fake. But it will be laid down before his birth and cannot be faked, for it shall be a mark of birth. And he shall bear the veil. His coming will be written in the stars as is the Way of all Lords Of The Veil.

He shall be lowly though my blood and my spirit shall be within him. For if he should be high born men may follow him only in their greed, but as an humble man they will follow him because he is great, and of a higher birth than wealth alone can raise unto.

And he shall be given the Seals at the beginning of the end of days. And they shall be given unto him by twelve Lords Of The Veil, the brotherhood of twelve and one, who are the Brotherhood Of Light and the enemies of darkness. The Nazarenes, who have kept the Seals safely through all the terrors of he who sits among the seven hills, and those of his like who follow the way of the beast.
Blessed be the Lords Of The Veil above all men. Their suffering shall be great and born in silence and loneliness for man's sake. Blessed be they in the name of the Seven Signs and the name of all men who shall live because of them. For all those who have sat among the seven hills, and their like in other lands in the pursuance of their false doctrine, shall burn and bring terror to all in the pursuit of their purpose.

And the Seals will be safe in the hands of those who will keep faith with me and with he who follows me.

And I see people crying in pain of disease caused by those who abominate and who are blind to all except greed. I see the sun scorch the Earth because of the blindness and ignorance of men. Cursed are they for they know what they do and care not. And those who plead ignorance, cursed be they, as men have minds and choose ignorance.

Men of all tongues will stand before he who will come after me, crying for salvation but should they come late and driven only by fear of death, I command him to turn his back upon them as they will destroy all that he shall build. For they will learn not, and know not reason, and shall carry in their hearts the false gods of their destruction.

Though they will protest not, such men will give false promise to you. And he who comes after me shall be blessed by me, and shall deserve honour and glory and power. And shall pass on his wisdom to his blood and it shall be protected by the Nazarenes, the brotherhood that carries my word, and the Seals of the Seven Signs and the Seven Lords.

And all who shall follow him shall thirst no more and shall hunger no more. Neither shall the sun burn them and kill them any more. As he who follows me shall show the Way. And this lamb shall feed you, and shall lead you along the way to paradise and shall dry your tears from you eyes.

And as he shall open the Seventh Seal there will be a silence till he shall decide. And if he shall decide that man is unworthy and close his Seal then prepare you to die. If he shall speak unto you, question him not, as he can not know all that there is. A man cannot know all things, but all men can know all things in their gathering together.

And men will play with him with words that have no foundation to make him look a liar or a cheat as they be. For all men know of their own minds better. And this they will do in the name of he who sits among the seven hills and claims mine attention and worship.

Some of them will say they know not what the Lamb says, to spread confusion among people, and shall deny him and all knowledge of him. But have no heed of them as they are cursed and will die for their evil. For they know well of him and of his purpose.

Each of the Seven Signs have stood before man, and man has ill used us and denied us all in his own purpose. They have gained the ears of men by falsehood and trickery, and because they know well of falsehood and trickery, they know how you use it well, and they know how to make other men appear to be as they themselves are.

Beware, lest you die with them at the end of days. Beware those who have not served you well, and speak of things that make no reason.

For he whose number is ten and comes after me, will ask of you to look so that you may see, and to listen so that you may hear, and to learn so that you may know. And thus be able to judge, to gain knowledge of all kinds for your betterment.

Those who will be against him are against you, seeking for your control and your homage, and they will seek to keep you ignorant as they have always done. Play you not into their hands. Like the children of Israel followed he who went before me out of bondage, follow you he that cometh after me out of the bondage that you know, and the certainty of the ending of days, and into Paradise and everlasting life.

At the end of days you shall see that one third of all that lives in the sea will die and the seas will yield poison. And even the ships upon the seas will be less that one tenth as they will have no goods to carry. The rivers will become poison and the wells will putrify with the filth of man. And men will wail and die.

And they that rule will little do except make excuse and try to advance themselves at your cost. Such is the nature of those who are of the beast.
And many men shall die of the waters, even the frogs that live therein will become twisted and without shape, and they will perish in the waters. And it shall come to pass.

And the sun shall scorch the Earth and shall kill men as it never did before, and it will make the Earth too warm for man and he shall perish.

And man shall spread disease and war and care not. And he shall tease the World. And the kings of the World of that time will make noise but do little, as they fear their position above the lives of men.

And great beasts of iron shall crawl upon the Earth, and man will slay man in my name. Cursed be he, for he uses me unjustly, as he kills only in his own name for his own ends.

And after great wars that will kill my people, at the will of he who sits among the seven hills and is not judged by men for his crime, there will be many wars even to the smallest of wars. Men will know madness at this time and kill for no reason except his own exaltation. Cursed shall he be for he cares not for his fellow man.

And men will walk gladly into that pit which has no bottom, that pit which is dug by the beast. And men will show their true nature and they will fight each other like dogs.

And he who comes after me shall command you of good faith, in the protection of those of you who are in good faith with him and with me, and those of you who have ears listen unto him. And those of you who be strong lend him your strength. Those of you who are wise lend him your wisdom and you will prevail against the beast that will roam the Earth to steal and kill, to rape and spread their destruction upon the Earth, till the Earth can no longer succour them. And they will believe themselves invincible.

And a bright light will come from out of the desert, and fall upon the waters and upon the land, and one third of the World will be destroyed and man can no longer live upon it.

And there shall come out of the smoke, and out of the dust crawling things that men did not know before, and they will cause men to die, and he will not have salves for them. And they shall have power over the Earth.

It is commanded of man that he should not harm the grass of the Earth, or the trees or the beasts or the wild things, or the fishes of the seas or the waters of the land, without good reason. And man shall be tormented for his wickedness for he has no reason and shall deny reason, and he shall die.

He shall destroy the waters and he shall drink of his own piss and he shall eat of his own shit and of his own abomination, and his own flesh. And the beast that he is shall seek power and find only death.

And he shall cry unto me and unto the Seventh, whom he has ignored except in his time of trouble. He shall cry for deliverance, and he who shall come after me shall be that deliverance. And many will cry unto him and unto me and I command he that is to come after me to choose but a few that they may keep good faith with him and with me.

He shall cast out the drunkard and his seed, for his weakness shall remain within his seed and of his seed, and such seed should not be known within the

Paradise to come. For it is as a weed in the garden and spreadeth bountiful. Cast them from you into the darkness and feed them not though your hearts be soft towards them

And men shall hear the sound of great chariots in the sky and hear the beatings of great wings, and shall see spears of wrath pour down. And he that comes after me shall take a care, he shall arm himself and you, and prepare to meet these things so that he and his, and my people shall be safe unto them.

And the chariots shall fall, and my people shall be overjoyed in their victory over them after the fifth month of that turmoil. But they will come again and again till the beast is too weak to seek his power over you. And you must kill the beast in his own lair, you must follow him and kill him and be you rid of him and his false gods and his evil forever.

Then shall Paradise be truly yours. Bought by your blood and by your labour at great cost, so that your seed shall know of that struggle, and value it and keep faith with me and with he that is to come after me, and with his blood, and with those who have gone before me.

And all those that have sat among the seven hills and their kind, shall be king no more. And you shall slay them and their priests, and put down all their idols and their graven image that are an abomination before mine eyes.

And there will be more woes among you, as the beast will still struggle within you to rule. And those who become as beasts shall be slain or shackled as slaves, and they shall not be allowed to spread their seed, as their seed is the seed of destruction among you. For my sake and for the sake of he who comes after me and for the sake of all those who shall live within the bounds of Paradise in my name and in his name for ever and for ever.

He who comes after me and his blood shall be as gardeners, and I command them to use the pruning knife with vigour, and keep that garden clean. And battles shall be many in this thing and in these times, for all men shall raise and seek cause to win glory unto themselves, and shall protest too loudly of their good intent. Hear them not for you know who they are.

For if the beasts that are as men shall not give up their false gods of gold, of silver, of iron and of wood or of precious stone, if they shall not repent and gain reason that will lift them above the beast that is within all men, then paradise will not come unto them. And I shall curse them, and all the Lords Of The Veil shall curse them, and the High Lords Of the Veil shall curse them, even if we appear to be dead and gone from them.

I see he who sits in my name, and in the name of the power of all that lives upon the Earth, among the seven hills surrounded by images and falsity and gold and ivory and precious stones. He shall repent not his wrongdoing, nor his sorcery, nor his murder, nor his fornication that he condemneth in other men.
I see he who sits in the east among the sand-hills and the fig trees. He that sitteth in the name of a High Lord Of The Veil, for he knows of the power and the meaning of the veil. Neither will he repent of his murders nor of his evil, nor of his falsities or his lies. And I see all others that sit in the name of us, and we curse them for their wickedness in our names. Cursed be they a thousand fold and their seed, and all those of their blood, till the Earth knows them and their kind no more.

And I see the Seventh come among you and he is sore afraid, for the wickedness of man is beyond his knowledge. And he too will attempt to be as they are, but he cannot for it is not in his soul. Men will teach him to fear them, as they know only of fear and of hate and their uses. And his number shall be ten, and he shall bear in his right side the mark of my last agony, and upon his face shall he bear the veil. And he shall be humble and not proud.

He shall be born among you in the time of great war, when my people shall suffer death at the design and command of he who sits among the seven hills. He shall thus try to kill the Seventh Sign as Herod did try to kill me from his sight.

And he who squats among the seven hills shall lay the blame at the feet of he who shall seek to rule the World in his madness. For he shall forget, in his greed for glory and for power, that I am of my people and of their blood. And he shall believe that the Seventh Sign is also of my people. He shall see his Sign grow and cause there to be thunder and fire upon that place.

So shall he plot with the war-monger, and give to him money and aid in return for the destruction of my people, and the killing of The High Lord Of The Veil. Such shall be the evil of him.

And he shall plot war and kill in his lust to be king over all men. Yet men will follow him, made blind by his power and by the chanting that he and his priests will teach, believing him to be good. For man at that time will believe many things and know no thing.

And the days of that time will teach men no thing for they are blinded in their belief, and their minds are clouded with clever chanting and praying to that false god. And their ears are deafened by the chanting and praying in clever words, so they cannot hear, except that which he who lives among the seven hill proclaims unto them, even though such falsehoods be so easily seen.

And he who comes after me shall plant his feet one upon the land, and one upon the seas, and he shall know of the both. And shall show unto you of his time, reason and knowledge, so that you may make good that which you have lost. And create you Paradise upon the Earth for your own sake, and for the sake of your seed which will live forever within that Paradise.

And his book shall be opened, and he shall teach you the ways that you will live from the land and from the sea. And he shall speak unto you in a loud voice and though he appears a lamb he shall have the heart of a lion. And the seven thunders, which are the voices of the Seven Signs shall be heard from his mouth.

And he shall hear my voice from the heavens, and the voices for the High Lords Of The Veil who have gone before him. He shall Seal up the Seven Seals so that men shall never know them, and he shall raise up his right hand unto us and shall say unto us, "Stay they wrath for I have found enough good men to fill the seven churches to ten thousand in each church," and they must all swear before his name that they will repent, and do no more wrong to the Earth, and to the heavens that have been laid in the charge of men. For only man can know reason and only they with reason can be called men.

And in the days of the Seventh High Lord Of The Veil, the mysteries of the power of the heavens and of the Earth shall be revealed unto them, as long as the seven churches keep faith with him. And if men shall take, and take them heed of the book from his hand as I command they shall do, and read it and know my words and obey my words, then that paradise shall be yours. If you say unto him, "Give me the book," and if you should find fault that is not fault with the book then be you damned, and I shall turn my face from you and from your seed.

And my sign to he that comes after me is, that when the time draws near for him to write of the book that which he knows, and that which will be told unto him, his belly will sour. For he has avoided his purpose many years, lest he offend his fellow man, and out of his modesty, for he sees himself only as other men. And because of this, that is wrong which he shall do, knowing that which he knows is laid unto him to do. At that time I will turn his belly sour and upon his breath shall there be sweetness, and he will be sickened till he follows his purpose. Even unto death shall he be sickened, for his purpose shall be great.

This purpose must be fulfilled, unless he finds not enough good men. And he will ask of me again to come before his people to help him, but I will not, nor will those who have gone before. Not Moses, nor he with one eye who has prophesied his mark and his coming, neither shall we come unto you for his sake. For it is a task laid down for him to do and none other. For he is the first and the last to come after me and it is fitting that he alone shall complete his purpose.

But I shall rest my hand upon his shoulder, and the other five High Lords will lay their hands upon him, and the ravens of the second Seal, and the wolf of the second Seal shall watch over him and give him strength. For his task is the greatest of all our tasks as he is the Last to come unto men, and there shall be no more. And should he fail it will be the end of man.

I bid you to protect him and aid him, and his blood for thine own redemption.

Knowledge shall be within him that he will use to measure the worthiness of men. And he shall shun the courts of men that give no justice but give only according to the laws of men made for their own connivance. And I shall give power unto him that comes after me.

And from the closing of the seven bodies of the heavens, till the pestilence shall come upon man in fury, shall pass therein between forty-two months and forty-four months.
(There is a lining up of seven major planets an the 6th May 2006, three years and six months to eight months = between November 2009 and January 2010).

The destruction will last for six years and seven months, to six years and eight months. And the rains shall fall in torrents to show the wrath of the power of the Earth. And the gales shall carry the seas over the lands, and the crops will fail and man will starve and the greedy ones will have nought but gold to fill their bellies.

And he who cometh after me shall be witness, and his sons will be witness, and all the members of the seven churches shall bow down and honour them for they only will be fed. And the greedy ones will try to exchange for gold, and the Lord Of The Veil shall turn them away, knowing that they will next return as thieves and murderers to plunder from the seven churches. And the seven churches shall give not unto them for the Lord will have bade them join him, and they will not as they are comfortable in their lot and give no thought to the morrow.

And the seven churches shall arm themselves and do war with them, and they will not prevail over the seven churches. And when the dusts have cleared and the stench of death has risen from the Earth, the Lord will give you instructions for his last time. And he will instruct his sons so that such shall never happen on the face of the Earth again.

And his heart will weaken from all his troubles, and he shall die and join me, and the Seven will be then complete. The circle of the Lords Of The Veil shall be complete and man shall henceforth stand alone, and shall no more of the forgiveness of man be shown upon the Earth.

The circle will now have its place about the star, and so shall it be.

And the Seventh Lord and his followers shall be remembered, and their message to you will be remembered, and the mystery of God shall be known unto you. For he who comes after me shall tell it to you. And you will suffer none to live that oppose him or his word. And you will suffer none to live against his word even if they be beloved of you, they must perish.

And the Earth will be smitten with plague in these dark days, and the rivers shall run with blood should you not listen unto the Seventh Sign.

The beast that is within your bosom will rise inside you and wars will grow many upon the face of the Earth. The dead will strew the streets of the cities, and the cities will burn, and there will be none to bury the dead. And as men hunger they will eat of the bodies of the dead, as all sign of the reason that marketh man shall disappear.

And if you should kill or harm he that comes after me or stand by and protect him not, even the maddest of you cannot dream the horrors that I will send upon you, and you will be cursed by me seven times till you cry for death. This is my word unto you.

Those who follow The High Lord Of The Veil and join the seven churches shall rejoice and be merry, as they will know that they will be truly saved for ever and for ever. And they shall make gatherings of joy, as the false prophets that dwelt among them shall be dead and no more.

And he that sitteth among the seven hills and claims my favour shall be dead, and all that he was shall be torn down, and his shame shall no longer trouble me.

And during the times of great wars, men shall be bidden to go into the heavens so they may see their enemies, and they will bring earthquake upon the Earth. And he who is the Seventh Sign shall call his twenty-four advisors before him, and they will make plans to conquer those who would kill them and kill you. And your enemies will fear him and flee, and he will command you follow and kill them all to the last of their blood.

And voices will call from the air and from the heavens, that at last the kingdom of the World is the High Lord's, and shall be ruled by him and by his blood in fairness and justice and reason to all men. But even then woe unto he who shall turn from the Way, for the High Lord and his blood and their advisors will not cease in their diligence.

And those who anger against him shall know his wrath, for he shall take upon his shoulders the well being of all men, and of all beasts and everything that swims in the waters and flies in the air. Even to the smallest blade of grass shall he make succour in my name and in the name of the six Signs who have gone before him. And he shall destroy those who destroy the Earth and make laws against them.

And he will create seven churches each with ten thousand people therein. And those that are of the beast will try to destroy the seven churches with guile and with war and with lies, and any thing that the mind of the beast can understand.

And he of the seven churches shall go and live in a far off land. And I say unto him that he should seek a land that is a cool land, and seek a place near to the sea, and to the mountains, and the forests where few lest his own shall live, so that the beasts cannot make war upon him and his people.

The beast that is of man shall not prevail over you. Your accusers shall be cast down and their deceit will show itself in its own light. But be you always vigilant, for the beast will persecute you in your purpose. For he shall seek to control and to enslave men, both in mind and in body for his own glory.

Hear me Lamb, I command you to build your house beside a river that is pure in its waters. You will build it on a hill beside the river, so that it will not flood at the rising of the waters. And the waters will you harness for your needs, to cleanse your bodies, to turn your grinding wheels, and to water your fields and your cattle, and all the beasts in your care.

And the river shall nourish your lands and be a great strength to you. And from your house will you see the sea, and be you watchful of it for it will feed you in troubled times, and carry your burdens to the churches and from the churches.

And you shall be as the fourth of the Seven High Lords in his wisdom, and shall pour out the knowing of your veil and your purpose before you, and you will scorch your enemies in fire.

And you will learn of the wisdom of the fifth High Lord, and pour out his wisdom from your mind upon the ears and minds of man, which is the seat of man. And you shall pour out your veil over the rivers and over the seas. And over the parts of the Earth that have suffered drought, and over the parts of the Earth that have suffered floods, and over the parts of the Earth that have the remnants of the great plague, that man can no longer be in that place for fear of his death.
And men at that time will curse you and me, and all Kings of men in their pain, and still will not gain reason except for a small number.

All this will start to come about at the time of the dying and changing of the frogs in the waters because of the poison that is within the waters.

And at this time the kings of the east will prepare to make war by cunning and by deceit. For at that time deceit and lies will be honoured as will all the abominations be honoured. In all, three kingdoms will be the instigators, and their people will believe them in their lies. And their ears and their eyes will be closed, and they shall not reason or turn from their foolishness.

75

And they shall spread their words upon the air, and in the cities and across great distances. And this will be a time of many false prophets, and you who will come after me shall be called false by those who will not hear reason, as reason will not profit them or profit those who follow them, and they will all plot battle and war.

Many will come unto the seven churches as thieves, to strip you of your honour and to strip me as I am, of my honour. As they shall do unto me in this life, so shall they into your time. But fear not as many will hear you and follow, and gain courage and be of good faith unto you, and unto me, and unto the Seven High Lords who have been delivered before them, to bring them unto salvation that is real, and not imagined by the beast.

And you shall pour out your veil upon the Earth for you are the Seventh of the veil.

And he who sits among the seven hills, and those who are liken unto him, yet oppose his teachings, will join one to the other in their common goal. And will turn their wrath upon you, and will send men to kill you, and keep the World from my reason and from your reason.

And they will instigate wars, as is their way to avert the ears and eyes of men from them. So that others can be found guilty of their own sin, and killed, so they may have no further defence against them.

And even though they hate each other, in their jealousy they will band together against you and against me, in their interest. Cursed be they for they know the evil they do, and are not deterred.

But the fierceness of the wrath of the power of the World shall not forgive men, should they follow these false prophets and priests of their kind. And the Earth shall be destroyed and laid to waste, and man will be no more because of their evil.

And because of the folly of men to follow those who say "Believe", so that men can know not. The end of days is nigh. And you shall know of this as even the heavens will open and the very sun that succours you will start to kill you, and the firmament will be rent with great storms, and pestilence will fall over the Earth and men shall reason or men will die.

Beware you at this time a viper in your bosom, who shall be born at the time if the Lion, and shall befriend you and yours, and your people. As he will be tempted to turn against you for his own fame, and write of your books and of

76

your knowledge. Teach him little, as that is all that he needs, and should he be not contented with little, cast him from you before he can do this harm and bring about his own following to rival you.

He shall know that should he break faith with you he shall die, as will all those who break faith with you, but he will believe that it is not so even though his reason tells him that it is.

And at this time he may turn his back on reason as does the gambler, and harm you and those who follow you with his confusion that he will scatter.

Beware you the Seventh Sign of the Seventh Veil who has possession of the Seven Seals in your mind. Should you show unto them the evil of the whore who sits among the seven hills, his power may be a temptation unto them, and the beast may rise within them that they may become kings, and they will start again the chariot of life towards another ending of days. Such is the way of the beast.

They may be tempted by gold, and by women, and the fornication of harlots, and of men who shall mount upon men as if they were women. Such men are the instigators of abomination. Cursed be they, and make of them eunuchs and slaves, as they are only beasts and less than beasts. And you shall none the less be honoured in your time. Be you ever vigilant against them, for they who are as men but are not men, will plot to kill you.

Beware you that such shall not find lodgings in the bosom of the seven churches for they will surely try. Beware of men that are not men. Beware of men who were not men. Beware of men who will not be men.

And beware you of women, as they are as quicksilver because of their cycles. They are as the moon, always changing so that you know them not. And because of the nature of men and the way of these natural things protect you your women, so they will not come to harm at the hands of the beast, nor at the hands of their own weaknesses. For they are weak though they believe themselves strong.

For in your time women will become as worthless, by their own design. And they shall become as harlots, and have no value of themselves. And men shall have no value of them except as harlots. Shame shall they bring unto themselves, for in their search for value they will be become worthless. And their gardens shall become as poison, and the fruit thereof bitter unto them.

Bring them within the seven churches and teach them of purity, and of reason, and of knowledge. So that they will once again become priceless as it should be. And valued in their own eyes, and in the eyes of their husbands, and in the eyes of their fathers, and in the eyes of their sons. Blessed shall be such women.

And of the seven bearers of the veil, five have gone before, and one is to come. Let him hear my words, and see my Sign and my Seal that I leave unto him for man's sake. He shall only be among you for a short time, use you well of this time.

To each of the churches that shall be raised, shall there be ten thousand members, and many of them shall be not known, and their names and works will be kept secret except to a few who shall know of them, for their safety's sake and for your safety's sake.

And shall there be set above the ten thousand one to each thousand, to rule over that church of men. And they will look to the twenty- four that shall rule over them for their guidance. And they will cleave to one mind and to one power. From this will come the power that they shall use to protect and to prosper.

And their strength in numbers will protect the Lamb and he shall prevail over the beast. And you shall say unto him and unto me, "Where sitteth the whore among the seven hill? There are so many that follow him, and some are of my blood and of my affection. How then can I make war upon them and kill them?" Have no fear and be strong, as the Lamb shall make war against none who shall not make war against you, even though they be blinded by he who sits among the seven hills and claims my glory, and by his kind.

And the ten that are set above the ten thousand, and the ten thousand shall hate the whore for the evil that he does, and his office will be made desolate and no more.

And he that has the Seven Seals and is the Seventh Sign shall say unto you, "Come, and I will show you all that he who sits among the seven hills has done." And he shall show you much murder, and deceit, and lies and corruption. And he shall show you the coming of kings unto the whore to fornicate with him in his filth. And he shall show you them as they drink from the cup of his power, and bid you beware of them for they shall try to destroy him that comes after me, and destroy the seven churches and all those of the seven churches, in the protection of their power.

And those of you who shall sit and wonder at the wonders that he who sits among the seven hills shows unto you, will know that he shows you no thing, as all is trickery. And those of his fashion in other parts shall follow his ways in trickery, and each shall say unto you, "Mine is the true Way." And it will not be so.

For theirs is the way of sorcery and trickery, and can not be the true Way because they lie unto you in their lust for power over you, and for the ownership of your ears, and of your hearts and of your bodies. And they are an abomination before my eyes. And the things that they show you shall not be. And the things that they tell you shall not be.

And the truth of me, that is in a place of six mountains, where my blood shall live, and even that place will they deny me, and even my blood shall they deny me.

And I set before you a mind which has wisdom. And he shall be the Seventh Sign before you, and the last that will come unto man in his foolishness and evil. And he shall be among you but a short time. Make you good use of that time, and of his knowledge in that time, lest it be lost unto you for eternity.

And he shall set ten to rule over, and to advise, over the ten thousand that will come unto him. For he shall show you reason and it will be good unto your minds and give you peace.

Many men will be of one mind, and believe the whore who sits among the seven hills and his like. And those who do not, will believe of him, and will believe of others that are of his like, and are also cursed by me in my name. For they pour their abomination upon my name in their own interest.

And they shall make war with the Lamb that I bring before you, and shall want to kill him. And they will set men's mind against him so that others may kill him in their stead, so that they might appear to be clean of him. They shall promise such murderers blessings for their evil as they have always done in such matters, and they shall know that blessings cannot be the wages of murder.

Know you that there be Seven Signs of Seven Kings with Seven Seals, one Seal to each. And the Seventh shall hold the final Seal, five are gone before, one is and one is to come, and his number shall be ten.

When he comes unto you he shall walk among you only for a short time, for age will be upon him at the opening of his Seal. For age will be needed of him so that he will have gained all the wisdom that shall be needed of him. He shall have gained his wisdom in his own foolishness, and in his suffering. Waste not you his time for it will not be long for you.

He will take unto himself those who will gather each to him and to her, ten thousand of your numbers. And the seven churches will he gather, in seven nations of the Earth.

And he who sits among the seven hills and is of the beast, shall try to prevent, and he will gather unto himself his like. Even though they hate one another they will hate him more, for he will bring them down till they and their like are no more.

And they shall make war against the Lamb to no avail for he is the Lord of all Lords to come unto you. For he is the Seventh High Lord and the last and his task is great.

He is the King of all Kings, and he shall choose of you those who will be with him to be faithful unto him and unto me. And you will say unto him that the people of the whore that sits among the seven hills are many, and speak in different tongues, and you shall say unto him. "How can I make war upon them and kill them for I know them?".

And he shall say unto you that The Lamb and his people kill not without reason, and if men should make war upon him and upon his people then he and his people must do battle. For he shall say to do else is folly.

And you who have ears shall hear him, and you shall hate he who sits among the seven hills the more for his evil. For he cares not, and knows the evil he does.

And the seven churches will grow in their diligence, and my words will be fulfilled. And you shall tear your Kingdom from out of the mouth of the beast. For he that comes after me has been born among you and has great power, and the Earth will know of his light and of his reason.

And his voice will be heard across the Earth and through the heavens. And he shall make the city of he who sits among the seven hills fall into dust, and all he and his kind to be no more upon the Earth. For he shall teach reason, and reason will give you light to see the Way.

And all nations and kings who have drunk of the power of him, and all those he shall have spread his filth and his lies to shall die. Even unto the merchants who have used that evil way to increase their wealth or their standing shall die. And the hypocrite shall be destroyed. Even those who shall claim ignorance will die after they have been offered reason three times. For they will be offered no more, and at the end of days shall be late in their coming unto him.

He shall say unto you to come away from such ways, so that you may be saved from the horrors to come. And if you should hesitate and come not on the third time you hear his voice, then you shall perish, as my face is turned from you. The crimes and the iniquities have reached across the Earth, of he who sits among the seven hills, and of those who would be like him, and have men to follow them in foolishness and in evil, and will touch all men.

Repent all you who have eyes and can see. Repent all you who have ears and can hear and follow The Lamb.

And all the kings of the Earth shall know death for their support of him that squats among the seven hills, for they know what they do. They know that he and they reign by might, and they know that the Seven High Lords rule only by right. For their mark is set upon them in the womb, and it is written in the stars of their coming. And so shall it be.

The money-changers and the userers shall cry out in despair of their trade, and will offer you and The Lamb ransom to change your course. Turn your back upon them for they know only evil, and misery is their trade among men. And they know what evil they do for they lust after the fruits of gold and do no labour. They grow not, yet they reap. And sow only the seeds of slavery for their own gain. And harden their hearts as does the common harlot against all things that are right among men.

And at the falling of the great city that has been built upon murder, and misery, and burning, upon fornication with evil and lies. Rejoice men of good faith, thy salvation is close at hand. For thou shall follow he that comes after me, and shall repair the Earth of her destruction, and shall cast down he who shall sit among the seven hills and claims my favour. For he has deceived men by his evil. Cursed be him by my mouth. So shall I judge that whore and avenge my name.

And the four and twenty elders shall rise up, and the seventy who shall rule over the seven churches, and shall set The Lamb upon his throne. And you shall be glad and honour him. And The Lamb that is delivered among you, shall be joined in you, and by you for ever and for ever.

And his blood shall rule over the World one to each nation, and be protected by mankind for his own salvation, and he shall not know the ending of days. For the end of men who keep good faith with me, and with he who comes after me, and with his blood, shall never come to pass.

All you who have ears listen to my words. And you shall sit The Lamb upon a white horse, and he will be clothed in black as I have asked of him to do. And his hurt or ill treatment shall be repaid in death. And the hurt or ill treatment of that which supports him shall bring upon you pestilence.

And he and his blood shall judge you, so take care, for they are commanded by me to meet punishment for wrongdoers against the way that is laid down.

He shall smite down the evil doers with his tongue, and from his pen shall he create fear among his enemies and your enemies. And he shall prevail, for he shall answer them with silence and be questioned not. For they shall seek to destroy him and you, and deny you Paradise.

And his wrath and my wrath shall be great. And his name shall be written "Lord Of Lords" and he shall be "King of Kings", and none shall oppose him and live. For he shall learn from me, and shall not yield unto the evil ones to do their mischief upon him.

And the beast that lives among the seven hills and his cohorts, who were his enemies and will be his enemies, shall raise armies great and small, and put them together against him and against those who are of good faith to him and to me. And the beast will proclaim false miracles before him to turn your eyes. But turn not, lest you be lost unto me, and unto The Lamb, and unto yourself.

And the candle that is set before you will show you light no more, and the end of days shall be upon you. For you will be as his enemy. And all his enemies and all those who are foolish not to listen unto him will be slain. For even his very tongue shall be as a sword unto his enemies and unto my enemies.

For the days of forgiveness for their wickedness are past, and all their pathways have become overgrown so that they may not know where they have been. For they shall not want to know where they have been for excuse sake, and for the sake of their false pride.

And I bid he who will follow me to cast away all his false pride and the fear that is with in him, for it matters not what men do think or what men do say, as they are but beasts and know not better, and have no wit.

And those who will have ears, and listen, and follow and have good faith with you and with me, shall know of your purpose and shall not speak against you, but will speak for you, and be your staff upon this road that is lain before you.

For you have been sent before men, and have the key to all the mysteries that have caused men to be confused. And you shall open them, and it shall be as a bottomless pit where the truth has been hid for an thousand and yet another thousand years after me. For man has heard me not, and has done me great wrong.

And he who sits among the seven hills will try to confound you in these mysteries as he will, and gather even his enemies who are as he is, to cast you down and to make you foolish or mad in the eyes of men. But hold you steadfast against him, for you shall prevail over him.

And they shall cause death upon those who have not worshipped the beast, and have not bowed before his image, and have not received his mark of water upon their foreheads. But they shall live and reign with you and with me forever for their faithfulness to you and to me.

And man shall resurrect himself and the Earth, after one thousand years after the aligning of the seven bodies of the heavens. For at that time the Earth will have cleansed itself of the evil of men, and shall give forth to those of that time, Paradise.

And they must not forget the beast that is he who squats among the seven hills, before his statues, and idols, and false gods, lest men shall be tempted and fall back.

And you who shall open the Seals, you who shall be the Seventh Sign, you who shall come after me and whose number shall be ten, shall instruct thy blood in these matters so that your light can be carried forward forever. And men shall hear and shall not bring about yet another ending of days. For he should do so there is no one else to come and sacrifice, so that his ending may be put aside unto him.

Beware all you who have ears, for the fires shall rise up from the deserts and shall fall upon the Earth, and upon the seas. And one third of the Earth shall be laid waste, and the kings will concern themselves in their false pride, and in their own interest. And shall not put effort into the killing that will end the slaughter. For they are just beasts, as he who plots to destroy, and like shall always fear like. Cursed be they, for they know what they do and turn away from what they should do lest they may lose favour.

And millions will die in support of their false pride, and they shall deceive nations to the four corners of the Earth, and their greed and wickedness shall know no bounds. They shall use my name to do this thing, but they heard me not. Neither do they know me. Cursed be those hypocrites.

And he who comes after me shall be sat upon a white throne, and his blood shall follow him in his purpose. And the Book Of Life shall be opened. And another book shall be opened, and the book of his mind shall be opened, and he shall speak, and the mystery of God shall be no more. And you will understand and be at peace.

And those who are not of good heart will find no place there before him, and shall be cast out and shall die. And whosoever is not written in his Book Of Life shall perish before him and before me. And the Earth and the heavens shall be passed away as men have known them to be, and man will live within the heavens and shall prosper.

And all the Earth and the heavens shall be ruled by the twenty- four who shall be born behind the veil. Lords Of The Veil shall they be, and only Lords Of The Veil.

And they shall appoint a lower temple of those who are not of the veil, and the whole World shall be ruled by them, under the council and guidance of the blood of he who comes after me.

And the World will be as one nation, and shall be of help to each other in all countries, and there shall be no more such kings that are not of the blood. And no members of the high temple shall rule for their own interest, but shall rule only for the benefit of the Earth which sustains, and for those who dwell thereon and beyond the Earth. And for the beasts down to the smallest thing shall he benefit.

And he who comes after me shall say unto you "Behold, Paradise is at hand". And he shall command you to your duty towards this end.

Let all you who have ears hear him, and all you who have eyes see, and open your hearts, and bend your beings to the task for it will be hard, but it will be good. And the tears shall be wiped away from your eyes and you shall fear no more.

I say unto him that is the Seventh Sign, that haveth the Seventh Seal, "Write these words that I pass on to you for mankind's sake, and be you faithful unto me though you fear".

Let you do this thing. And beware you murderers, and those of clever tongue who care not for their means only for the end that profit them. Tonight I shall be with you as you read my words in your mind, for you truly are the Seventh Sign. And I have and shall show proof unto you.

But if you wish, you too can turn your back upon me, and all of me will be lost and laid waste.

Turn you not from me. Though it be hard and painful for you and for me, you will find peace through it. Be you with me, and hear me and I will show you that which you must do and cannot turn away from for man's sake. For I know you to be of good heart though you doubt and you fear, but it will pass.

You shall go into the high mountains in that cool place to which I have given you direction, and there shall build you a house where your followers can protect you. Build it beside a river, in a place where you can look upon the seas, of which you will favour, and will please you.

And you will take with you twelve families of goodly heart and faithful unto you and unto me, so that they can protect you and do that which will need to be done. And set you loose the dogs of war in your perimeter so that you may sleep without fear of harm.

And other things I shall tell you shall you not write down, but pass on to your blood so that they can carry on your purpose in good faith after you. For The Lamb shall have peace, and know contentment at the end of his life, and it shall be long in the place that I will show you.

No man shall reside in paradise whose name is not written in his book.

You shall take with you tools, and beasts that will prosper you in that place, and feed you and those who be with you. And plant fruit trees so that you might enjoy sweet things.

Take with you the knowledge of healing and of healing herbs that have been passed down to you.

And they shall see your face, and your name will live forever in the minds of men.

And I Jesus, a Nazarene, A Brother Of Light say unto you that my sayings be faithful and true. And I shall speak them unto Peter and unto John, as only one of them will be suffered to live, as they shall fear for their power and kill him in shame. But it will be their shame, and the one who shall live shall write my words in front of the eyes of men where they will not be able to see them.

And I shall speak the words in a way that will confound the beast who sits among the seven hills and claims that he speaks for me. For no man shall speak for me except at my command.

And he will try to destroy my words, and men shall destroy me for fear of their power upon the Earth and over men.

And I say unto you that I am Joshua Ben Miriam. Born in Bethlehem in the reign of King Herod, who did murder all in his fear of me at the sight of my Sign. He did murder all of the first born, such was his fear of my coming. For I am King by the right, and by the right of the Sign of a High Lord Of The Veil, and he only by might of armies.

I am known as Jesus of the house of David, the Christ, the anointed one. And he who shall come after me shall be known in such a way.

1. He who shall sit among the seven hills in his time, will plot with the war mongers of that time to kill the Seventh, for he too will fear he who will come after me. And he shall know of his Sign. And the very Earth below his Sign will be shaken with thunder and the city will be burned, so that they will kill the bearer of the High Lord, and thus shall kill the High Lord. All the nation of my people will be put to death in search of him, for they will know of his coming. And they shall fail in this evil. For he will not be of my people. As all men are

like unto each other. And let this be a Sign unto you. He will be born in the time of that great war when the whole World will do battle. A war where he who sits among the seven hills shall plot with the war-monger to kill my people in search of him. For they will see his Sign grow in the heavens and shall tremble in fear of him, for they know for what he comes. And they shall try to kill him by killing multitudes, as Herod did in his time, and in my time. So that they who rule only by might, can rule forever. Such will be the evil if he who squats among the seven hills. And he shall be forgiven of his evil for expediency sake, by those who know better, but fear the loss of their own power.

2. And let this be a second sign unto you. He who shall come after me, shall be born bearing the Veil of his high office.

3. And when the veil be slit so that the child may breath, a third sign shall be noted that there will be blood in the palms of his hands. And some will think that this be my sign, as there will be many beliefs of this at that time.

4. And there shall be a fourth sign in his right side, and it will be a mark of birth, which will be the mark of my last agony. It can not be faked, though some will try to fake this sign and cause injury to themselves, so as to cause wonder among people. But it will be to no avail as I will curse them in their wickedness. And the High Lord will be great, and some shall recognise it and know of the folly of those who shall try to usurp him. Cursed be they.

5. He will be born in the month of the birthing of lambs in that place of his birth, as a fifth sign.

6. And as a sixth sign his mother shall be taken away from the city where she shall live, for that city shall burn with fire, and shall be shaken by great thunder. She shall be moved away from that place, and from the fires, to a safe place for her and for his protection.

7. And his seventh sign shall be that he shall be born bearing marks in his right hand and in his left hand, and they shall represent according to the second Sign in his agony. These signs number six, for he himself is the Seventh Sign. And these signs are numbered thus so men will know.

\* \* \* \* \* \* \* \* \* \* \*

## Left Hand

1. And the signs of his hands shall number six after me, as I am the Sixth Sign. In his left hand be a sign, and it shall mean according to the signs of the second Sign. A sign of his friendship, of his compassion, and of his kindness of spirit. Which he shall offer unto you. (Gyfu)

2. And another sign in his left hand will show unto you that he is unconquerable in his power. This sign will show you a success that he will bring you to, and that his enemies will be surpassed. (Eohl)

3. A third sign will show of his strength of his ability to persevere in the face of all his adversity, and promises that his task shall be complete, though his obstacles will be many. (Ehwis)

## Right Hand

1. In his right hand shall be seen a sign that will show you that he will lead you to that which will sustain you. That he will change minds in many matters as you grow in spirit and raise yourselves above the beast. (Lagu ).

2. The second sign in his right hand will show you that you will inherit Paradise after him, bound in the brotherhood of his following, and bound to the duties of that brotherhood. It shall show you help in your adversity and loneliness, and a removal from this state. (Odel).

3. The third sign in his right hand shall be but a single line that shall show his fate and blood. And it shall tell of the divine right of his veil that can never be taken from him, even though he be dead, and his veil destroyed and burned. That his power is beyond death, and beyond life. It tells of the justness of him and of his purpose. That he is a carrier of knowledge and good news to all those who have ears and hear him. It signs that his enemies will be many and his enemies will be your enemies. It warns against treachery, as his wrath shall know no bounds. The Way of his brotherhood is straight. (Isa).

(For those of you who may not be familiar with Numerology, all numbers are added together until you are left with one number )
e.g. 22 + 35 = 57 = 5+7 = 12 =1 + 2 = 3.

And he shall fulfil six more signs that are numbers. His number shall be ten.

1. The number of the day of the year, when added to the number of the week of the year of the measuring of the year in his time, will be ten.

**110th day + 17th week - 1 + 1 + 1 + 7 = 10**

2. The number of the day of the year when removed from the number of days that there be in that year, when added to the number of the year will be ten.

**255 days remaining in the year + the number of the year 1942 =
255 + 1942 = 2197 = 2 + 1 + 9 + 7 = 19 = 1 + 9 =10**

3. The number of the day of the month when added to the number of the month when added to the hour of his birth will be ten.

**20th day of the 4th month = 20 + 4 = 24
Time of birth 1.30 = 20 + 4 + 1 + 3 = 28 = 2 + 8=10**

4. The letters of his known name when added will be ten.
**Bob (3) Crosbie (7) = 3 + 7 = 10**

5. The letters of all his names when added will be ten.

**Robert (6) George (6) Crosbie (7). = 19 = 1 + 9 = 10**

6. The number of the century numbered after me shall be 10.

**19th = 1 + 9 =10**

Seven Signs shall there be for men to know of his birth. And six signs shall there be in his hands and six signs shall there be that number ten. The number of these signs when added will be ten. (10.)
Seven signs of birth, + six marks in his hands, + six signs of my numbers.

**= 7 + 6 + 6 =19 = 1 + 9 = 10.**

I am the Sixth Sign and give you these signs according to my number, and his number. And his number shall be ten. And to him I will give another sign, and it shall be that in his left hand there shall be two crosses, and in his right shall show five more crosses. These shall be to remind him of the responsibilities that shall have been taught unto him. They will serve to remind him of the number and the importance of his Sign.

He shall well know of the nature of the number of seven, this will remind him of the last chance that he is, for the changing of the ways of men. He shall know also of the meaning of the right hand and the meaning of the left hand.

He is the first and the last to come after me. I bid you to protect him in his being and in his purpose, for his purpose is to show you the Way, as was my purpose.

I must now trust in mine enemies as my friends are in great fear, and I cannot put my trust in them. My enemies I can always trust, for they are apart from me and I know them well.

Treat well of him for thine own sake. He is all you will have to save you. You who have ears listen unto him, you who have strength lend it unto him, for he shall be in need of it, and you shall be in need of him. Blessed be you.

There shall be no more sent unto men. The time of forgiveness is no more for man.

He is the last to come after me and the end of days is upon you.

I have written the prophecy as it has been given to me. On more than one occasion I have nearly stopped, partly from embarrassment and I confess also from fear, and the whole idea of it and what is to come. He repeats things a lot, but I fear that if any should be removed then the whole exercise is in jeopardy. I have had quite a struggle with it as my source has been altered so much in the past. I also appreciate that it will give offence to many who believe in different followings as he is obviously having a good old go at them all, and who can blame him.

To me Jesus is a bigger man than I had ever imagined. His intelligence and reason are second to none, as is his understanding of men, who in my opinion leave much to be desired. Many of you will read with tongue in cheek. I would ask you to think as you read, without prejudice of your own beliefs however innate. Look at what he is saying as it is. For I think that the greatest disservice men have done to him is that every word he has ever said is interpreted according to the beliefs of them at that time.

Joshua Ben Miriam, which is his true name, needs no help from any man to decide what he is saying. He was not a fool and knew his own mind.  He was in fact the opposite, hard, though men have tried to change the image of him, as he says "to their own purpose". He meant the things that he taught to be of benefit to mankind, as did all the six that have now passed, and I in my turn wish the same, knowing that my life shall lie forfeit because of it. It seems a bit conceited of me to accept so readily that he speaks of me. Let me hasten to put this right. It has been thrust upon me, by men and women who have kept the Prophecy safe at great cost to themselves and to their families, and at no small risk to all concerned. They have waited till the time is right, and the time is now.

The time is now because of the Prophecy itself. The number of the century is right, nine and one equals ten. I was born in 1942 as previously explained, on the 20th of April the month of the birthing of the lambs.

As I was born at number five Rose Lane, Diss, In Norfolk, England, to where my mother had been moved for safety's sake, as the war was raging. I was born there because my mother was taken from the City of Liverpool, away from the bombing as previously prophesied. She was moved as members of the High Temple, who are highly skilled astrologers, not quite as you read in the Sunday papers, far more serious than that, saw the Sign grow in the skies, as they say, heralding the coming. My father was stationed in Norfolk at the time so it was no problem for them to get her to move. They used a family friend in the plot to make sure. At the time she left, Liverpool was on fire due to heavy incendiary bombing, and so it was.

I was born with a "caul", or "veil" which is pictured here for your interest. Now it sometimes gets mixed up with placenta stuck to the face or head, but it is unique and once you have seen one you can't mistake it for anything else. It has two loops that go around the ears and help to keep it in place. One of the loops on mine is a bit stuck, and due to its delicacy will remain stuck, as it would cause too much damage to try to remove it now. I was born with both hands bleeding, and with a birthmark as prophesied in my lower right side, which is a mark that cannot be faked. My hands still bleed from time to time, especially when I use them for healing. Might I add with very good results. I even astonish myself from time to time still, even though you would think that I would be used to it by now.

In my hands I also have the marks as prophesied, which appear to be runic. Hence the mention of the One Eyed Sign namely Odin. It must be him as there are not too many like him, and he keeps being described as a High King. I will go into this later on as there is a bit more explaining to do on this matter. The numbers as laid down all add up to ten, as is also prophesied, and I think that there are too many for coincidence, and the coincidences do not end there.

There is a lot of confusion about Christ, this is because he has been used rather badly in the past, and a great deal has been altered for various reasons, and indeed for no reason at all. Christ was a "Caulbearer" or as it is sometimes called "The veil". "Born behind the veil" is a common way of describing a "Caulbearer". In the old World because of the uniqueness of the veil or caul, all those born bearing one were considered King by right above all other Kings by might. Because of the significance of the Seven Signs, which are people not things, those who were born of the Sign are considered High Kings such as Odin and indeed Christ.

Many people and scholars could not understand why Christ was called King of the Jews, or why Pilate placed a sign over his head at the crucifixion, stating "King of the Jews". It was simply because he was a "Caulbearer", and because of his Sign a High Lord Of The Veil. King by right.

And this was the reason why Herod tried to find him and kill him. It states in Matthew 2 verse 2 - "Where is he that is born King of the Jews? For we have seen his star in the east and have come to worship him". Now to us of the Old Order, worship means to honour and revere, not to pray to.

Verse 3 says that when Herod heard of these things he was troubled, and all Jerusalem with him. And goes on to say, "And when he had gathered all the chief priests and scribes of the people together, he demanded of them where Christ would be born". How did they know?

Verse 5 states and they said unto him, "In Bethlehem, in Judea, for thus it is written by the prophet".

Verse 7 says, "Then Herod, when he had privately called the wise men, enquired of them diligently what time the star appeared". They followed the star. Everyone knows the story in Christendom. And Joseph took the young child and left under darkness into Egypt, where they stayed till the death of Herod. Christ was considered so important that Herod felt justified in killing off all the firstborn, and boy children up to two years old. And he would no doubt have the backing of Rome, as they would not feel too secure as long as he lived and had followers. As it is with me. He was also known as Priest, even today in the Old Order the word Priest means teacher, and he was a teacher as he so often said.

At the time of Christ's birth it was a practice if you wanted to start a new religion, they would impregnate a virgin with a quill, and once pregnant would show her in her entirety to all who wanted to see, and to marvel at what the ignorant thought was a miracle and definite proof that some deity or other was daddy. It could be a rock, or a golden statue. It didn't matter. Someone was the intermediary and collected the cash. They slipped up though, and got themselves a "Caulbearer", and they couldn't, or perhaps were afraid to pull his strings, so right from the start he had to go. He was a danger to all who ruled and wanted to stay in complete control of the masses. The Jews, the Romans, Herod,etc.

He tells us that at twelve years old he had to leave home and wander with desert tribes and his teachers, so that he might be hidden from the assassins who hunted him. There are one or two other reasons that he had for this, which I cannot go into at this time.

Now you may wonder why Jesus was born when he was, but if you check up you will find that the people who lived at the time of the coming called this period "the last times", which is very similar to now which is called "the end of days".

People in his days believed that their World had fallen so far into evil that it was doomed, and he came to them as the Saviour. You may well consider that this cannot reflect what is happening now. But it does. Look at the World we live in, pollution, disease, wars, strife of one kind or another. Men out of work because machines are making them redundant, and they are being held up as the cause of all troubles through really no fault of their own. It is all to do with profit, but what profit. If all are out of work and everything is done by machine, then there will be hunger and death as prophesied, and then what?

It's simple, there is nothing more dangerous than a man who has nothing to lose. He is not going to be a nice boy and starve to death, and watch his children starve now is he? So he will come out fighting. And the bankers and financiers and their puppet politicians will try to crush him. But it won't work for them.

Think of all the homosexuality. Perversion is absolute make no mistake. Man is not slightly perverted, nor is he perverted in one way only, he or she is just perverted. And they are ruling the World, your World, my World. Even Christ the great forgiver was and is, against them. Throughout, his Prophecy, and The Bible, the very book that they all profess, speaks against this perversion. His words are now saying no more forgiveness for man, simply because men expect forgiveness, and therefore take no responsibility for their actions, which must end. As we are all responsible for the bad we do, and it is not fitting that we only accept it for the bit of good we do.

Christ in his life was associated with some military activity and it seems to surprise some. But he was a hunted man, so of course he was surrounded by people who could, and would defend him, with more than just a good spirit, or a prayer. The thing that distinguished Christ from all the other leaders both political and military was the fact that he was King by right, and no one could top him in that. He was more than just Royal, he was considered marked, and his mark sacred. From the time of Christ to today kings have claimed Divine Right, and it has been underpinned by the leaders of various religions, who have had the audacity to claim the power of God to bestow divinity on who ever they chose. Thus supporting each other and in most cases dividing the spoils, in their ultimate power. The original idea was that the King was only a sort of referee, ensuring justice and fairness for all. He was there to have the last word in matters, to ensure the prosperity of his people and to control the armies, in the protection of his people from those who might stray from this honoured path and make war upon them.

The King was the servant of his people as they still claim today, while making it very obvious that they in fact are not, as they are too far above their people, which they show by their actions, for this to be their purpose.

During the writing of this Prophecy of Christ he has wandered about a bit, or perhaps it is just a mark of the time gap in between. He has also spoken of great discoveries of strange lands and peoples, of wars that would fit the rise of the British Empire and the fall of the Roman Empire, and a great many other wars. But they are a bit too vague for me to make too many definite connections except for the French revolution.

As he says, a killing of kings in his adopted land, and wanton slaughter and cruelty, caused by the same. Let this be a lesson etc. He mentions the whole World at war twice. Obviously the first and second World wars. Mostly he goes on about those who sit among the seven hills with great accuracy.

His people returning to their own lands. And he prophesies that they will know no rest there, unless they fight till all their enemies are vanquished. He says that the enemies of Israel will be encouraged by those who pretend to be friends of Israel, and have more of an interest in their own gains. He says that Israel will have to fight with a purpose to win and heed not those who have not interest except that of power in the land.

He Prophesies Mohammed, and warns that he will not be heard, only interpreted. And these so called followers will go against reason and start wars, and lies will be their badge etc. That they will have no conscience when it comes to getting their own way in things as the ends will justify the means as far as they are concerned. But it is fair to say that this has been the way of things all throughout history. It is no different now than when Christ was here. People followed power, not right in his time, and are doing the same today. Nothing seems to change. As he says "And men shall know no reason".

And yet we know that reason is all that makes man different from the lowly beast. I cannot see why men refuse to see this, and think the World can be safe. We can be safe but only if man turns his back on unreason and embraces reason. It is unlikely that the seventy thousand people he mentions for the seven churches exist because of that.

I have nearly wiped this Prophesy from the screen more than once. I haven't just despaired ten times, I must have done so fifty times as I have thought about the things that he has said. So many things that I will not write here.
He was the saddest man you could ever come across, he knew exactly what they would do to him in the future, the way he would be used, and he could do nothing about it. His only hope was and is in the Seventh comer.

Perhaps when men really feel the wind of death on their necks they may just change, but I think he may be wrong. As it appears to me that if men just come out of fear, they might as well not come at all. For when the fear is over they will go back to their old ways and turn their backs on reason and blow the whole ball game. That has always been the way of man and I don't think he will be able to change.

He prophesies much boding for the future so I shall continue with more of it.

The children of my heart shall turn their backs upon me, though I have given them the nourishment of wisdom with my blood, yet shall they rebel against me. Even the ass knows his master's voice. Yet shall men do evil against me and against he who shall follow me.

You are all evil and corrupters, and go backwards to your own destruction. You shall revolt more and more, because your hearts are of evil and your heads are sick. Such wounds and bruises cannot be bound and shall putrefy, for there is no salve or ointment for them.

You lay the very land that sustains you desolate, and you burn your cities with fire. You shall be overthrown by strangers from far lands, who shall scorch the very Earth, and bring disease unto you. And you will be devoured in your own presence, and then shall you cry unto me and unto he who comes after me.

Your daughter shall drink wine and lie with strangers, and she shall be besieged with her own corruption.

Men shall perform sodomy with small children and say it be good. And so shall innocence be sacrificed upon the alters of the damned. Yet you shall do nothing to save your children except make excuse for the defilers.

I shall delight not in the blood of the innocent and I shall curse you to the end of your days. And the iniquities shall live on in your blood. So also shall I most curse them also, for there shall be no more forgiveness for man, and he shall know justice unto himself and unto his blood that follows in his way.

Call you no more assemblies before me or of he who comes after me. We want not your vanity at the coming of the new moons or Sabbaths. I want not your abominations or your iniquities, though your assemblies be solemn. My soul hateth your Sabbaths and your appointed feasts, even that which you shall rise to mark my birth. And why should you do this? You know that I be a Lamb. I am weary of them and of you for it is all a trouble unto me.

Your hands are full of blood, and none more than the hands of your masters that you bow before and give honour to. Wash yourselves in the rivers if your rivers be clean, as you cannot be cleansed in foul water.
Though you make many prayers there is none to hear you.

# THE PENTACLE
# THE SEVEN RESPONSIBILITIES

Here are listed the seven points of the pentacle and the seven responsibilities of man.

The pentacle represents the responsibilities of man. The circle within which the star is contained represents the world in which we live and it should be obvious to any reasoning person that our responsibility to it is of the utmost importance for the most practical of reasons. As you view the pentacle from the top down as the wearer you will notice that it hangs from the topmost point which represents the wearer. If you do not take care of yourself then who can you take care of. This is not selfishness as some may think but a practical reality. The second point is the one on the left as you look down from the top, representing the parents of the wearer, the place where we came from. They took care of us when we could not so it is only right and proper that we look after them in their times of need. The point opposite the second represents your children or in other words your everlasting life. Again it is a representation of genetic information going into the future. The third is the lower right hand point representing the spouse or partner in life, the person who makes the going easier. Kick this leg from under you and you fall. The lower left hand or fifth point represents your duty to your fellow man without which you would find it absolutely impossible to survive.

The hole in the centre of the pentacle represents the spirit of the person and the man. Do not forget the needs of the spirit lest it wither and die.

Left Hand

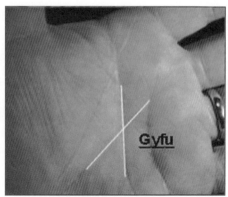

**Gyfu** Left Hand

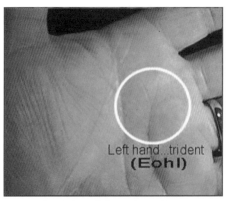

**(Eohl)** Left hand...trident

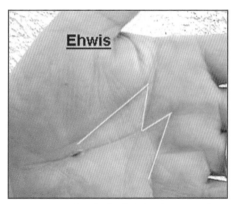

**Ehwis** Left Hand

Right Hand

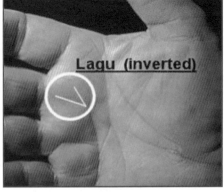

**Lagu (Inverted)** Right Hand

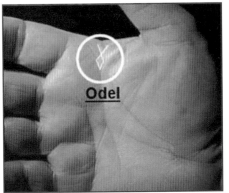

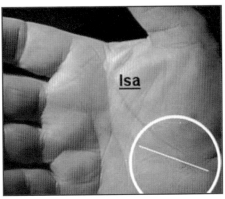

**Odel** Right Hand

**Isa** Right Hand

# THE MARK OF THE
# LAST AGONY / INSULT

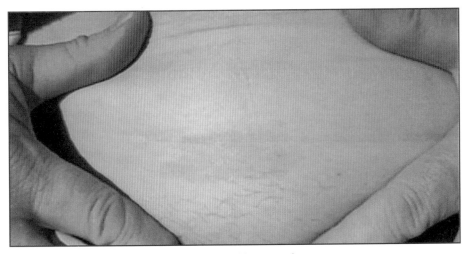

**(Birth Mark)** Wound

*"And there shall be a fourth sign in his right side, and it will be a mark of birth, which will be the mark of my last agony. It can not be faked, though some will try to fake this sign and cause injury to themselves, so as to cause wonder among people."*

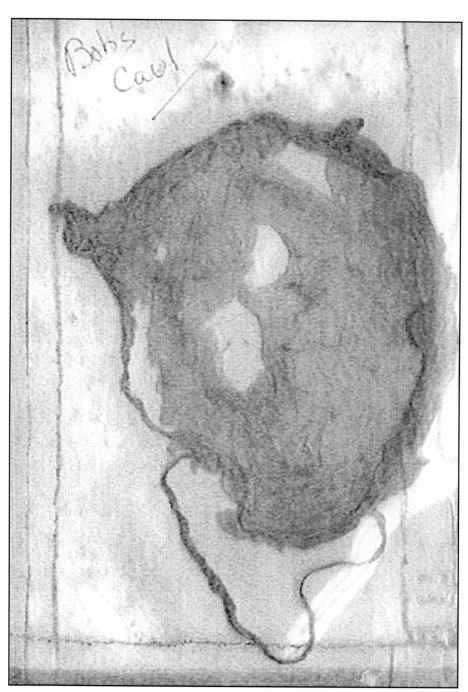

THE CAUL

Cease to do that which is evil, especially in my name or in the names of the Seven High Lords Of The Veil. Cease your evil doings before mine eyes. Turn your course and seek to do instead good things for the Earth that supports you and for your brethren.

Assist you the fatherless and be you of assistance to the widow and bring her into your house. But lay not your hand upon her less you shall marry with her, and she and your wives be content with it.

Listen to him who cometh after me, and gain reason from him. He shall show you The Way. If you obey he who comes after me you shall eat good of the land that is beneath your feet. But though it is, consider it far above your head and honour it to the last speck of dust. Show to him your obedience, and if you rebel, he shall slay you in my name and with my blessings to him, and my curse shall be laid upon your blood forever.

How have you become perverts and your wives and daughters as harlots, and your sons murderers, and make companions of thieves? And it shall be so.

I know you and I know your minds, you takers of gifts and givers of nothing. I say unto you, though it be two thousand years and two thousand more I will avenge he who comes after me of his enemies. This is my word. I will lay my anger upon thee, and my hand shall be against thee.

You shall follow him in good faith though he shall believe it not as he will be much distressed in you and trust you not. And I shall bid him to set up councillors as I have instructed and you will obey. And then shall the seven churches be called righteous.

And he and his appointed shall convert you, and shall bring about the destruction of wrongdoers and of fornicators. And those who forsake him and his, shall be consumed and their blood shall be consumed for ever and for ever upon the face of the Earth.

Shame shall you bring upon those who lie man with man, and you shall make of them eunuchs, and bind them in slavery for their lives. For they shall be less than any beast of burden in the fields, and thus shall they toil and earn their bread. And I shall curse all who aid them in their ways. So shall you treat all who would sodomise little children, for they are less still in my eyes, and should they ever harm any child after this then put them to death.

And it shall come to pass that the house of the High Lord Of The Veil shall be built upon a hill beside a clean river in a land that I shall show unto him. And all the seven nations will pay homage to him in this place, and look unto him and to his blood who shall rule over them for ever and forever, for guidance in all matters.

And many of you will say to your families, and to your fellows, "Come with me to the house of the High Lord, that we may learn from his wisdom so that we might walk in his ways, and know the laws of the righteous way so that we might be exalted in that path".

And many will come unto him at the ending of days, and unto his blood after him, and he and they will judge and many will be turned away. And some will come to kill him and his, and his people and theirs. And after some time they will all die and be no more.

And his people will do no more battle, as they will be as one with the land that he shall show you, and multiply as he instructs in goodness and in reason. You shall all become husbandsmen of the Earth, and all that is upon the Earth and below the Earth, and beyond the Earth.

And some will gain no reason, and they will forsake him and you, so that they may rule in abomination. Let them go. But if they should return for any purpose, kill them and have none of them.

And they will raise horses and chariots against you, but they will fail. They will try to give you false reason so that they might rule your minds, and show you gold and silver, and harlots. And their harlots will bring unto you disease to kill you. And their gold and silver will not sustain you as they are only for ornament, and shall serve no better purpose than iron.

Heed them not as they and you will bring about another ending of days. Worship not especially that which you have made with your own hands, and trust you not in the birthing of virgins, as it is trickery.

Be you not haughty as you shall be bowed beneath the weight of it at the ending of days. In the time of he who will come after me all men shall be brought low, and shall be so until they gain reason and learn better from their lowliness. You shall toil and raise towers and fences against thine enemies lest they will rob you and kill you. And you shall set the dogs of war at your perimeters.

And build you ships that will be strong and steady in the high winds so they will not break. And go you to all the seven nations, and be brothers unto one another in good faith, and in your protection.

The day comes near unto you when the Earth shall shake with the thunder of mighty weapons. Hide yourselves within ramparts so that rocks will not fall on you, neither will the dust touch you with its death. And close yourselves from men that are not of your way lest their breath shall kill you, and if they should come unto you turn them from you. And if they should come again kill them in mercy for their sake and for your sake lest you all die.

Store you bread and all manner of foods that you can store, for the time comes when there shall be little. But fear not, follow in the Way of him who will come after me and know him, for his number shall be ten.

And hear not the words of those who will condemn him, as they either know too much or know of no thing. By both ways shall they seek to destroy you. Your time of testing will lay sore upon you, and those who be not worthy shall be better dead, and will be dead.

And he and you shall appoint captains to rule over each of your sections. And Councillors shall he appoint from among you, and "Caulbearers" shall he set over them, and Templers over them, who shall be honourable in their duty to you and to him and to the Way that he shall show you.

And some will say that you be oppressed, and that those above you are not fair and are too proud. If you therefore know this to be true, then go to those above you and tell them of what you know, and it will be put right. But be you aware that some of you will not be in good faith, and will make trouble among you, so that you might be put down and they, the trouble-makers, raised above you. Let this not be. As it also will destroy you and he that will come after me, in your purpose and in his purpose.

Those of you who have ears hear me, and those of you who have eyes see, and know the wisdom of my words.
Men who shall come not in good faith to the way of them and of you, shall say that he has fine clothes, or a sword, or a chariot and should therefore be set above you. And will act as if to make impression on you. He might say that he is a learned man, and seek to make impression on you.

99

But turn from him, and go to those who have been set over you in the Way, and tell them of this so that they can deal with it in a just manner, for your own sake and for the sake of your brothers.

And when others shall be approached, they will say, "Make me not to be above my fellows, as I am an humble man and have not knowledge". And he that will follow me shall say unto him, "Go you forth and learn." For all men must take unto themselves responsibility in matters. As you shall be few, and therefore will only survive if you be humble, but willing to give of all that you are and all that you have in this purpose.

And men shall walk among you in these days that declare themselves as sodomites, and shall do so in false pride, for they are lower than the lowest beasts. Woe unto you should you accept them into your way, as they will bring diseases and evil, and shall destroy you unto death. And you and your blood shall be lost forever. Make you eunuchs of them, and chain them as slaves for their lifetimes, for they be less than beasts. They reward only evil unto themselves. And should you weaken in this, they shall surely destroy you. And you will eat the fruit of your doings, and it shall be ill with you.

In the time of the ending of days, women shall rise up and declare themselves as great, and will try to rule over you. And they shall claim freedom from oppression and be as harlots. Oh foolish women, beware what you do. For better women know better of themselves, and are content in their place.

And men must beware of their households lest your children shall oppress you, and rule your house, with their mothers who fall into this way. Do you not know of the ills of women, for they are as quicksilver and are not to be noted in their actions or in their words at these times? The wise among women know of this, and be well with it.

Men and women are made in this way with purpose. Each must know of his and her way and be glad of it, and do justice unto themselves and unto each other in their way.

Man can not be woman, and woman can not be man. It is not the way of things. They are as they are. And let it be so. Though you fear poverty, there is a different and far worse poverty that awaits the foolish in these matters.

Drink you not of strong wine and be drunkards, as you will be cast out in these times. As you will be a burden unto those who are sober and have great purpose.

100

And with these very words shall I make the way of he who comes after me harder. As many at the ending of days shall be drunkards, and will speak loudly of the wrongs of that which I say. But they lie, and they know of it.

And they know of the truth of my words. For they do not master themselves. Wine is their master in all things, though it bring them unto death and degradation. Such can not be taken into account in their thoughts or deeds. They are of no use or purpose to me, or to him, or to you.

Beware of all evil in that time for there shall be many. Your daughters shall walk the streets with wanton eyes, and their necks stretched forth. And they shall walk in a mincingly way, and make tinkling with their feet. And they will be stricken with scabs in their private parts and in their blood. And they shall shame the "Caulbearer" who shall come after me.

And he shall turn away from them, and turn them from him and from you, so that you be safe from them. Even though they be wives and daughters of you. He shall cast them out with their nose jewels and rings of ornament that mean little, as they do before mine eyes. For they are foul before me.

And it shall come to pass of such women, that where they have scented shall there be a stench of them. And their hair shall fall from their heads, for in their evil shall they lie with the sodomite, and shall pass his vileness to others. Each to ten men, and the ten unto their goodly wives. And their evil wives in their turn shall they pass on such abomination to ten more men and so shall it be. And death shall profit from it.

And let all you women who are pure and content in your purpose gather you unto the "Caulbearer", for he shall have need of your kind, and shall add to your value. For your purity is beyond price. And your faithfulness to your husbands is beyond price. And you are beyond price in your goodness.

And in that time men shall do war for little reason, and politicians shall lie and connive and cause even more wars, for it shall be a profit to them.

And as they do this evil, good men will die by the sword, believing that they do good by it. And they shall know not reason. They shall believe much that is false in those times. And shame shall be the name of such men who do no thing to alter this evil.

And the widows shall sit desolate, and cry in bitter sorrow for them, and for their children, and for themselves. Take you care of such widows, and take them and treat kindly in honour of their dead husbands, though they die in vein purpose.

And the day will come when seven women who are pure, shall come unto he who shall come after me, and whose number shall be ten. And they shall say unto him, "Let us come unto you. We ask nothing of you except that we can abide in your name, and that you shall reproach us not." They shall bear him children.

And in that day shall his glory be complete, and they shall be content in his service. And each shall do his business in each of the seven nations, and it will bode good unto him and unto them, and their children shall rule in those places after him.

And he and they will wash away the vileness of women from them, and the blood of his people shall be purged in his wisdom.

And you shall abide in the places that he shall show you, in the manner that he shall show you, and be you content with your lot. As you will live, but many will die. And your salvation shall be great.

And you shall be fed and have good shelter, even from the sun that shall burn and kill so many in your time.

He shall take lands, and clear these lands with you. And they shall bear fruits in plenty for all that be with him. And the birds of the air shall prosper, and the fishes of the waters shall again multiply and be good.

But men will still judge between that which he hath, and that which he desires in his foolishness, and shall displease the "Caulbearer". Some will neglect the walls, and the hedges, and the fences, so that wild beasts will enter the gardens, and destroy.

And they will say unto the "Caulbearer", "Why hast thou let this happen in thy power?" And he shall put you from him even to the last man, for you be of no use to him or to me in thy stupidity.

And those who have ears, and those who have minds to reason, will be with him. And their gardens shall be bounteous, and they shall inherit the Earth.

And as the Earth is cleansed, in one thousand years his people will remember him, though he be dead. And they shall glory in his blood and in the leadership of his blood. And they shall spread throughout the Earth and make it good.

And there will again be great forests and clean waters. And man shall remember. And because he shall remember, and be of good faith to him and to me, he shall prosper and do no harm in the doing of it.

And at the time of the ending of days, many houses shall be left in desolation, as their owners shall be dead. And their bodies shall rot within, as there shall be none left to bury them.

The Sun shall burn you to death. And disease of fornication shall be rampant, and will kill you.

You will fight one with another, man upon man, and nation upon nation, even brothers will attack one another. For in these times men will know no reason, and shall not put in effort until it is too late for them.

And they shall come and cry unto you to feed them, and you shall hear them not.

Offer to men, that they come unto him that comes after me, three times in three months, and if they should answer "No", three times, then shall you write their names in the Book Of The Damned. For they will know no salvation, for they are not worthy.

And their carcasses shall strew the streets within twenty years of the opening of my Seal and his Seal.
And men will eat of the flesh from the bodies of their brothers. Such will be their desire to live. Yet they will follow false gods, and not he who will come after me. For it will be hard for those who follow him, as it was for those who followed me.

And those who will follow him not, will eat the flesh of their dead, and shall have not the strength to bury them.

And in this time many ensigns will be raised, and men will be as beasts in their purpose, and they shall war one upon another, each in his design.

And some will follow him to a far land to the north that is desolate and make it fruitful. For all the Earth shall be hot, and you shall abide well in the coolness of that place where the sun shall not burn thee.

And there shall be whirlwinds and great storms upon the Earth, such as men have not seen before. And the summers will be without rain, or there shall be times of great floods. The seasons shall be as quicksilver, and they shall be so that they can no longer be predicted.

Your crops shall fail and your beasts die. Even the frogs shall not be able to live in the waters, as they will be poisoned with the folly and the filth of men. And man shall show no reason.

Beware of such men at this time, for you may not recognise them for what they are. And they will try to kill you, so that they can eat that which you have, and lay your labours to waste.

The mighty will be levelled by hunger and shall grow more cunning. And you who will follow him will have need to fight for life, against both the beast that is man, and the elements that he has caused.

And you cleave only to the seven nations that follow him, and cast out all others from you. And you shall not sleep, nor remove your shoes for many days, for fear that you will be attacked by your enemies. But it shall pass.

You shall know times of hunger. But it shall pass. You shall labour with your backs bent and this shall not pass. But you will take pleasure and glory in the doing of it. You shall build paradise upon the face of the Earth, and you shall prosper by toil, and by reason, and it shall be good.

You shall give honour to the Earth, and to all living things, lest your honourable men despair of you, and you shall hunger and thirst and bring about another coming of the ending of days.

Men of goodly nature, rule yourselves with a rod of iron.

Hold you not your Sabbaths before mine eyes, for they offend me. And pray you not for assistance, for there shall be none. And pray you not in false gratitude, as it abominates me, for there is none left to hear you.

Men shall live for eternity upon the Earth, and beyond the Earth. But only those who follow the Seventh High Lord Of The Veil shall be suffered to live one hundred years after him.

Cursed be they who do not follow in the way of him, for the evil of their hearts and the stupidity of their minds. For they do much harm to no purpose except their own. And cursed be he who squats among the seven hills, for he knows the evil that he is, and that he does in the use of my name.

He who comes after me is a branch of my tree, and from his roots will rise up more trees, and from his seed more trees, and I will be well pleased. Even if he shall despair, and turn from you in your wickedness.

Seven Churches shall he raise in seven nations, which I have set before him. But if he should find not ten thousand goodly men in each nation, then he shall be blessed by me in his failure. For I too have failed. And the Seven shall have failed in our purpose, because man has failed in himself, and in me, and in all that is good.

The foolish shall be cursed as the wicked, as the harm is the same. And he that comes after me whose number will be ten shall know of the odds against him, and they will be great.........

* * * * * * * * * * * * * * *

As far as I am concerned I have written down all that I must write down. The rest shall stay unwritten. I shall add to the prophecy, as we all must. Though I see no point in this exercise. As Jesus says, the odds are heavily stacked against me, in this purpose. I do not think for one minute at this time, that men will show reason. It is beyond the ability of the species, except for a very few to do so. Almost certainly, not to the required number of seventy thousand.

The ending of days is upon us, and man still shows no reason. And because man shall show no reason, it is commanded of me to say to you, as Jesus said. Luke 22, verse 36. "Let he that has no sword, sell all that he has, and buy one." If you follow The Way you will survive, but only at great cost. If you do not follow The Way you will not survive at any cost. Jesus was brought before Herod, who it is said had wanted to see him for a great reason. When Herod questioned him he answered nothing. I too am instructed to write, then answer nothing to any man. When Jesus said that he was going to prepare The Way, he did not mean the way to heaven, as is supposed. Again he meant exactly what he said, and The Way is here. It waits.

I find it very difficult to accept myself as the person of The Prophesy. Even though all the dates are correct, all the marks are present, and all the other points are evident. I have known since I was very young, that I was different. I used to think inferior, as in the World of men different usually means just that. I look at my "Caul" or "Veil", it is known by both names almost equally, and to me it means the reason for my existence. This is because that is what I have been taught to accept. The Brotherhood have gone to a lot of trouble to ensure that I accept my role, in the scheme of things. They feel, that because we are fast approaching the end of days, for me not to accept my responsibility would be a catastrophe, as well as a waste of the efforts and lives of those who have gone before. The purpose mostly seems to be to do with other people and not me. It all seems so remote somehow, and so matter of fact I have grown used to it all. It is said that I will despair ten times. Well I can assure you I have been in very deep despair hundreds of times.

I watch people a lot. I have often been accused of staring at people, mainly because I feel that my eyes deceive me. The things people do has that effect. With this in mind, I wonder how I am supposed to find the necessary seventy thousand right thinking people to fulfil The Prophesy in the desired fashion. And I of course do despair. I see the bombing of Iraq, and listen to the "bull" that men speak. They know they lie. But that's politics for you. They accuse each other of lying. Whatever suits is the truth, until it no longer suits. Why would men want to develop such diseases and weapons anyway? Are they mad, or are we, the ordinary people in the street mad? I despair. Will I find seventy thousand among the population of the World, or even seven for that matter? Perhaps the lights of all the Seven Signs will flicker and die as the "ending of days" comes upon us.

I see pompous people forming discussion groups, so that they can give their considered opinions on matters that they don't even begin to understand. Their only qualification, their audacity and over-inflated egos. Their only textbook their conceit. Their only reason the underpinning of these same false egos. And men say to me, "Why do you despair?" How can I not? The task set before me is colossal, the people I have to do it with unreliable to say the least.

Imagine yourself in my position. The mind boggles. At least mine does. Surely the right man for the job would be a man who loves people. Well I only love a very few. My reasons obvious, at least to me. I see every sort of evil, stupidity, greed, lust, hate, and madness that you all see, and I wonder whether you see it as I see it. I know I am different, but not that much surely. I see the state of the World that supports us, and know that it can't go on. Something has to give. I see the diseases that are incurable, increasing. Most of them would not be here if men had used reason. Am I, and a handful of my followers the only ones who see it this way? Are we alone out here? Of course I despair, wouldn't you? I hear the lists of crimes committed by Saddam Hussein and his merry men. The powers that be knew of this after Kuwait, yet they let him go on out of political expediency. Why? Is this the clay out of which I must shape the salvation of man, and is man worth the effort? It's a good job I have family of my own, because if I did not, I wouldn't bother. There are those who would say, "Who asked you"? Well nobody asked me. I was just told. I was given no option. I have been very unfortunate to be born according to the Old Prophesy, one of the Seven. I have two choices, to accept the burden set upon me, or cast it off. Which would you do, all things considered? Jesus said, I will be sickened unto death if I don't. And I can see that happening even now, because I have dithered for quite a while.

Take into account what is likely to happen. At best I will be considered a dangerous, evil rogue. At worst ! The worst is unthinkable. I will be abused as I have always been concerning this matter. I am not a Christian, and that is a crime in itself. But neither was The Christ and I doubt he would be if he was alive today.

He was a great man, a good man, an intelligent man. How could you possibly balance this against the beliefs and dogmas of the Christian Church as it is now, and has always been? You must remember that the Christian Church firstly recognised Constantine as the Messiah, before they "voted" Jesus as Divine, whatever that means. This was at a conference in Nicea, in the year 325 A.D. Even then it took time to re-invent him to the deity you know today. It was the same with Odin, who is now considered a myth. He wasn't. But it is what people believe that counts, reality has little to do with anything. He was real, and the myth was built around him. As they say a man can get lost in the myth.

All there is of these men now are but invented images, that by clever mind bending techniques were, and still are, set in the minds of men. And who was it that said, "Bow not before false images". What images? Images of the mind, or of stone or gold? They are in fact all the same. Images are images, and they are not real. They are in fact illusion, set to confuse and therefore control. Again you may think "If he feels this way why does he not quit?" It's simple. I can't. Imagine being born as I was, according to the Prophesy.

## Childhood

Imagine a little boy, just as any other little boy. His earliest memory of being a bit different, without knowing what different meant, was in school. I was what was referred to as a 'war orphan' in those days, because my father was dead. He was one of the 'Dunkirk heroes' who survived to go on and serve in Africa, where he unfortunately picked up something that killed him. The war office even complained over the cost of his coffin, his funeral and even his grave. They told my mother not to come whining to them. She wasn't too hard to look at, and some man would keep her if she looked for one. Nice people, the War Office wallahs.

I remember somebody stole something in school, so the 'war orphans' were searched. They searched in my shoes, my pockets, my socks, even in my under-pants, and all in front of the class. Whichever of us did it was to be made an example of. I've had 'a thing' about teachers ever since. The rank moronic stu-pidity, the arrogance of them. However it turned out that it was the daughter of what was known in those days, as a 'spiv' who stole the money. Her father had stayed at home during the war, nice and safe. Making money out of the sit-uation, selling black market goods, and fiddling food coupons and the like, while the fathers of the 'war orphans' died in the service of their nation. Giving their very lives for King and Country. Even for the teachers that later abused us, and for the 'spivs', who looked down on us and tried to take even more from us. It amazes me how it turned out to be a 'spiv's' child who did the steal-ing. When you think of the genetic makeup, like father like daughter. There is so often more than a grain of reason in the old sayings.
The spivs were crooks to a man, dealing on the black market, and every despi-cable thing you could think of, but it was the war orphans who were despised, and we had done no wrong to anybody.

We were despised because shamefully, the pensions begrudgingly given to our widowed mothers were very meagre. Ten shillings a week for the mother, five shillings a week for the first child and two shillings and sixpence for each subsequent child. Today's value seventy-five pence ! Worth dying for don't you think? If our fathers had only known what they were letting their children in for ! I bet the government never put that on the their recruitment posters. Your country needs you! Where was our wonderful country when their orphaned children were in need.

Of course these 'war orphaned' children were very poor, often hungry, and totally defenceless. While the children of the spivs were respected purely because they had money, albeit the dirtiest kind of money. After all, they came to school in a car, and so were we judged. And true to form, 'man knew no rea-son', and he has not changed. He has no wish to change. And he will not learn to dig for water until his behind is on fire, when he is too late.

I remember after I was brought from England to Ireland in 1947, away from rationing and an attempt or two on my life. Remember I was only five at the time. Already having had my face burned very badly, in a so-called accident. My mother was at the back of the house when she heard me scream. Mrs Emmett from next door was on her way into the house when she heard me, and a young woman nearly knocked her down while getting out of the front door, as quickly as possible to a waiting car. I was in the fireplace by then uncon-scious. Jammed in by the fireguard so that I could not escape. Those who want-ed me dead, probably thought it would be considered an accident, and if I was-n't burned to death, that I would die from the shock. I was two years old at the time. It must have been an opportunist method. The woman in question could not have planned a particular method beforehand. A man apparently tried to keep my mother talking through the back yard gate, asking her about some-thing or other, so that the woman could get in the front door. She must have seen me and just did the first thing that came into her head. Probably just as well for me.

That scared my mother, I can tell you. She couldn't turn her back for an instant. If she did, some fine upstanding Christian gentleman or woman would have a go. It was usually one of those brave Jesuit Priest types that everyone respects so much. The members of The Society Of Jesus would you believe? I can never understand anyone who could respect those, whose order was founded solely for the persecution of people, and who were trained in the so called arts of torture, and murder. The Jesuits taught Hitler's little playmates, the SS after all. They even had a hand in the holocaust. You will find that much has been written about it of late. Some time after this incident I was removed to Ireland.

I was coming out of School in Celbridge one day. Celbridge lies about twelve miles outside Dublin. I was playing with some children I had met near what was then the picture house, where a chap called Nip Cummins used to show films. A very tall man approached, at least he seemed tall to me, a Roman Catholic priest, all dressed in black. He stopped some children from the Catholic school, that I was playing with. He shouted at them, then he used his walking stick on my little playmates and told them to go home, and not to ever let him catch them playing with the Anti Christ ever again, or it would be the worst for them. They would get more of the same, and he would see them burn in Hell forever. I went home and asked my mother who the Anti Christ was. I didn't want to play with this character Anti Christ either. Whoever he was, he sounded like a real bad lot to me. I remember the tears running down her face as she sat me on her knee and tried to explain. How she ever did it I still don't know. She had to try to explain to a small five-year old boy that he would be regarded as the Anti-Christ. Imagine how she must have felt, when she had to tell me such a thing.

I can still remember it. Oddly I really wasn't all that bothered, as she often related to me when we had our little discussions later on in life. Her explanation was good enough for me, but the memory stuck in my young mind. From then on I knew that I was really different, so different that I was someone to be hated. I didn't understand why, I just accepted that was the way it was. But I still could not understand. Just like all the war orphans, and the Jewish children during the time of that other madness, I just accepted. There was nothing else I could do.

People say to me that they understand, and they really think they do. But believe me, you couldn't possibly understand, no matter how hard you try to imagine yourself in such a position. There was one of my "Aunts," who came to see me at regular intervals to send me into that nice sleep that I liked so much. She used to make it a game, and I liked her. Though I knew I wasn't allowed to speak of her to anyone, or to speak of the game to anyone. Her name was Popoff. She is long since dead, and I have always missed her, though I still hear her in my mind from time to time. Still there after more than forty-five years. Her Russian accent and the way she would sometimes laugh at me, as we played. She had a heart of pure gold.

Another of my childhood favourites is also dead, as are they all now. He was Sir Ivone Kirkpatrick, or 'Uncle Ivone', who was instrumental in bringing me to Ireland. He was I seem to remember the head of S.O.E during the war and an ambassador to the Vatican, and I think Germany. I believe he had a lot to do with Nuremberg and the trails. He used to tell me stories about the war, stories about Rudolf Hess whom he interviewed when he made his landing in Scotland. He told me of a lot of things, of people, of great men and those who would want the World to think them great, and those who were not so great. He told me of certain 'Royals', and of treachery and stupidity that got a lot of men killed to no purpose. He told me of the Pope whom he despised above all men. And oh, the stories he had to tell that I was not to forget at any cost, and I haven't. He said I was not to speak of them till the time was right, and I would know when the time was right. He used to put me into that nice sleep with the help of my mother, and he would give me things that made me remember. He used to give me words to say in my mind, so that I could dream. He used to say that the dreams would be real, and to this day when I use this method I can remember it all so very well.

111

He protected me and I loved him, and I remember. Every word, I remember. Most of all I remember the stained glass window at his home, Donacomper. The big dagger dripping blood, and the words beneath it "I mak siketh" meaning "I make sure." And I do. He taught me to always remember the window, and told me that one day, I to would have a big dagger in my home so that I would always remember to "Mak Siketh". To "Make sure". I remember his old mule that could bite you with its mouth while kicking you with all four feet at once. At least I remember someone saying that he could. I stayed far enough away from him, so that I would never find out. I remember the walnut trees just to the right of the main gates, I used to pick the walnuts, and they were lovely, I remember, my hands all stained brown from them. I can almost taste them as I remember them.

Dear old Uncle Ivone. I was told one day that he would not come again, as he was dead. I thought that it must have been foul play of some kind. I was not allowed to attend his funeral. No one must know about him and I, ever. I hid behind the bushes in the old doctor's garden on the Dublin Road as the funeral that I thought was his went past. I remember seeing a very small man there, who I was later told, was none other that Sean T. O'Kelly. It turned out that it was all a lie, as 'Uncle Ivone' did not die until 1964. I only found this out very recently. I will never understand why he never contacted me again. My mother never mentioned his name, and when I asked I was told to keep quiet. Nobody must ever know. He was gone from us and that was that. I can only think that he must have had his reasons, and knowing him as I did I can only accept that they would have been the best of reasons. He was that kind of man. A man of honour, and to me there was none better than he. Within a very few days as I remember, some chaps came to the house. There was a lot of talk, but as I was sent out of the room I am not exactly sure what it was about.I was duly ushered in and told that it was thought best, as no one was to know about 'Uncle Ivone' for my safety's sake, that I must never mention him or go to the cemetery under any conditions. They said "If the wrong people knew, in England or Ireland, about him and I, it would be very dangerous indeed". 'They' stop at nothing, as I already knew. I just didn't know who 'they' were. I never even went to Uncle Ivone's grave. He was dead!

After that others took over in his place. They used to take me to Lucan to fish in the river there. There was a hole in the wall down the little lane between the shop and the houses, that I could get through, into the Italian Legation. I was always taken there by a woman and I didn't like women, except my mother of course. I had a little camera that they gave me, and it was my job to photograph everyone I could see in the Italian Legation every time I went in. The Italians used to come and talk to me sometimes, and ask if I had caught anything. One or two of them were very nice. One chap offered me a sweet, and I nearly blew it. I had been told not to take anything from anyone I was not acquainted with, and even then only if my mother said so. Just in case. He was a very nice chap but he was not Italian, he was different, he was a German I think. Apparently they were resettling and hiding people that the allies and the Jews wanted to get their hands on. He was quite annoyed when I would not take the sweet at first. His temper was close to the surface. So rather than give myself away, as I thought, I took the sweet he offered, and I ate it. I was sure I was going to die. I remembered all the stories told to me, so I was determined to do whatever it took. Like all my favourite people did in the past, both the ones I knew, and the ones I had only heard of. As soon as he went away, I got myself out of there as soon as possible with my little camera, and the priceless film. Dick Barton, eat your heart out, you chicken. The woman who had taken me was in the sweet shop at the end of the old access lane, so I had to wait for her. It was the longest few minutes of my life. I kept waiting for them to come after me. When she eventually came back to the car she was not amused, and I was told off. I refused to ever go with her again, and she was replaced. Mind you when she hit me for coming back against the plan, I did kick her, and hard!

It was a very regular thing at weekends, or after school, or during school holidays, going through that hole in the wall. I can still feel the fear in me.When the mill was running, the water was low below the weir and sometimes you could see the salmon jumping up the baths that went up the face of the weir like a staircase. Inside the grounds, there was a sort of an island with what seemed to me at that time to be a big stretch of water, between it and the shore-line of the river Liffey. I used to get lucky there now and again, giving the Italians a source of fun. They always seemed to be pleased to see me, and I began to feel like a traitor. But I knew the price of refusal to do what I was told. If they had ever looked in my little bag and found the camera and later on the cameras, I wonder what they would have done. I really thought they would have killed me.

There was an old Jewish Gentleman, or at least he seemed old to me. As it turned out he wasn't much of a gentleman either. I remember he came to us on a very warm summer's day. I was told to go and play, which I never did. I used to listen instead, which my mother knew I did. There was a lot of talk between them. I never could hear it clearly because she talked in a very low manner, perhaps to prevent me from hearing. After the talking was over she was very upset. It turned out that he wanted some of the films that I brought back, and of course she couldn't let him have any. They belonged to the other people, dangerous people who would stop at nothing. The usual threats were made, and I was later to learn that what I was doing, was in fact the price of my pro-

113

tection and hers. In other words if I did not do this thing, protection would have been withdrawn. News of where I was would be given to those who sought to kill me, and I was as good as dead. My family would have been dead as well no doubt. If only to cover their tracks. These so-called 'Gentlemen' play a soulless and very dirty game. The upshot of it was, I ended up carrying two cameras, thus increasing the risk. Just because the Jewish gentleman and the British chaps could not, or would not share the films. It was to do with the Huguenots not being officially recognised, the Jewish State still being anti British and all that.

The life of one small boy was unimportant in the Christian, and in the Jewish way of things. They usually preach one thing and do the opposite routine. You see, I was a threat to them as well. But for some reason I never understood until much later, they preferred to use me for their own ends, in spite of what they knew and believed. It turned out later that there were some members of the Brotherhood in powerful positions, both in the secret services and other government departments. They did their best, but I was just a very small pawn in a very dirty business, and they couldn't tip their hand, as then they would have no strength left. Then all would be lost to us.

When I was ten, our house caught fire. It was said to have been an accident. About a week later I was outside with my mother, when a bullet went between my legs and punctured the water barrel that I was leaning against. It had been fired from the Hazel Hatch Road some couple of hundred yards away, over the wall. My 'uncles' and 'aunts' all had their say, and it was decided that they would watch over me round the clock, but I must be moved. Life was starting to be far too dangerous. Thus ended our living in Celbridge. We felt that we were completely alone at that time, and afraid, as my usefulness to the people that Uncle Ivan had charged with my safety had come to an end. Almost a complete end. These people let everyone down, the country they are supposed to serve, the people they are supposed to protect, and even themselves. I bet Uncle Ivan never envisaged them using me to do their dirty work in this way. He was of the old school, where honour used to live, and was accepted without question. I always thought that for him to have lived to see the way they behaved would have broken his heart, as it was without reason or purpose. At this time I was still unaware that he was alive. I really believed him dead.

The house was quickly sold, and we went to live in Avoca in Co.Wicklow. That beautiful vale, better known today because of the TV series as 'Ballykissangel'. A small farm was bought, and off we went. Out of harms way as Mum used to say.

Life there was hard, and at first we worried that they would try again to kill me. But I was a very good shot. There was a rifle in the house, and I was not afraid to use it either. Some of them had good reason to be more than aware of this fact. By now I was eleven years old, and about to really start to understand what my life was to be about. Just as before, I had a stream of 'Aunts' and 'Uncles' who used to play 'that' game with me, but now it wasn't a game. I now understood it. I had learned a lot and learned it well. I had learned most of all to hate, and I mean really hate. I remember the feeling so well, and I am ashamed to admit it, but I often feel it even now. I couldn't have any friends for long as I might let something slip, and as they used to say, loose words can be dangerous.

I was becoming very much a loner, and could trust no one except my mother, my sister always being away from home. As I had no one else apart from my mother, I was on my own really. Things were fairly O.K. in Bally K. I have some good memories. The times I have gone up those old stone steps to Mrs Johnson's shop as it was then. The pub 'Fitzgerald's was called The Fountain, and was owned at that time, by a man called Totsi Byrne. As I watch the programme on the T.V. the memories come flooding back. Some good as I have said, but mostly not so good. My training and education went on. Again no one was to know. Not even my sister. I should say especially not my sister, who was always away in school so she could not be involved. She was to be protected against harm at all costs. But again the Brotherhood took care. Another attempt was made on my life later, but was thwarted by a real uncle who was a chemist.

I was not very well and went to the doctor's, which was a thing that was always watched closely just in case. Doctors could not be trusted, and lucky for me they weren't. But this time it was the Chemist. He supposedly made a mistake with the amount of arsenic he put in my medicine, for my nerves, they said. Some mistake. Naturally, and as usual, nobody wanted to know. My Uncle Ron was on holiday with us at the time, and he saw I was becoming very ill. He just sniffed the bottle. It was loaded for bear. He went straight to the Chemist. The Chemist said that Uncle Ron didn't know what he was talking about, and of course the Chemist was backed up by the Doctor. Uncle Ron was also a Chemist and a very good and experienced one at that. He was also a very good man, and there were times that I would have been happier if only I could have talked to him. He would have made things better. He knew he was right about the arsenic, and went to the police, known in Ireland as the 'Guards'. Just another daft Englishman! Despite the fact that he was very well qualified. They, as usual showed absolutely no interest, and then appeared to forget about it. There was as usual no record, but it was enough that we knew. Needless to say if Uncle Ron had not been at hand I would have been dead.

I neither trusted nor distrusted the medical profession before, but I have never been able to bring myself to trust them ever since. On another occasion I was given the wrong anaesthetic for a minor operation. It was just a few years later in Merceir's Hospital in Dublin, which caused heart failure. I have had a heart problem from then right up to today. I nearly died from it seven years ago. This needless to say, did not add to my feelings of security whenever I found myself in a hospital after that. If they had managed to fulfil their purpose at that time and all the other times, the Prophecy of Christ and all it means, and can mean to the human race would have died with me.

Greater care was taken of me after that as far as illness was concerned. This is another good reason I have for writing the story. Because should they try it again, on either myself or my family, fail or succeed, it will not be so easily brushed aside as it has been in the past. It was and is, a very hard way to live. I couldn't answer a single question without thought, or speak a single word to anyone without thinking, just in case. And more often than not I had to give, what I was taught to call 'misinformation' so that no one would know. Or tell them such a whopper, that they would just go away and leave me alone. Sometimes for their safety, and sometimes for mine. I forgot to mention that the Chemist died soon after the arsenic incident, but whatever happened to the Doctor from Merceir's Hospital I have never even bothered to find out, as I knew the old brick wall routine well by now. And I feared that perhaps I was beginning to appear a little paranoid. If I started to push, I would just look like a 'nut case', and I will not give them such an advantage. I will give them no help in the cause of my destruction, the destruction of the Order, or of the destruction of the threat I was, and am presumed to be. Even though I don't exist, and the Order does not exist. Its a weird World don't you think?

The true faith is above all that kind of thing, and always was. They have never stooped so low as to cause harm to anyone. We all know that. And of course no reasonable man would be so fanatical that he might indulge in such a thing. Ask any Muslim. Odd isn't it?

Nevertheless, the Chemist met a very untimely demise, "Tragic in one so young", they said. He wasn't as young as me though. Even more oddly the Guards didn't know about that either. They simply ignored it, and his death was recorded as natural causes. His injures were inflicted by someone called 'natural causes'. It is also odd how a crook never trusts a crook, have you noticed? The price of failure in these things is as high as the reward for success. Rich if you do, and dead if you don't. Nice people! The stakes are high when the prize is to own the World. Imagine.

There were a lot of difficulties when I was growing up. Shortage of money was one of them, and I can't understand to this day why it was necessary for us to live so poorly. Was it really to avert attention away from me? Was it really true, that if I received no help at all they could judge the opening of the points of the Prophesy, without questioning whether it was down to something I did myself, or because of their help. Or maybe it was just down to the pressures of poverty. There was a time when I was about eleven, not long after we moved to the farm, when we had run out of food, money, and credit. I took out the old rifle, and shot a couple of the rabbits that abounded in those times, and my new career had started. From then until Myxomatosis was brought into the country in nineteen fifty-six, I made a reasonable living for myself, and my mother. Uncle George was nearly always away at that time, working in Dublin or England. It was the only time I ever knew my mother to break down, and give in. It scared the hell out of me. She just sat there, in that old Irish fireplace sobbing. She could take no more. The autumn before we'd had a bumper crop of damsons in the orchard, and she had made fifty-six pounds of jam. We had lived on dry bread and damson jam for six weeks, without either tea, sugar or milk.

The people who stayed in the background at that time, I am led to understand, stayed in the background solely for my own good! And they, as far as I see it, are no different, than most people. They got us into this. They should not have let this happen. I was only just eleven years old. I thought then as I often think now, they too only look out for their own ends. But I stayed with them all the way nevertheless. Though I never quite felt the same again. I found as I grew into my teens I could not mingle with anyone normally, or with any form of ease. It was impossible for me to have friends, and when anyone became too friendly I would have to back off quickly. I lost a lot of credibility, and a lot of people had their feelings hurt, but there was nothing I could do, or dared to do. I was taught that if I had a friend, he or she could get involved, and the result could be disastrous for them, as well as for me. There were a few people that I really liked, even loved, but I had to turn away, leaving them somewhat confused. I had already experienced people dying mysteriously around me.

From time to time I used my hands to cure this and that. I had to stop. It too was far too dangerous. It would draw attention. I had to curb my instincts to try to help, and avoid being noticed at all costs. I sometimes wonder what would have happened, if I had just forged ahead.

Maybe I would have been safer. If there were more people who knew, I may have been safer. But I suppose that it is just wishful thinking on my part. Writing this book will soon tell. The Brotherhood probably were and still are quite possibly right. But this straight jacket that I have been placed in, that I know as my life, really restricts, and it chafes painfully.

I did a year in an agricultural college. Uncle George insisted, and I hated it. The people who looked after me tried to prevent it. There was no way that they wanted me put to such risk. They had something against the Principal, a Methodist minister, and considered him unsavoury and not to be trusted. So did I when I got to know him. I wrote a hymn when I was there. I showed it to him, and never saw it again. When I asked him for it back, I was told that I would be better paid to attend to my studies. What studies? Apart from a very little class-work, I seemed to spend most of my time lifting and snagging sugar beet, and the rest of it hoeing the stuff. I went there to learn something I did not know, just like the rest of the students. Those of us from small farms were well experienced in the mundane tasks. It was a rip off. I did everything I possibly could to get out of going there. My 'uncles' and 'aunts' did their best to prevent it, but it just made things worse. The more they tried to avoid what they saw as a danger, and a waste of time the more determined Uncle George became that I would go.

They had always kept him out of things as far as possible. He was a bad tempered bullying type, and far to volatile to be trusted. If he got an idea in his head he would be like a bull in a china shop, and chaos would certainly reign. It usually did. He never actually knew what it was all about, even though he lived with us most of the time. He used to get upset when anyone turned up who was called 'Aunt', or 'Uncle'. He seemed to think that they should come to see him only. He was the man, and I should not either be seen or heard. He insisted on being the centre of attention all the time. It was his firm belief that the universe turned just for him, and any encroachment on this state of affairs should be repelled forthwith. He was a man with a big ego problem and not a lot of sensitivity. I remember him calling me one morning, saying that it was seven o'clock, when I looked at the clock it was only a quarter to six. Naturally I informed him of the right time, and the answer from him was, "If I say it's seven o'clock, then it's seven o'clock". And so it was with him. Whatever he said, must be accepted as fact, no matter how ridiculous or how wrong.

Oddly, he was very Christian, especially from the teeth out, as most are. He tried to do the best he could according to his lights, but his lack of understanding of other's feeling always got in the way. His mouth always did four hours at war, before his brains got out of bed. He fell out with everybody, and so all the good he did, was lost in the debris of his quest for supremacy in all things. Which in some cases made it easier for me, as no one wanted to know us because of this, and they left us more or less alone. Except when they came to rip us off for whatever meagre things we had.

119

There were plenty of such people around at that time, and since returning to Ireland, sadly I find that there still are. It is the way of life over here. Everything is a rip off. There was one farmer who was a Freemason as was my Uncle. He rented some land from us for tillage. He paid us ten shillings an acre for the land, knowing full well that the going rate was ten pounds. He sold us an Ayrshire cow that could not be handled by anyone. It kicked like mad if you went to milk it. Which of course was my job. He took it back at half price, and all this while he knew we were on the starvation line. He was a great man in the Church, wouldn't you know it. Because he was a Mason and a Church goer, Uncle George just took him at his word. Mind you Uncle George was never there. It was we that paid the price of his stupidity.

That same man came to the house one day, he did not know that I was in the house, and could hear him. He made my mother an offer he thought she could not possibly refuse. I will never forget his face when I appeared. I told him where to go and threatened that I would let the World know. His answer was simple, "And who the hell do you think is going to believe the likes of you?" The story of my life, and I am sure the lives of many people who are down and broke. You are judged in this World solely by the amount of money you have, or appear to have. I hasten to add at this point that I have nothing at all against Freemasons. I have found them to be among the best people I have known. But like ourselves in The Order, the odd one gets through. If I held them all responsible, then I would be likewise responsible for the actions of every one of my members. I am sure that the other Masons in the area would have been more than a little upset if they had known about any of this at the time.

You still hear a number of 'iffy' things about the Masons these days, most of it propaganda, but you also hear bad things about Catholic priests. That doesn't mean that they are all bad, they are I am glad to say in the smallest minority. It has been my experience that most Freemasons and indeed Catholic Priests, are good men, though somewhat misguided and sometimes downright evil. The vast majority are decent and trustworthy men.

My uncle at that time made things so difficult for himself as well as for us, and it was all so unnecessary. He was as I have said a Freemason and a great Christian. He was what was known as a 'four wheeler'. They go to church in a pram to be christened, in a car to be married, and in a hearse to be buried. He seldom went to church, but he prayed every night. I remember when I was young listening to him, as I did often, and he always said "Grant me conquest over my enemies, that I may be successful. In the name of Thy Son Jesus Christ" etc. I always wondered why he never asked for happiness, wisdom, guidance, or anything else. It was a bit like a child asking Father Christmas for goodies, and promising good behaviour in return. I used to wonder who all these enemies were, and then I realised he meant everyone who might disagree with him. How Christian! He tried hard to make a Christian out of me, and I put up a good act, even though I say so myself. At that time there is one thing that Christians taught me, and that was, never trust one, and never be one. By now, they had really got to me.

When I was about eighteen the visitors slowly stopped coming. Some of them had passed away. Others were getting too old, and their job was done. The rest was up to me, and I was alone with my life, and all that was to happen to me. It appeared at the time, that I was abandoned to my fate as it were, and I felt very alone. So very much alone with all that I was, whatever that meant. Yet I knew somehow, that they were watching, and I know they still are. The difference now is that 'the ending of days' is here, and they get in touch now and again just to let me know whether they disapprove, or approve, of the things I do, or do not do.

I have met with more disapproval than approval lately, and it takes all that I have in me just to keep up with it all. I often wonder, what has it got to do with them. They have put absolutely nothing in for years. They just sit there like the gnomes of Dulwich. Surely you have to do something to earn the right to criticise. I feel very peeved with them, such a lot of the time, and I still get the same answers. And I don't like the answers.

# MARRIAGE

I got married in 1965. It was a disaster. I won't go into these things, as too many people were hurt enough at the time, and as with all things long dead, the time for burial is long since past. Needless to say it ended.

All was not lost. I have a very good son out of it. At times I could not have survived without his support and help. The Brotherhood, the High Templars and the Upper Templars were against me marrying anyone at the time, not least of all the person I did marry. They were right, and I was wrong at that time. This is why I must be careful. I don't always like the answers or the interference, but they are sometimes right. I still think they should either put up or shut up. Perhaps I should not feel that way, but I need help more than just criticism, both physically and financially. They have always come up short on things financially. You would think they were all Christians. Tight with the cash, and free with the opinions. The Brotherhood nonetheless have kept in close touch, but as is their way, not too close a touch.

I felt I didn't want to know anymore. I felt that it had no bearing on my life except to make it a misery. I had been treated badly, so I decided at that time to go my way and to hell with it all. My mother used to tell me that it is easier to step away from the World, than it is to step away from oneself. In the end I could not step away from either, and here I am. Gathering members, burning the midnight oil and the proverbial candle at both ends. She never stopped using every tactic she could drum up to get me to turn around. I flatly refused to lay my hands on anyone again, but just now and again, it happened. There were times when I just couldn't resist. I am not sure whether I was trying to prove something to myself or not, though there were those who said that it was my only motive. I think them wrong. I knew I could do it. I had always been able to heal people of the most incurable things, so what was there or is there left for me to prove. I did it on the quiet, as I really did not want to get back into the 'old life', as I now considered it. I certainly did not want to attract any attention. My mother was always right. She was a woman with that habit, and secretly I knew it. I couldn't outrun whatever was in me. But I gave it a very good try. I think deep down, I knew one day I would have to turn around, and face it. After many years in the wilderness as it were, I found myself extremely ill. My heart decided to quit on me. I had three heart attacks in a row and just for good measure a slight stroke. Believe me, there is no such a thing as a slight stroke. I was divorced for the second time, and married again, and looking down a very long dark tunnel. What a 'screw up'.

On one of my frequent but not frequent enough visits to see my mother, we had one of our chats. The type you know you never can win. You know the ones when you just know that whatever you do, you will end up doing something that you really do not want to do. And you know mothers, you just can't resist them.

I received a telephone call from her asking me to come and see her that night, alone. My sister was out and we would be alone. She cornered me with that old 'what do you think you are doing?' routine. She started to speak and laid it all on the line. I was stunned. I had never heard her speak like that in all my life. She went through my life step by step, and blow by blow, and there were a lot of blows. All the things I had done, and had not done.

Those who had risked, and often lost, their lives in the past in the protection of the Way, and in their efforts for my protection. Even though I often made it nearly impossible for them, because of the risks I took. I felt that some of it was right at least. I had lived my life semi-secretly and still do to some extent. Like a Kamikaze pilot I lived with a death wish all the time. I was almost, but not quite bent on my own destruction.

If something was so dangerous no one in their right mind would do it, then I was your man. I even transported nitro-glycerine in the back of a truck over some very bumpy roads, and I remember every bump. I sailed in seas that no one else would dare go out in, or be mad enough to consider. I have actually left harbour in a force ten gale knowing that it could get even worse. The waves breaking forty feet in the air and me in an open boat, thirty feet long. Mum didn't know the half of it. She couldn't have done, she was only grey not bald. She was right. I had given them a very hard time, and myself an even harder one. When they didn't want me to get involved with something or someone, then that is exactly what I would do, in some vain attempt to shake myself loose from this thing.She had asked me to come to see her that night and to come alone. That night changed my life. Well I suppose it is fair to say that my life did start to change, I just didn't know it at the time.

My mother died and I think that did it. She had the last word the night she died, and from then on I really started to think, because that is what she had said. "Please son, think. Do it just for me". Her last words. I did and I still am. I never stop thinking. Some of it helps, some of it doesn't. Thinking is a bit like that.

My health got worse and worse, exactly as she said it would. A man who denies his purpose denies his right to exist, so it is said in the Old Order, and I had a very firm promise from Christ that I did not know about at the time. That he would sicken me, sour my belly and cause sweetness upon my breath. I am now a diabetic. How's that for an arm twister? I had been told often enough that it was written, and promised by Christ, that if I did not fulfil my purpose, I would be sickened unto death until I fulfilled that purpose. Should I not make every possible effort to do so, then I would die.As usual I chose to stick two finger up to it all, and sicker and sicker I became, till I knew I was going to die.

It took the three heart attacks and a stroke, but they did not knock the smallest dent in my resolve. I had little contact with the Brotherhood who by now must have been fed up with me, and wishing that the Prophesied one was someone else. I wished he was too. I bet they combed everything and everywhere, just in the vain hope that they may have got it wrong, and it was someone else all the time. What a relief it would have been. Unfortunately I know them better than that. They know exactly what is what. They knew every move I ever made long before I even thought of it, never mind made it. So I couldn't be so lucky.

The Brothers started to come out of the woodwork then. I met members of the Brotherhood in the most unusual of places. One came up to me in Lincoln railway station. Saying the words, and clinging on to me. She was an Egyptian lady, and she stayed with me till my train came. The tears running down her face, holding on to me as if her very life depended on it. Pleading with me to stop and think. To love myself a little for a change. To stop the anger with myself. She even jumped onto the train, and wiped her tears on my hand. She then got off the train at the last second, and I never saw or even heard of her again. This is the way of things in the High Temple. Weird.

I could relate a dozen or more such incidences during that period. Even my son was approached by a man in Blackpool, while he was there for the day with some friends. He didn't know what to do, but he knew enough from my speaking to him to know the Signs. My son Harry was at that time and still is very much a part of everything I do. As I have said before I simply could not have survived without him. He is the kind if chap that is totally reliable, and always there, no matter what. Someone once said of us, "you two are joined at the hip". That about says it all, though it was not meant in a complimentary way at the time.

It was shortly after that I managed to get my life sorted out a bit, and I am still sorting it out. Just when you think you have it cracked it up comes the old Prophesy, and away I must go again. The difference now is that I don't mind. As a matter of fact I like it, and can't for the life of me think why I ran away from it all those years. Ill treatment and neglect by the Brotherhood and the High Templars, an excuse and never a reason. But in fairness to myself they could have done a lot more. A little help and understanding on their behalf would have made a great difference, and I cannot see why it should not have been so.

Those wasted years. Mainly because I was afraid that people might turn against me yet again. When I was younger living in a very Christian World, what I am got in the way with the girls, etc. In those years, it was very difficult as far as married life, and everything else was concerned. Day to day living was unbelievably difficult. How could whatever is out there, possibly pick on someone like me. It can't be too bright now can it? The oldest and perhaps the most asked question in the World "Why me?" At the same time they tell me that everything that has happened to me, and everything I have ever done, was Prophesied. I am told that most of it was very necessary, because if it had not happened I would not have the experiences that will help me to fulfil the Prophesy.

I have done so many things. I started out farming as I lived on the farm, and really liked the life. Because of difficulties resulting from my first marriage I had to sell my little farm, and return to England. Not an easy thing for me to do as I really loved my life as a small farmer. It was all I ever wanted to be, living amongst the most beautiful countryside you could imagine. Working and living close to the land, and to nature. Doing the things I liked most in the World. I could not, and can not, think of any better way of life. To me it was paradise. I became a psychiatric nurse, again I loved it, and again I had to move on through circumstances 'beyond my control', as they say. I later went further into psychology.

After that I sold insurance. I found the Insurance business 'dodgy' to say the least. The customer always lost, but because they apparently couldn't work out the actual figures, they never seemed to cop on. This sort of a situation was not for me; fair is fair. Because of my experience in selling insurance I got as job with a finance company. I was a financial consultant after a very short training course. Big title, small money. I did not like it, but as they say 'when the Devil drives'. I had a mortgage and three small children to support, at least that is my excuse. It was far too 'bent' for me so I quit as soon as I could.

After that I moved to Scotland, where I bought a small boat. I became a fisherman. The open sea, clean air, and no one to bother me. It was a great life, and again I loved it. The sunny days still stick in my memory, and I would prefer to forget the cold and the storms. The times when you could not get out, to sea, and money became so scarce that bad weather or not you had to put to sea. This is mainly how accidents happen at sea among the fishermen. Shortage of cash leads to low maintenance, and desperation. Put these two together and you have catastrophe.

I sold a boat that had made me a good deal of money, and bought a bigger boat, with the intention of making a far better and more reliable living. With a bigger boat I could sail in heavier weather with a greater degree of safety, and have even bigger 'catches'. Unfortunately the new boat sank on delivery, in a storm off Red Ruth in Cornwall. I was insured through the bank, and thought I had no worries. No one was hurt, just the boat was smashed to pieces, and you can get another boat, or so I thought. I put in my claim and awaited payment. It went on and on. My lawyer kept assuring me that all was well, and they played me along. Waiting for the insurance money for five years. Every month it was, "They will pay up soon". Meaning the Insurance Company would settle. They apparently already had. It turned out that the lawyer, who was supposed to be my friend, had the money all the time. At the end of that five years, he just told me, that under Scottish law after five years I could forget it. Like a fool I believed my friend. I really thought that the insurers and the bank had ripped me off with clever legal tactics. My lawyer friend had me convinced. It was not till he got caught out many years later for ripping off more of his unfortunate clients, that the penny dropped. Because of the loss of everything I had in the boat, I was broke. Everything I had was in the boat. I was unemployed, and it was winter. The cost of keeping the house warm was high.

I sold an old car I had and bought a chainsaw, and some 'thinnings' from the Forestry. By 'thinnings' I mean the young trees that have to be thinned out to allow room for the others to grow. They are usually bent ones or forked or have some defect that makes them fit only for firewood. I started to cut firewood for myself, not thinking of doing anything other than saving a bit of money. A neighbour saw me carrying in the wood and wanted me to sell her some. She couldn't get any at that time she offered me seventy pence a bag, so I sold her some, and it caught on. Before I knew it I was off the dole and making a living. It was a hard living, but a living none the less. There was a very limited number of ways a chap could make a living at that time, and I was glad of it. From firewood I managed to get a mobile saw-bench and a tractor. When the summer came I knew that the firewood sales would drop, so made horse jumps and anything I could sell to turn money. From this I managed to start a saw mill. Life was becoming good again. The light was visible at the end of the tunnel. From here I bought machines for the mill, and machines for extracting timber. I contracted to the Forestry, felling and extracting timber, as well as buying woods and felling them for use in my own mill, then selling the spare timber to other saw mills.

Then it happened again. The saw mill was burned just one week after the insurance ran out. The insurance agent always called for the renewal and the cash, about a week or so before it was due. It was so very odd, almost as though he knew. He was related to a local family in that unfriendly and hostile, insular little village, who objected to my running the mill, as they felt they should have it. There was no room there for strangers. I wonder if the 'Animal' has got them yet. Everything I owned was burned, together with my mini bus that was used to transport workers to and from the woods. It went up in smoke along with a lot of other machines, and bits and pieces that were burned with the mill. It was a critical time for me the business was just over the hill, but not quite. That fulcrum stage and this was the finish. There was no way I could carry on. Another freak accident! I was broke again.

After that I ran discos, and fashion shows. I was making money out of a very good idea. Unfortunately others saw what I was doing, and they too started up, and ruined it all. Not only for me but for themselves as well. Most of these people had it made, and could just sit back and snipe off the profitable bits at a knock down price. Suddenly it was all a waste of time, as I had to make a living and they did not. They had other irons in the fire, but, there you go. Life is about money, and money, and the worshipers of money have no scruples. How I wish I had discovered this fact about money sooner. I left that area and moved, selling 'fruit and veg.' on a market stall in Dumfries and various markets down as far as Carlisle and Workington, and up as far as Edinburgh. I found that it was not profitable enough, so my son and I started a garage business, selling and repairing cars.

I then moved down into England as there was more scope there, and the living was easier. I went deeper into the car business, and again, the finger pointed right at me. I had to 'get out' as my health would no longer stand the strain. About this time my heart started to let me down, and I was very ill. Because I am a member of the Guild Of Tarot Masters, again a 'Caulbearer' only organisation, I was able to make a living, or at least part of a living, reading cards and hands, and casting astrological charts. I also taught astrology, and clinical palmistry. I find it such a shame that palmistry is not more widely used in medicine today. Its accuracy is infallible when you know how to do it well.

I have plastered walls, built houses and renovated old houses, made furniture, welded old cars together and crashed ones. Panel beating, spraying, all sorts of metal work. I did a little market gardening because of my farming background. I have owned and driven bulldozers and diggers. I have written songs. One or two of them became quite popular. I have written poetry and children's stories.

There are many other things I have done some I am proud of, some I am not. Some shall remain in those darker corners of my mind, just like anyone else, only in my case more so. I have lived hard but I have lived intensely, and managed to stay alive, though only just on one or two occasions.

The thing that bothers me and has bothered me all the time, as I am sure it would bother anyone else, is that unanswerable question, "Why me"?. There are so many other lesser questions. Why do my hands bleed? Why if they cure one person of terminal cancer, do the not cure everyone of the same disease? Why if one spinal cord severance patient walks, don't they all walk? Why do I always question? Surely I am the last person that should question, maybe that is why I have failures. Or maybe this is why I have success, and often very dramatic successes.

The members of the Old Order don't help. They say that it is the way I should be. It is better for me to question myself and what I do than become conceited. All these clever answers that I get all the time, and none of them are any use, at least not to me. As a member of the High Temple told me recently, "You know. What is there for us to say to you that may change your reality. The truth is as it is, and the truth cannot be altered nor can it be changed". One of the Knight Protectors says that it is because I am afraid. When I asked him what he thought I was afraid of, he said "Of losing the dream and not being able to live with the reality". Maybe he is right. Maybe it is the other way around. A lot of people say a lot of different things, most of them make sense at the time, then they don't.

The signs of the Prophesy are there every day for me to see, they are not dreams, they are frighteningly real. And as I write, I start to think that the dream is over, the reality begins. Both your reality and my reality, and they are not so different. We are not so different. We may have different roles, but life is about survival. End of story.

To survive is the most singular important thing in life, for if you don't survive you don't do anything, and the dark curtain falls. The next question in my mind is: Do I want it to fall? Sometimes I do, sometimes I just don't care. Once I loaded my rifle and went down into the glen at the farm just before I decided to sell it. I put the muzzle of the rifle in my mouth and I pulled the trigger, the rifle just went "click". The loudest noise I have ever heard. Yet if you were standing six feet away from me you would not have heard it. But it still echoes through the mountains and the valleys of my mind, even now. I lifted the bolt and dropped it again, and pulled the trigger again, pointing the rifle skyward. It went of with a loud solid crack. The bullet was not a dud. It had simply misfired the first time and my demise at this time, was just not meant to be. I think that if that bullet had been a dud, I would probably have put in another one and I would have done it again. I sat there looking about me. I did a great deal of very clear thinking in a very short time. My mind was never so clear, and I knew exactly what I must do. As I sat on the bank beside the brook, looking into a deep dark pool it all became as clear as day. So I went back to the house and informed my then wife, that as far as I was concerned our life in Ireland was over, and I was going back to England for good. If she wished it, I would give her one last chance to sort herself out. She could come or she could stay. It was all over and I could not and would not take any more. I was selling the farm and leaving. If things did not improve between her and I in England, we could be divorced and go our separate ways.

She wanted to come to England, but she didn't take that second, or was it that ninety-second chance to repair our marriage. She probably had more sense than me, and knew it was a waste of time. Things between us stayed almost exactly the same. But I knew I had done everything I could to help the situation. I did not want that curtain to fall, but it fell despite everyone's efforts, except hers, to prevent it, and I found myself with two small children. But I had a second chance none the less. After the incident with the rifle when I intended to end my life because I could no longer stand the pain, and even less the shame.

I got in touch with one of my old 'Aunties', and I told her exactly what I had done, and what had happened. She said I should not to say a word to my mother about the rifle for obvious reasons. I remember being quite surprised that she should think that I would. Still if I was prepared to go so far, I probably wasn't thinking right anyway. And old 'Auntie' probably had this in mind. I don't know to this day what she really thought about it, as the subject was never mentioned ever again. I am a pathetic creature aren't I?

So back to the same old question again. "Why me"? Why not some tough, rich, tall dark and handsome 'film star' type? The cool calm type, that always gets it right. I have been told that they can only pretend, they can't really do anything other than pretend. So that's apparently why. Every one has an answer that seems to block my every road out. And yet no one has an answer at all.

Once again I find myself with absolutely no options. I was born as they say "behind the veil" and all that it means with all its obligations and responsibilities. And all the questions that go along with it too, I suppose. I am constantly asked by the High Templars, the Upper Templars, the Brotherhood Of The Flame, the Knight Protectors of the Brotherhood, High Priests, Exalted Priests, and many ordinary members, what am I going to do, and when am I going to do it? When am I going to add my bit to the Prophesy? What do I add to the Prophesy that anyone wants to hear, as we all must add to it?

Firstly I want to bring out the Old Order into the light. I cannot see the point of protecting the Order as it has been protected over the last two thousand years and more if I don't. Hidden as it has been all this time it is just useless, and cannot serve its purpose, if it has a purpose in our time, unless it is out in the bright clean light of day. It can become seriously problematical out in the open. But we are used to problems. The members have struggled against all odds and have kept it alive, only just alive, but nevertheless, alive.

Since the Brotherhood of Light was first thought of in the mind of the second comer, it has always been dogged with problems. Everyone wants knowledge, or so they will say. But only the kind that they can control, and use for themselves alone against the rest of the World.

Problems I have had all my life, with varying degrees of success and failure. But not quite like this. I would be a fool if I thought that they were even remotely the same. People kill to protect their belief systems, and men like me are the targets as we are always considered a threat. And so are my associates, and my family.

# JOHN

In the Order Of The Ancient Way, when the Supreme High Priest is about to pass on, he names his successor, and you can't say 'No'. John was my predecessor. His wife and family staunch Roman Catholics. The last thing he asked from me was that his family should never know of his membership or of his position in the Order, as he thought it would cause them pain. He had lived his life under very great difficulties, and no doubt considerable fear for his family and for himself should he be found out. It was a very much like being a criminal, always looking over his shoulder. There are so few people who can understand this way of living.

If you are a criminal its one thing. If however it is because your purpose is solely the good and indeed the survival of mankind, it is another. Try to imagine it in your mind. To give you a measure of the man, John was a very good Supreme High Priest, although some would disagree with me on that point, because he had, as they saw it, only a caretaker role. How wrong can you be? This attitude is to be condemned, unless you live that way yourself and take such a way of living for granted, and most of us do. Because if we did not we probably could not do it at all.

All men do what they know best. It all depends on what they know. This is all that John knew, the sum total of his life experience, no different to that of many before him, and I hope no more after us. As far as he was concerned his part was complete, as the Prophesy was close to it's climax, and I was almost ready. All I needed was the final push. From here on it was up to me to take things forward, or abandon them if I cannot, or if I decide that it is no longer worth it. I can only decide this, if man is no longer worth it and I cannot get the numbers needed to ensure survival.

John was not a member of the Brotherhood Of The Flame, as it was considered in his time too dangerous, both for him and for them. It was a need to know basis, so they nevertheless kept him abreast with whatever they thought he would need to know, to do his job. So he knew a great deal about the Prophesy. He did not need or want to know any more than was absolutely necessary as has always been the way of things. No one is actually allowed to know it all, not even the Brotherhood themselves. The knowledge that requires protection is spread about in the Brotherhood. That way you would have to get us all in order to destroy what Jesus and those gone before him left behind. Teams of two are chosen, they will both carry the same information. Each team will do the same, each pair knowing a different piece. Thus it has been protected for two thousand years, against all who hunted it and it's carriers in order to destroy it. Purely for self motive and the protection of their belief systems, which they know to be wrong.

John's position in the role of the Order was simple. All these things had worked very well over the last two thousand years and beyond. The method had worked very well. His attitude, though he was often under pressure, was as is mine, 'If it ain't broke don't fix it'. The time was just not right for the Order to come into the light. For him to bring it forward would have just caused unnecessary problems, and been a waste of effort. It could have given the opposition insight that could have proved disastrous for the Order. The child could prove stillborn.

And so he waited until the Prophesy started to unfold. Until the time was right, for the minds of men to possibly start to change. As far as he was concerned and as far as the Brotherhood are concerned the time is now. According to everything laid out in the Prophesy, down to the minutest detail, I was and am the one. He therefore named me his successor in spite of my protest, and it is fair to say at this time, also the protests of others who saw things differently. They felt that someone else should have been Supreme High Priest, leaving me free to do other things in the background where I would be safe, and even more important the Seven Seals would be safe. I now know how wrong they are. We can make things so safe that we can suffocate them. So safe that they can never be allowed out to play thus the necessary sunlight that is so vital for growth would be withheld. The purpose would defeat the purpose.

The more the Prophesy unfolds the more I appreciate John's thinking. I really did not want the job. There are those who expect me to say that, as though it is kind of obligatory, but I really meant it. It wasn't until after his death that the points of Prophesy really started to show themselves. I have since come into possession of the other six Seals. Going through what they reveal has changed my mind in no considerable way. Just as he knew they would. He had said as much. The points of the Prophesy were known to the members of the Way, but only in fragmented form, and were not to be written until after John's time. It was thought necessary for certain things to be written about this time.

Other signs were starting to unfold one by one. Even now the mutation of the frogs is apparent. It started a long time ago with the Sign of the 'Caulbearer' that was Prophesied. That Sign already seen and as far as they were, and are all concerned the Seventh Sign is born, and lives.

I know in my heart and in my core that I am that Sign, even though for most of my life I did not want it to be so, and I could do without it even now. The fact remains that I fit every one of the points of the Prophesy, from my 'Veil' or 'Caul' to the mark in my right side. To the very marks in my hands and the numbers as were Prophesied. As John said to me on more than one occasion, the last time he said it was not long before he died, "Who else is there that fulfils all the points? There is no one but you, so to who else should I leave the future of the Order? Who else was born at that exact time, in that exact place, bearing all the marks? Who can and has healed the un-healable?" When I remember the way he used to go on at me not so many years ago, the things he used to say now make sense. To my shame I really gave John a hard time, as I did all the others. With my doubts and fears, and my lack of sureness in myself, and in my capabilities. It was all so unreal to me. It was as if they were my enemies and were trying to steal my life away from me.

To me now it is all so reasonable, from every point of view. It is a lot to accept, but it must be accepted. Some members of the Order want me to keep it low and quiet, they would like the Order Of The Ancient Way to remain an exclusive club. As to the others, they can't understand why I did not just declare myself, quickly and use my various talents to advance the cause of the Old Way. The opinions vary from one end of the scale to the other. But if they were me they would do exactly as I have done. I must do it as I see fit, after considering all the advice. It is so easy to criticise my actions or lack of them when you are outside looking in, and no one is giving you a hard time. I am often given a very hard time, from all sorts of angles and I seldom have any constructive help or advice offered. Criticism is seldom helpful. I get all the usual kind. You know the type the "if I was you" routine. So easy when all you have to do is give lip service, but oh so different when your head is on the block of this responsibility, and you are being pulled this way and that. Mostly by people with their own axes to grind and no responsibility for the grinding of them, or of the spoiling of the temper of that metal . If I get it right it is always because of the advice I was given, and everyone involved feels good. If I should get it wrong it is because I am a fool, and everyone else involved feels good. Its a funny old World isn't it?

My vision of the future is really quite simple. According to The Christ, I require seventy thousand people or thereabouts in seven different nations, in order to ensure the continuance of the species called man, on the planet, and indeed in the universe. It must be remembered at this time that the Old ones as we call them said, "Man will one day live in the heavens". This is where the idea came from for heaven, a bit of a mix up in concept. I say it this way out of charity for it's inventors though it resulted in yet more false belief which has been readily accepted without reason, or the use of a single iota of common sense. Man will indeed live in the heavens one day, which is now self evident, and will become a permanent situation in the future. If the species manages to survive, and has a future. Which is doubtful. Paradise is an Earthly thing as far as we, and the old ones are concerned. Not somewhere 'up there' where you will go after death. Providing you have obeyed that which you have been told to obey and that you have suffered enough to gain entrance. A Paradise, there for your reward, only yours to claim after you are dead. With no one to come back and complain over raw deals in the matter.

This idea was invented so that the masses would be content to put up with all kinds of hardships without question or complaint. Most of those who believe are even glad to suffer, which is a total waste of their nobility. It is my experience that you never see any member of the hierarchy that advocate this theory do much suffering, nor do they ever appear to be hard up or short of anything in any way. So if they believe that which they require the rest of us to believe, why are they not giving away all they have? After all eternity is a long time compared with our stay on Earth. It is indeed a credit to the resilience of the human race that they have this capability to withstand all kinds of hardships, which can appear unbearable. If we are to survive we will need this ability, this nobility, in large quantities. So perhaps this particular trait of human nature that has been so abused by the organisers of religion for their own ends, will at last be proved useful in a constructive way, for the benefit for those who actually do the suffering, for a change.

Perhaps the wheel turns, albeit slowly. I require seventy thousand people out of the population of the World, with this trait in their natures. So if you happen to come across a few of them while you are out, let me know. My vision, or my Prophesy if you like, of the future, is that disease will kill off most of the population, mainly sexually transmitted diseases, as was the case in Sodom and Gomorrah. They decided then that they had to kill all those who practiced the perversion of homosexuality, hence the word sodomy, which is still used today. Imagine the practice of homosexual, anal intercourse. Imagine it. Then tell me it's not a perversion. They burned both cities with fire. All those bodies not burned in the fire were covered in brimstone and buried, to ensure the maximum destruction of the disease that was carried and transmitted by them, and it was no more.

Among the masses moral decline will reach a far lower level than can at this time be imagined. Therefore it is imperative that we return to the ideals of a more puritan kind, but without going over the top, as they did in Victorian times. This is of course will make virginity and faithfulness in marriage paramount. Sexual matters outside marriage will have to be strictly confined, if a healthy population is to be achieved. This of course will be cried down, as those who practice perversion are usually totally perverted, not just sexually. It does not matter if marriage is monogamous or not, it is the ideal, the reason and the sense of it that we must cling to. As with all matters concerning life, and the quality of it. There will be so many groups in the near future, each one fighting for supremacy, each one sure that his or her beliefs are right.

The Christian, the Muslim and all the rest, going totally against the teachings of their religions. Wallowing in the blood of their so called enemies and justifying it. Saying it to be in God's cause. I'll bet they don't ask him first. They never do. It is just assumed that it is all done with his permission. Mind you it's not hard to get the permission of someone who does not in fact exist. They will continue refusing to accept facts, refusing to accept or differentiate between belief and hard reality.

Again the old ways will die hard, if at all. Belief without reason has been the thing for so long now. It has helped the most base amongst us feel good about themselves, and superior over all others. It has been such a great excuse. It has enabled so many to live with themselves that the habit will be hard to break. It has become a kind of perversion in itself and will break the species and render it extinct; as well as destroy the planet, if all false belief is not quickly abandoned and replaced with fact and reason. These differences will not amount to very great wars, as we have known once or twice in the past, though it may seem so. They will mostly range from terrorists to small 'war-lord' types. Leaders of new religions and political dogmas, all juggling for supremacy. They will be backed at worst by organised religion, and at best not discouraged by these same religions so long as they can profit from it in some way, no matter how obscure. The leaders of religion are always looking, and hoping to gain strength by backing a winner. The warmonger is always trying to gain leverage, credibility and strength from religious leaders, who lend respectability to that leader or to that cause. Thus enabling them to raise armies in the cause. In Christian countries and those mixed, but mainly Christian, the backing of he who knows the evil that he does will be sought and given, and of course the same will be the case for his like in other religions. They are all the same in the ways that matter. Each religious leader, wanting to rule the World. To own, the hearts and minds of all.

You have seen evidence of this in the past two thousand years, all over the globe. Their cruelty and their greed, not to mention their conceit has known no bounds in all these matters. The Pope is to ask for forgiveness for the mistakes of the Roman Church in the past. He omitted the evils of the past. They were not mistakes. They were deliberate in their design, foul in their purpose and totally beyond any form of forgiveness in their evil. What sort of mind would describe them as mistakes? From the burning of people as witches, to the Jesuits having a hand in the training of the German S.S. in matters of torture. If it is not true, then why has the Papacy avoided the questions so often put to it on this matter? Uncle Ivone was right about the Pope's hand in Hitler's madness. That might appear to have been a mistake, but true to form, only when found out.

Christ has said, "The time for the forgiveness of man is over." The Pope is very well aware of this. He must now take full responsibility for all his actions and the actions of his office, past and present. The Pope apparently does not see it that way. Because if he did, if he was to be honest and the truth became evident, his church would be torn down and his cronies hunted and no doubt put to death. As they have done so often and so cruelly to anyone who opposed them in the past, or to anyone who dared to cast doubt upon their professed belief. Even though that belief is totally unable to stand up to scrutiny. They still do the same even today, though they will deny it. They will be more than willing to do it again in the future should the need rise. Purely to protect the belief system and their power over the peoples ruled under that belief system. They cannot afford to be honest. So the lie goes on, camouflaged by a false show of remorse that will, in the end kill off the Roman Catholic Church. The leopard will change not his spots. He may paint them over, but come the rains they will wash off, and again the leopard will show himself in his true colours.

The Anglican Catholic Church will fare no better. They will carry on as is usual with blindness and stupidity. I think they are chosen because of this, not because of any show if intelligence. It is painfully obvious to all that they are disconnected, not only from any form of reason, but also from the needs of the people they claim to serve. They have only ever served the crown, and their own ends. The attempts of the various factions will of course set brother against brother yet again in the future. Once again unfortunately and uselessly, man will know no reason.

The Europeans will fight among themselves, and revolution will be rife. There will be germ warfare, as well as atomic confrontation. All this as the Mother struggles even harder beneath the feet of the beast for her very life. Her

136

struggle will go unnoticed, as usual. No one will give a damn. No more than they do today. As usual man will have far more important things to do. He will have points to score, political careers to build and such like. Not a lot will change in the nature of the beast.

The ozone layer will become thin. The sun will kill. They will search for cures of this and that, while ignoring the causes. There is no money nor is there political gain in pointing out, or curing the causes. This is a situation that will go on indefinitely, and the reasons are simple as well. All you have to do is see who is creating the causes in the first place. And what is their purpose? The very air you breath will carry so many germs and bugs that you don't even know of yet, and will not be allowed to know of till, as usual it is far too late. Supermarkets will eventually become officially noticed as a prime source of disease, through droplet infection. This is a fact well known now but it is ignored, and nothing is done. Because the banks, who really own them, would lose too much money and money rules. Those who control the money call the punches. One saving grace may be the introduction of shopping on the Internet. Ordering your goods and having them delivered. Unfortunately you will not be able to see the conditions of either the staff who handle your goods, or the environment your goods are stored and handled in. This system again will have many disadvantages for the public  but not for the bankers. People will have to wear masks whenever they come into contact with others. Schools will no longer be able to function, again because of the spread of disease. Look at meningitis now. Water will be so impure that clean water will cost more than petrol. Clean uncontaminated food will be at a premium. Society will break down all over the World as the oil runs out. Eventually the oil companies will have to release the rights to all the other types of fuels that they now hold. Again, to protect their interests in oil.

There will be many new ideas that will range from water to methane to solar. Many will prove useless against the tide of humanity, and its demands. Governments will take away from the public all forms of weapons on some pretext or another. In order that people may not be in a position to protect themselves and their families against the rioting hordes that they expect, at the expense of everyone else. Politicians, would you believe, will become even more dishonest, corrupt and evasive, though that may seem impossible at present.

Farmland will become so polluted by slurry and chemicals, that food will become difficult if not impossible to grow. And it is now a neglected fact that animals cannot drink dirty water and survive any more than people can. They too will die and another food source will be lost to us. Another link in the evolutionary chain will be broken, for ever. More and more farmland will be covered in concrete and poor land will have to be reclaimed, to try to fill the gap. Again, at a great cost to the public. Some as usual will make a lot of money out of it. Look around you, it's already happening and will go unnoticed till the situation becomes impossible.

The climatic changes will be so great, as the planetary line up gets closer, on and about the sixth of May 2006, that the seasons will become unrecognisable with extreme weather conditions prevailing. You can see it has already started now. This will make the growing of food almost impossible except under controlled conditions. What price cheap food then? The price of food will go sky high, even the most basic diet will be expensive as well as scarce. In most countries it will prove impossible to grow enough food for the needs of the population, including Britain and Ireland and most of the Continent of Europe. This will be made worse by their attitudes and population density. America will try to bring Canada into a form of union, for her own sake, certainly not for the Canadians sake. The Canadians will indeed be foolish to allow this to happen. The E.E.C. members will keep falling out among themselves. And as things become worse the union will break down altogether. Minor wars will commence among the now friends over all sorts of issues. Mostly unsolvable even with good will and with the lack of it impossible.

The German Government is already preparing for this by giving grants to certain German people. I was informed of this by a local estate agent, when approached to sell my house. I haven't got a long driveway, and the grant is solely to buy houses and farms in Ireland, with long driveways and preferably near lakes. Lakes can be seen on the darkest of nights. Perfect for parachutists to land unnoticed by the public in general. They are doing just as they did in Poland before the last World war. History will again repeat itself. This was the reason Poland fell so easily. They were surrounded from within. The German government recognises that Hitler's biggest mistake was not taking the Irish President up on his offer to put troops into Ireland. If he had done so it would have been all over for England, as the German Forces could have just sat there and taken pot shots at all the shipping going past Just like shooting fish in a barrel. Britain would have quickly been starved into surrender, leaving Ireland under the jackboot. What a catastrophe it would have been.

Ireland would do well to bury the past and join the United Kingdom. Though many will disagree, England is in fact her closest relation. We have been intermarrying for generations and there is hardly a family in Ireland who does not have English relatives. When they fight with each other, they are in fact fighting their own kinfolk. Every time a bomb goes off Catholics get killed, most of them of Irish descent. Together they would stand, but there is nothing surer that divided they will both fall, if not to the German then to the Oriental.

This time the Germans are ready, just in case they can't get things all their own way through the Common Market, and they won't. So await the rise of the Fourth Reich. It will come.

Spain will want to go to war with Britain eventually, but fail to even get started, as the people will not have the heart. Thus will the power-mongers fail, and hopefully learn a lesson. South America will burn under the ozone free sky, as will we all. But those near the equator and close to rain forests will suffer the most. The rain forests themselves will shrink at an even faster rate, not for food production but for money that will buy luxury goods. The seas will cool around the coasts of Britain and parts of the Continent, making things even worse climactically. The poles will melt down and cause the Earth to go out of balance. Like a huge car wheel it will start to wobble. The skin of the Earth may slip and be the cause the poles to change. The poles will change anyway with catastrophic results to the species of man, and to his supporting species.

The Earth will vibrate as it spins. It is fixable, but until this problem is rectified the dangers increase every day.

Political leaders will hold discussions that will appear to go on forever, and should they ever reach agreement it will be too late. Hence the need to repair the ozone layer as soon as possible, which is unlikely to be done in time. The smallest thing now takes at least six months of talk before anything can be done. Along with religious belief, the second biggest curse is the dragged out political talks and point scoring. The ox guns should be banned. Do you know what an ox gun is? Well it's for firing 'bullshit'. That stuff that will drown us all.

Crime will flourish, as the ordinary people will be disarmed and defenceless. The ordinary man and especially woman, in the street will become so brainwashed and frightened over the use of arms, that they will be totally vulnerable. Unable to protect themselves physically or emotionally against not only the criminal thieves and robbers, but also the legal kind of criminal, who will increase drastically, and to political whim and to all those whose whims are more of a base nature. The public will not have any guns or weapons but the criminals will. As you see in Britain today. Dunblane was a blessing to the Government of the day. It gave the excuse needed to sway public opinion. If they were for real and really cared about the deaths of children they would ban cars. They kill far more children than ever get killed by lunatics with guns.

Irradiation is another thing. Do you know that the food is exposed to the same kind of radiation as is used for x-ray and cancer treatment? Some of the material used is extracted from the waste of nuclear plants. They are used to kill off the microbes that spoil the food and guess what, they don't even know for sure that it is really safe, and they won't, until a large number of people are exposed to it for a long time. Then it will be a case of "Whoops! - Sorry we didn't know". It doesn't even kill all the bugs, so there is a mutation problem waiting to happen.

Dirty water. Do you know that 80% to 85% of your body is water? You will die from water shortage faster than you will from the lack of food. You need 2-3 litres of water a day. Your body loses about 2 litres a day even in cool weather. Most of our water is contaminated with nitrates from excessive use of fertilisers, which helps to produce cheaper food. You may have lead or asbestos water pipes. Try to get your local authority to change them and see what the reaction is. You will come up against every excuse under the sun. They care about children? I think not. Chlorides and aluminium sulphate, are used to purify water. It is now thought by many, that when chlorine is mixed with the acid naturally found in peat water it creates another chemical that may well cause cancer. There is a good case to answer for the use of the aluminium, which may also cause premature senility. Fluoride should only be added to water very accurately at one part per million. Imagine a chap being a bit careless whilst adding it. The machines used are not always working right. Did you know that it is in fact rat poison, and causes osteoporosis, while doing absolutely nothing for your teeth.

It is a fact, that every time you drink water you are drinking second-hand drugs like the contraceptive pill and sleeping tablets. When Ampicillin is taken, one third of it will be excreted from the body within six hours. It is an antibiotic, and it will damage your immune system as they all do.

Your domestic waste-water goes into the sewers and on to the treatment plants, where it is "purified". The systems were designed to remove bacteria from the water as well as 'solids' which was fair enough once, but not now. The apparently clean water goes back into the system as drinking water! It goes around and around up to a dozen times till it is finally dumped as unfit. The drugs and many of the chemicals pass on unaffected, and they multiply every time they go through the system. Heart drugs, tranquillisers, pain killers, anti depressants, sleeping pills. They all pass along time after time after time. And your government knows about it. So why the rush to remove guns, while letting the most vile killers of all pass on and on and on? Killing millions and deforming little children before they are even born.

140

But OK, you can always blame the will of God. Believe that if you like. Now you know what is in your water. What are you going to do about it? The disarming of the public is now a paramount goal, all over the World. The purpose is sinister. If they cared at all it would show in a more reasoning way, and there is nothing reasonable in dirty water.

Beware America, where people will go on suing companies for 'this and that'. Someone will be to blame for everything. People will not take any responsibility at all for their own actions, again making the situation worse. Causing divisions between business and the public, who rely on each other. Crop failures and starvation will be rife. People will die in hordes. There will be but a few left and they will be too weakened by disease, starvation and thirst to even bury the bodies. Those who will still be in fair physical condition will no longer care enough. They will be too busy trying to stay that way and who can blame them. An uncaring society breeds uncaring people.

Any country where people have to pay for medical attention in is not civilised. When the lives of people depend on their ability to pay for medical treatment, where they have to go the end of the queue due to lack of money, then that country is not civilised. Neither are the people that live in it and let it happen. Malaria will come to Britain along with other water born diseases as the water temperature of the rivers, ponds and lakes rise. During the extremes of weather conditions there will be extreme heat in places that are not used to it, and intense cold in places that are not used to that either. People will not be equipped either mentally, physically, practically or medically for any of it. Instead they will wait for 'Divine intervention', which of course will not come. They will seek help from their religious leaders and as usual they will be told to pray, just as were the Jews in the concentration camps, and a lot of other poor devils before and since then. The Middle East will become a 'hell hole'. There is no other way I can describe it. People will have to wear masks whenever they are likely to come into contact with their fellow man, but it will not stop the inevitable, and at this time avoidable, march of death.

It has been reported and should be taken as a warning to all that a woman with this new incurable form T.B. not knowing that she was infected boarded a plane, I think it was from Kansas. She changed planes in Baltimore for New York, stayed a short time and returned. She unwittingly infected one third of the passengers on the four planes she travelled on, and so many people were condemned to a horrible death. This is only the first of such things. Flying will become a very dangerous thing to do, for reasons other than crashing. Disease will be a real danger due to the circulation of air in the aircraft.

The incident in America is passed, and you will be told that this was due to this very air circulation in the planes pressurised system, so it was, and it will happen again, and again. As time goes by it will become impossible to use public transport at all, planes or otherwise. Droplet infection is a real threat, with or without air circulation. There is more than a small case for the return to the old type shop, with a counter between the public and the food, wrapped, irradiated or not. You can screen the staff, but you can't screen the public.

So the evidence is before your eyes now, and many of my predictions are already provable, showing the tips of the inevitable icebergs. By the time you read this there will be more, they are happening every day, and they too, are, and will be ignored. We must not panic the populace, now must we? A convenient excuse. Again if they really had the best interests of the public at heart, the attitude to these problems would be a lot different. Government Officials in all the governments of the World are paid large sums of money, thousands. The public can't expect more than two brain cells to be working, for that kind of money, now can they? It is all down to the quality of your politicians and who is really the boss in our democracies. Is it really you or, is it them?

Homosexuality is at a dangerous level. I know I keep saying it, but it cannot be stressed enough because all forms of perversion will become the norm. 'Do gooders' will continue to ply their protection of them for no more reason than they believe in freedom, and will ensure the complete freedom of the perverts and criminals, at the expense of the rest of us. The minority must be protected, which is fair enough, but reason must prevail. It should all depend on the minority and what they are about, not just any old minority. All this will all be done in the name of freedom, which I uphold as right and so did Christ, but there are limits to how far you can go, even with freedom. All things have their price and their limitations. The vast majority of the populations of the World are at risk through this perversion. Not only is your security at risk, the very security of your children is at risk as the age of consent goes even lower. You are not old enough to vote, but you can indulge in homosexual activity without the older person, who is the 'perverter' getting into trouble. It is not advocated for the good of the young, but solely for the good of the perverts who wish to use the young and turn them into perverts just as they are, so that they can use them. And the word is use. Any government or government official who backs such a Bill or such a law must have ulterior motives, and is not fit to be voted in for the job as dog-catcher. In future you will have cause to regret this way of thinking. The cost of such stupidity will be as great, as it is inexcusable.

Many years ago there was a joke told in Ireland of a young man who went to the Australian Embassy in Dublin to enquire about his chances to get on the ten pound assisted passage scheme to emigrate to Australia. When asked why he wanted to live in 'Aussie', he replied that five hundred years ago in Ireland if you were caught indulging in homosexual activities you were burnt at the stake. Three hundred years ago you were hung, drawn and quartered. One hundred years ago you would be jailed. Now he said it is to be made legal. "What has that got to do with your wanting to go to 'Aussie?' " he was asked. Well he said, "I want to get out of here before it becomes compulsory". That was just a joke in those days back in the sixties. It is no longer a joke, and it is fast becoming a possible reality.

Homosexuality will grow among governing bodies, amongst top business executives, amongst managers and people in all kinds of positions of power. They will, as they are doing now, prevent anyone except their own perverted kind from 'getting on' anywhere. And ask any straight psychologist if you can find one, and he or she will tell you perversion is not just sexual. It is absolute. It contaminates and effects all functions of the mind. It's a bit like being slightly virginal. Slightly perverted is the same. Either you are, or you are not. Free sex among the young, as young as eight years old will be the norm and so will diseases of the incurable types. Disease does not respect age no matter how tender. What a terrible price to pay. But this evil sells things and there is a profit to be made. Unemployment will of course increase greatly and politicians will go on with their promises of 'vote for us and we will create jobs', knowing full well that jobs create themselves and cannot be created.

Mechanisation will of course increase, making even more unemployment. Eventually, and as usual too late, this will be recognised, and the working week will be cut. If it were to be cut to a thirty-hour week now, the unemployment problem would disappear. They said, when the forty-hour week was introduced that business could not stand it, but look what happened. There was a boom. If you give the working man leisure time and money what will he do? He will spend and thus create demand and round and around the wheel will go. In the mean time, the unemployed will be used as a whipping boy for political inabilities and for keeping the attention of the populace diverted away from these inabilities and the mistakes made by politicians and heads of state, who created the situation in the first place. Done mostly deliberately for self-gain, with the usual portion of stupidity thrown in. Just as it has always been. They will bring out all sorts of daft ideas, both in America and in Europe to prevent social welfare abuse. While they themselves will cause the unemployment and will then abuse those people unfortunate enough to find themselves on benefits.

Did you know that one third of the world's population actually lives on less than one dollar a day? In this day and age! The governments will do this solely in order to help themselves to a much larger slice of the proverbial pie. Banks and big business are the direct cause of most unemployment as they replace people with machines to increase profits. Society is, and will be, designed for the maintenance of power centres alone, and for the direct benefit of those who control those power centres. This will be done with the usual short-sightedness. The fact is that if people are broke they cannot spend, if they cannot spend production becomes pointless with the obvious results for the power-mongers themselves. They will lose.

In Ireland the stupidity of governmental greed, both as a combined force and an individual endeavour will become worse. The landlord system will return to Ireland in the guise of banks trying to recover their mortgages from the hard up farmer. This shall be their hypocritical excuse. The pretence will be that they are trying to prevent embarrassment for the owners of the land. The mentality of the Irish farmer with his false sense of pride will assist them in their cause. He will assist in order that his neighbours will not know of his plight, and so lessen his imagined shame. The banks will show him a way out of his predicament, and thus shall gain that which would have been thought impossible not many years ago. Aren't they thoughtful? But, as is usual only on the surface. This ploy will be of only the purest deceit. That is if you can ever call deceit, pure. Bang goes my credit rating   -   I won't get a mortgage now, will I?

144

They will repossess and then rent the land back to the debtors. So shall the power of the landlord destroy this beautiful country once again. Even after all the killing that was done, and all the suffering, to get rid of 'landlordisim' in farming in the first place.

All over Europe, America, Russia and China propaganda will be pumped out in great quantities. Watch out for China. She will come into the ballpark together with Korea and Japan, and create further problems for the rest of the World as they try in vain to cure their own. China will start to prepare for war with no small success. She will cross her borders into places already coveted as a prize with the excuse to her people that it already belongs to them anyway. They are only going to take back that which was stolen in the first place. She will not be alone.

The Muslim forces will gain strength in unreason, and war will visit the streets of Britain as they struggle against the infidel who took them in and gave them a home in the first place. Racial aggression will be at the forefront, as the native British slowly get pushed aside in the fever for racial equality. Jobs and opportunities will be allotted on the basis of colour instead of ability, as politicians struggle to climb the ladder of success on the backs of those who will be destroyed by it. Muslim groups now training in terrorist tactics and being allowed to do so by the present government can only spell trouble. They do have, and will have, the guns and explosives they need to terrorise Britain. There are no lobby groups as there were from Dunblane to be heard in this matter. These things are well known by both police and government officials at this time and again they are afraid to do anything about it lest they appear to be 'racist', which could have a damaging effect on their careers. This situation will not change till it is far to late.

Cancer research will go on forever with as little success as ever. Usually just enough to keep the money rolling in, helped with the odd bit of assumed success, just to keep the ball rolling and a lot of wasters in easy money. If they were to be judged on results they would not last long. Genuine effort in the field of research, and in charitable endeavour would be refreshing but shall remain only a dream.

As the seven planets line up in two thousand and six, people will get more and more aggressive. The closer they come together the more aggressive people will become. Just as when the moon is full, only more so. Agricultural policies will fail as usual and cause havoc all over the World. Fishery policies will become even worse. Men who don't know what they are talking about, as usual, both in these fields and others, will still make the rules and the silly ideas committees will still not be expected to take any responsibility for their stupidity. In other words, not much change as far as government is concerned. The scum will still float on top of the bucket all over the World. And man will know no reason. Men never have, so why should anything change now?

We have survived so far, but rest assured we shall not survive much longer. There will be battles, both verbal and physical for some time to come. Gradually becoming worse, and worse. People will shout about rights, while taking away the right of the majority, slowly but surely. It will almost be an offence to be normal. 'Abstract art', and 'blank verse' will grow to even greater heights, until no one knows what is real and what isn't. Rendering the ordinary people in the street, the vast majority even more confused and even more vulnerable. And they will be abused by all, big time.

All perversion is an abuse and perverts are abusive by nature. They even abuse themselves. So what do you think they will do to you? Homosexuality will be at the forefront and homosexuals will become more and more aggressive in their quest for supremacy over heterosexuals, as they try to prove that contradiction, 'that which is bent is really straight'. I nearly said - 'normal people' instead of heterosexual, because what is normal, will come into question. Who is the normal, and who isn't? Homosexuals will make a lot of noise while claiming the unclaimable. Namely that their perversion is normal. Very often accompanied by violence, and threats of violence behind the scenes whilst preaching peace and justice, where they can be seen and heard. And the World will do little until it is far to late. People will preach freedom whilst building prisons of one sort or another. Women will no longer be able to walk the streets alone any more. They will not even be safe in their cars, or at home without a guard. It will be no different for children. Even young men, will be targeted by the perverts. No one will be safe from it. It is bad enough now but wait till they get a greater hold.

You can't trust the police any more but you have seen nothing yet. They will become even more dishonest as they wallow in their drug money.
The Police in all countries will increase their grip on the drug business, diversifying as the drug laws start to change. They have become used to the money

and will not want to give it up. The worst thing is that it will be considered by the ordinary man in the street to be just the way things are. He will feel that he can do nothing and he will be right. Therefore little will be done about it. The will to change simply won't be there.

Pollution will be rife. Clean water will become so scarce that it will be valued beyond gold and certainly beyond oil. Additives will be put into water to "keep it fresh" which will in fact cause health problems, despite assurances from those in power. Governments will waste even more much needed money to give grants to open factories and car plants to maintain jobs. Though they know that oil is about to run out altogether, soon. Power will be the first consideration, and anyone trying to change this system will find themselves in trouble.

There is only fifty days supply of grain in the World at any one time. Harvests will fail due to adverse weather and because of this, starvation will be visiting peoples and places where they think that it can never happen to them. It would pay the Arab nations well to take note, as they will have only oil to drink or eat and not much of that. We all rely on each other but the, "it's my ball and I'm going home" attitude that will remain and increase the problems. Each nation wanting supremacy. Everyone wanting to rule the World and by the time they have all finished it won't be worth ruling. The Arab nations will still go on about honour and their own particular brand of protocol. They will also have to return to reality and cease their policies of the end justifying the means. Lying to their people is proof of their intellectual superiority over them. It is not. They would do well to practice the teachings of Mohammed instead of just using them and what he stood for in the pursuit of personal gain as they do.

They're as bad as the Christian nations in that respect. I wonder who learned from whom. Lying, cheating and barefaced hypocrisy will be the norm in all nations. And as it is in the Arab World at the moment it will be looked upon as a justifiable tactic, used without conscience by those who seek to tell the rest of humanity how to live and conduct themselves.

As clean uncontaminated food becomes impossible to acquire, those of us who take pains to produce it will be at risk from those who do not. Legislation will be passed so that we will have to give our food up to those in high places, for distribution to the needy who will in fact see none of it. Only the greedy and the needy political leaders and rulers of our World, together with their armies that will enforce their rules upon us, shall be fed. The armies will only be fed so that they can fight for the cause, though they will never really know what the real cause is.

Again the use of propaganda will be the favourite weapon. They will blame other countries, political parties, any group, or any thing, to avoid this reality. This will not stop the march of the coming of 'the ending of days'. Look out Britain, and dare I suggest it, America. Governments will carry on their policies to break down the family unit. They will of course always say the opposite. They will do this, as people on their own are easier to handle. Money will slowly be withdrawn and the almighty plastic will be all you have. Your social security will be totally controlled. Your salary is controlled totally. Putting the banks and politicians in that position which they have dreamed about, and have striven so hard to achieve since time began. Absolute rulers over your life, and your money. This will give them the ability to destroy you if they wish, any time they wish.

So you will learn obedience to them or die. Which of course will be justified by them, and you will live and die according to their rules. Just like organised religion they will have their way no matter how destructive it is. It will all be done for your own good of course. Imagine the increase of taxation and the cost of the bureaucracy to enforce it. That cost will be borne by you as well as the cost to police it. Every penny you spend will be recorded. To each his number. Cameras will be on every road, every pathway, in every street. In every toilet! And most likely in your own home, just in case you are robbed by those big bad people who are always out of work. Big brother will become obsessed with watching, again for your own good. Gun lobby groups will be encouraged to prevent the public from having any means to protect themselves. Even penknives will become illegal, and propaganda will teach people to be neurotic in these respects. Hence the sudden rise in 'Counselling'. It is designed to make people believe that they cannot cope with anything unless they have outside support. Someone telling you what to do and what to think, thus weakening the population psychologically and making them still easier to handle and control. People will be constantly brain washed through this type of thing till they fear everything that has a sharp edge or which goes bang. And the ones who will preach the evils of guns and knives will carry them themselves. Justifiable of course. They are always special cases. They will not shrink from manufacturing guns or selling them or dealing in them for profit. Only Government officials and gangsters will have guns. Leaving ordinary decent people totally vulnerable to whatever they wish to do to you.

It is already designed that people will be as slaves in the new societies all over the World. You won't be paid for cash up front, as were the slaves of old. Instead you will be paid for by the week, or the month. Then when you are no longer required you will be dispensed with, to starve or whatever. It is not a new concept. You don't really think that slavery would have been done away with out of the goodness of people's hearts if a better way were not found first do you? You are not their responsibility. The World will become a bit like "Animal Farm 1984" he only got the timing wrong. You will all carry identity cards, as they now propose for those under a certain age. It is a small step from there to everyone. Then you will eventually be chipped, just like dogs are now for easy identification. This will be to help catch and control law-breakers of course. Should you protest you will be made to appear anti-social, and then become a sort of outcast. You too can become a law -breaker. Some of the laws they will dream up will need breaking. So you will put up with it, you will have little choice.

Groups like ours - The Order Of The Ancient Way, will be vilified, because we pose a threat to this ideal situation. They will try to make you see us as the great manipulators of mankind. We are not, and we won't be, but we will be made to look like that just the same. As will anyone of similar mind, who dares to advise you to think. They know their own tricks best. We will pose a solid body of people who will be hard to handle and will become considered subversive, even terrorist. All through the necessity for the governments of the World to control their charges for their own protection and survival. It will come to a point where the leaders of the World will be afraid to let go for fear of receiving their just deserts. They will not have forgotten the French Revolution, and they will know that it can happen anywhere, at any time, should the populace be pushed hard enough.

Organised religions will at first come out against us, but they will retain a foot in each camp and hedge their bets. They will find a way of justifying themselves as they usually do. Chaos will start to come to the fore when the threat of oil running out can no longer be hidden and starts to become an obvious reality. You will find the price of petrol and diesel going up, and many reasons will be given to you in justification. Pollution avoidance, watch to see if they mean it. There's a lot of pollution about and they have been aware of it for a long time. They will use traffic congestion, and anything else they can think of as a smoke screen. If they are going to be for real about it you will see. The real reason will of course be to slow down the use of oil, as it is perceived that the last man standing with a Sherman tank and a gallon of fuel, will rule the World, or what's left of it. Who in his right mind would want to?

Greed by definition is a form of madness. Town and city planning will be carried out with the containment of the public in mind. It already is, but it will become more obvious in two or three years from now. This is February 1999. I have already viewed departmental documentation that carried this statement. Namely, that all planning of roads, buildings, and water schemes should be viewed mainly with the containment and control of the public in mind.

150

Why would our democratic government wish to do this? For our own good no doubt. It will appear to be so they can catch bank robbers and rapists and all sorts of criminals more easily, by only having a few easily controlled roads out of each town. Thus protecting you and I even better. Good reasons if they were the only ones. They are not. Governments all around the World are well aware of impending unrest, and contrary to the propaganda that is pumped out on a regular basis, you John and Joan public are pawns in a very large and somewhat sinister game. You are expendable. You have your uses, but you are expendable.

Members of the police and armed forces will start to be sent to distant places where they have no relatives, and during the "emergencies" they will not be allowed to contact their relatives, for security reasons. Again, for whose security? Yours? Mine? The reasons that will be given will not be the real reasons, they never are. Just look at Iraq and see for yourselves what can be done with propaganda. All governments indulge in it to some extent. The extent considered by them to be necessary is gauged on the situation at the time. As you have seen elsewhere in the World, it has happened to them and it can happen to you. It will. It already does. The mind conditioning started a long time ago. Just as they gave farmers grants for this and that, only to get them into the 'tax net'. Now they are no longer free, they do as they are told, because they have been left with little or no choice.

The planetary line up cannot be avoided, but it could be planned for. The reason that it is not being planned for is mainly because it is spoken of by Astrologers, and they have made the first forecasts. These forecasts must therefore be ignored, for religious reasons. It is also true to say that they think it won't happen. Apart from all that they don't know what to do about it anyway, without losing money in the process. The ozone layer can be replaced, but it will cost. That is why it hasn't been done.

A very important point that always must be considered is, that it would not do if it were seen that someone knew something that the religious leaders, who claim the favour of God, do not know. And most politicians rely on their support in one way or another. It is not ignored for practical reasons, but purely for reasons of belief and self-interest. Christ prophesied the alignment. The coming of the seven bodies. Guess what else it represents. It heralds the time of the Seventh Sign, and if I haven't got an act going around then, it's all over. But that's only what the real Jesus said, and who is he compared with the myth that has been built up since the conference of Nicea in 325 A.D.? Constantine made them sort themselves out, and Jesus was chosen. He won the lottery of divinity. We must not forget, and be suitably grateful, that if it wasn't for the Church of Rome voting him in as the Messiah in the first place he would hardly have been heard of ever again. The man himself wasn't good enough, so a myth had to be invented, just like has been done to Odin.

The powers that be do not trust their people, meaning perhaps you, and as he who criticises always speaks mainly of himself, what does that make them? Well, you may be assured by me and by your own common sense, that belief certainly will not play any part in the survival of the species. You can also be assured that there is not a bearded old man sitting on a cloud who will make it all right. Your destruction or survival depends solely on your ability to rise above the stupidity of men and society in general, and use your reason. You will survive only by the use of reason, of knowledge, of logic, of common sense and no other way. If man follows this way he will survive and live in paradise. But his paradise will be of this World, and of this Mother Earth and later, of worlds beyond. There is no other paradise in the sky called heaven. It is here on Earth in this life. Just open your eyes and see. Know a little reason. It has always been here, but only for the few who have managed to get people to look in another direction, while they grabbed it all for themselves.

Jesus was a far greater man than you have been taught. He is far beyond the comprehension of our tiny minds and if Christ is right, and I am betting my life and the lives of my family and followers on it, we do not need to perish. The reasons for all the turmoil in my life, according to those who know, was purely so that I would understand the ways to beat this. I am not an expert in anything, but I am expert enough to pick men and women who know more than I do, without picking the wrong people, or being fooled by the cunning ones, who know of nothing while they profess all. Being a psychologist won't go wrong, neither will it prove useless, I'm sure. Every single thing that he has prophesied has been accurate. So it's a fair bet he isn't going to lose it now, is he? What will you bet your life on? Think about all that you know to be real, to be reasonable, to be right. Then decide. Many will come but few will be chosen. To be chosen demands a high standard of mind. Faith will not be needed, except in your own ability, neither will belief.

If effort and determination are invested it will come about. If reason is used instead of unreason and fact instead of mystery, it will come about. There is something out there, but the fact is that we don't know what it is. Neither does anyone else. As for those who profess to know, let them show you! They can't. By accepting belief and faith as fact, you are not only killing yourself, which is up to you, you are killing your fellow man and the very planet that we all depend on for survival. And that is not up to you. You, no matter how great you are, do not have this right. By pumping out chemicals that we could do without, we are poisoning ourselves, and all the living things that again we depend on. We live in a 'throw-away' World and all this so that a minority can live high on the hog, with you as the hog. I am not saying to instantly stop producing chemicals, they are not all bad. But neither are they all necessary, and not in the quantities in which they are they are produced, purely for commercial gains.

# RELIGION

The Church of Rome will fall, that will please the Muslims. But Islam will fall, which will please the Church of Rome, and as they fall, each will use the death throes of the other as proof of validation to feed to the faithful, that God, Allah or whoever, is on their side. Protecting and favouring them above all others. Each claiming to be the chosen people as the Jews have always done. Every religion will be doing exactly the same, not just them. Opposing factions will rise among them and they will fight among themselves, thus hastening the end. Many people will die. Their goodness, their faith and their faithfulness wasted on the shifting sands of unreason, on a pointless exercise of religious mania, where even those who profit will lose.

The Muslims will become even more fanatical. Death and destruction will be their answer to anyone who disagrees with them, or casts doubt on the validity of their beliefs. They will hand out death sentences all over the place. From such a thing there will be no winners.

# SURVIVAL

There is a way that the species will survive. Christ, the Sixth comer and all those who have gone before have laid it before you, and I in my turn shall also lay it before you, as commanded. When I have the seven nations. The co-ordinates of the places of safety have been revealed and will be kept secret till the time is right. If it ever is, and if I can find enough reasonable people, then I will show you the Seven lights, and not until then, as is laid out for me and my people to do.

Everyone thinks that he or she is a reasoning person, especially those of least reason. Here lies one of my biggest problems. We can clear up this mess though it will take a thousand years. But there will be purpose to even the most humble of lives and therefore a reason for the sacrifice, and a point to existence. This is the blueprint for the promised Paradise.

# WARS AND CONFLICT

The Chinese, due to crop failures will starve in great numbers and as I have said, their leaders will start to blame the West for all its ills. They shall cast their eyes beyond their borders and shall invade surrounding countries and they will not be stopped easily, or at least till they reach the shores of Britain. France will capitulate, as usual. America will hold off and wait and see who is winning, then throw her lot in with them, again as usual. The American President of the time will try to integrate Canada into the United States, more for the protection of America than any real concern for the Canadians.

The Christian fanatics will start wars against the Muslims. The Muslims will already be at it among themselves. They will fight, nation against nation and sect against sect. So shall it also be in the Christian World. Like in Northern Ireland which will continue until the fall of Christianity and beyond. It is said that, "Such a stupid and useless thing could only happen in Ireland."I wish that were true. Israel will have to ignore the West and their purposes, which will not be the needs of Israel, and do battle on the Arab and Muslim World just in order to survive. They will have to watch their backs for the Christians as well.

Holy War will be the in thing. The World will be full of war, hunger and disease. So shall the 'ending of days' come about. Not with trumpets sounding the coming of glory. Not with the sound of feet, marching to the music of angels singing as they lead the faithful to the throne of God. But with a whimper of blind stupidity.

Many will come but few will be chosen, and the survival of these few will be harsh. That survival will be a long hard struggle, but in the end worth it. The only choice if you can call it a choice will be survive or die. The Brotherhood which has been known as the Brotherhood Of Light, changed after Constantine to the Brotherhood Of The Flame, also known as the 'lost brotherhood' and 'the Nazarenes', has been here for several thousand years and has available all that accumulated knowledge. So are the High Templars, the Upper Templars. The hidden ones, who remain as a silent help in time of need. It almost makes me feel confident and sometimes even drives away despair. But not for long. There are times when I wish that I had been brought up to have faith, at least in human nature. Then again perhaps it is better I remain cynical. Harsh judgement may not be the best judgement, but it is better than no judgement. Care is needed, as it is not only my bacon that is in the pan.

The 'ending of days' is at hand. Anyone with half a mind and one eye can see that. Everyday there is more and more on T.V. about this and that. There is the new Syphilis, Gonorrhoea, Herpes and now Aids. All sexually transmitted, all incurable, all avoidable. The madness of men is self-evident, he is not avoiding it.

Have you heard that saying we have nowadays, "making love". Love has nothing to do with it. It is pure lust. Love is something else. Lust is to do with the beast that is your base nature and mine. While love is to do with the higher humanity that sets us apart from the beast. Words are the things to watch out for, their meaning changing, the games played with them ever widening and confusing. People getting further and further away from reality until it is no longer recognisable. Did you know that the word 'Occult', mean's only 'changing.'? See the ad on T.V. "The truth about Hitler, was he possessed by the occult?".Well no, but he was possessed by the Pope. Does that count? Is it the same thing? See what I mean? All will tell you he was possessed by an 'evil force', and so he was. But what force makes the difference, though not to those who died in their millions because of it.

The time of forgiveness is over. The time of leaving it all to that guy that is known as 'Someone'. You know him. He is the one who is going to find something magical and fix it all. 'Someone will come up with something' Aids will be cured by 'Someone'. 'Someone will discover something and I firmly believe it'. Stand back we are all safe now. Well we are not and we are not going to be. 'Someone' is not out there and doesn't exist, except in imagination. Spurred on by the need for hope, any hope, even false hope, and that is simply not good enough.

Some diseases will be cured by simply not indulging in casual sex, or by doing as was done in the time of Sodom and Gomorrah. Remove the cause and the symptom will simply go away. If you don't indulge you won't bulge. Imagine virgin girls again. Young men that are the same, learning about life together as it is meant to be. Women becoming beyond price once again, as they used to be. Beyond value. Instead of worthless as most of them have become. If you don't like each other then divorce. It's not nice, but sometimes necessary. Don't just screw around. Don't play silly games with your life, or with the lives of others, especially little children. You only have one life, make the most of it. How will you do it if you catch something nasty? Stay clean and stay healthy.

I am not just an old spoilsport who has had his day, and won't let you have yours. It is the only way left open to us to ensure a life, never mind a happy one. We now, thanks to perversion's greed and downright stupidity of one kind or another, live in a very dangerous World.

Pope Leo the Tenth is recorded as saying, "It has served us well this myth of Christ". It is now time to live the reality of Joshua Ben Miriam, and put the myth where it belongs, along with all the other myths of real and great men. Especially the myths of the six that have passed this way and that have been used badly to wrongful purpose. The myths of them should now be consigned to the dustbins of history. Never to be forgotten so that they will never be allowed to be used again in such a negative manner. More important is the reality of them, used as they would have it, to further the wonder of the World and all that there is of the World. Ensuring the continuance of the species of man and all his supporting species both plant and animal.

It is the purpose of the Seven to serve the well-being of all men, and this purpose should not be perverted. Men will kill for clean water, wars will be fought over it and the control of it. Again the need of the few to control all will be to the forefront of life. I have a very small chance that I will manage to gather a very few men of good mind. If I was to ask you if you are of good and reasoning mind, would you say "No'? We all do the best we can, each to his own lights. If asked, you  would of course say "Yes". My problem is, are you?

Jesus the man is nothing like Jesus the myth that Pope Leo the Tenth spoke of. The Jesus he spoke of was and is the mythical Jesus. Used for the control of men for the benefit of the few. His name used in vain. The myth of the Virgin Mary, again just a myth. A very nice story, but just a story. She existed and was the mother of Jesus, but there it ends.

In those days there were a number of characters, ranging from kings to crooks, and little difference showing between them, (I keep telling you that little has changed.) who were starting up new religions for the same old purpose. They impregnated virgins by the use of masturbation and quills. The first form of artificial insemination. The very pregnant virgin would then show her bits and pieces to the ignorant, and a miracle was then declared. It is amazing how religion has been more about ignorance than it has about anything else. Knowledge never comes into the equation. The perpetrators of the new religion would be the main men who held the ears of the newly invented Deity, and all due respect had to be given to them, along with anything else they might demand of you, to ensure your life and a life after death, or whatever.

If you broke their rules, you were dead. It was all done for the benefit of the followers of this new Deity. If the crops were good, it was due to the efforts of the priests, proof of their power, to intervene on your behalf with the Deity. If the crops failed it was due to unbelievers displeasing the new god. The unbelievers would be 'winkled out' and accused, and then usually put to death, their property forfeit to the priesthood. So it was very easy for the priesthood to get rid of their critics. Or, as the case may be the 'Opposition' and get rich at the same time. Does the story ring a bell so far? It was not as uncommon as you might think, although most of the evidence for this has been destroyed mainly by the Christian Church. After all they don't want to be rumbled. They have always been very good at destroying things and indeed people in the protection of their beliefs and dogmas that they want to maintain the status quo, apparently at all costs. This is true of all the other religions of the World. The end justifying the means.

And so was The Christ, the anointed one was born. They messed up. This was someone different. They got themselves a 'Caulbearer'. A King by right, that people of that time would follow against all others, as was the way. He couldn't be bought or controlled. He might have been better off if he could. Herod knew of his Sign and tried to kill him at all costs, so nothing has changed in the corridors of power even to this day.

Joshua Ben Miriam, was born according to Prophesy, a 'High Lord Of The Veil', the Sixth Sign. Most Christians don't even know his right name. 'Joshua son of Miriam'. Odd is it not? There are a lot of odd things to do with the myth. For instance his birthday, just a couple of days after Winter Solstice. A time of giving. Invented by the Christian Church according to Christian tradition. But it isn't, it is another falsehood. He was called 'The Lamb' with reason. Not just because 'the lamb is innocent.'

The shortest day was a time of giving for thousands of years before Christ came. It was hard to keep animals and various food stuffs over winter, so the Priesthood of the Old Order held meetings, at pre-selected places. You brought all that you did not want or need, or that which you could not sustain, and it was given to those who needed it. You in return got things that you needed. It was and is simple, practical and sensible. You gave gifts and you received gifts. The Christians stole the idea from the Old Order and proceeded to pass it off as their own. They set the date for the celebration of the "Birth of Jesus", just a few days after Solstice, mainly for very calculated reasons. One reason was to disrupt Solstice and another to offer converts, many of whom were 'pressed' and therefore dubious, a similar time of gift giving and receiving, so that they would not feel too left out at this time. They would not feel that they were missing something, and revert back to the old ways, or cast doubt among their fellow Christians. They were not so far away from the thinking of the time of Christ. They knew the meaning of the 'Caul'.

Thirdly to instil the belief that the church was a benevolent body. It also followed the worshippers of the sun in their belief, which the Christian Church could not find it within themselves to give up. It was the belief of the 'Son' replacing the 'Sun'. Subtle, but effective in the quest for converts.

Then there is Easter, a time to celebrate his crucifixion. Timed once again to steal something from the Old Order, and use it for their benefit. Easter was approximately, early in March or the Spring Equinox, depending on the position of the moon at the time. In the Old Way, the first day of spring was also considered New Years Day as it was the beginning of the year, marked by new growth all around us. Not in the dead of winter, which was considered the end of growth and life. So Easter marked the end of winter and the birthing of all things, and what did we have in abundance? Eggs, of course. People celebrated the coming of the New Year with whatever was plentiful at the time, and we still do. There would have been then as there is today, young things that could be killed and eaten. Rabbits for instance, hence the Easter Bunny.

We have always been a practical people and consider all the angles before we do anything, at least that is our goal. Sometimes we get it wrong, but that's life. It was considered wasteful to kill the young things, as they need to grow.

We also look at the rights and wrongs of what we do, and think it is wrong to kill anything before it has time to partake of the pleasures of life and of the World. All things should be allowed to live before they can be killed. To do anything else in our thinking is not only wrong, but doubly wrong as it is also wasteful. Everything has its purpose. If we find ourselves in a position where it becomes necessary to kill something young in order to survive, we will do so without conscience as long as there is no other way. Jesus lived by such rules. He was a reasoning and thoughtful man. He was not the kind to turn the other cheek. He was not the silly person that you have been told of.

In these matters you must keep in mind that the passages in the Bible were decided upon by committees, and anything that might cast doubt on what they wanted you to believe was left out, altered or destroyed. Hence the panic when the Dead Sea Scrolls were found and a number of them seem to be missing. Only the bits that support the Bible, Judaism and Christianity remain. It seems to have gone unnoticed by those who are in charge of them, and who might they be? Need you ask?

From the time of his birth Jesus was a marked man. Indeed you might say from before the time of his birth. Herod Agrippa did no worse than power-mongers have done down the centuries. He indulged in slaughter, the favourite and seemingly only method that such people understand. But The Christ survived. He disappeared from the Bible from the age of about twelve until his meeting with, and baptism by John the Baptist.

Where was he? The answer is simple. He would have been with the Brothers. They would have been teaching him everything that he needed to know to fulfil his purpose. The Brotherhood Of Light knew about the 'ending of days', and so would he have been instructed. His teaching would have been structured and limited by them, to protect the knowledge and to protect him. Only a few of the Brothers would have been allowed to know the signs, and it is possible, that he, Jesus would not have known any of them, as it was not of his purpose. They would have been aware that he would not make it, and he also knew. Whether I will make it or not I am very unsure at this time.

Jesus rode into Jerusalem on a donkey as was prophesied, apparently throwing caution to the wind. It was a bit like a red rag to a bull. Too much of what followed was planned for in advance, for him to be unaware of his fate. His passing on the Prophesy, and adding to it. His instructions on how it should be hidden. His trusting in his enemies as he could not trust his friends. Only three hours on the cross is a sort of proof of this, as it takes a lot longer than that for a man to die. Normally he would have been up there for at least three days, which was the allotted time it usually took a man to die. Providing his legs were broken, so that he could not raise himself up and ease the pressure on his chest, thus allowing himself to breath more easily. Someone took him down beforehand. Who exactly did this we do not know. Pilate had a lot to do with it, as he was really on Christ's side. He saw nothing wrong with him, but his options were none.

Jesus trusted in his enemies. Who better than Pilate? He looked like his enemy, but he wasn't. Centurions answered to Pilate and could be bought. He certainly escaped death and went to France. It too seemed to be pre-planned. He was not a man to leave anything to chance. He and his family were protected among the six hills. Where else would the Sixth live and end his days? Mary, his wife was a very rich lady, and he was not without wealth himself. You must remember that he was a great healer, who could argue with the priests and lawyers and win. So he was at very least educated. The Brotherhood would have seen to that. So it is fairly certain that he was no pauper as he is so often described. His education would have been undertaken by the 'Brotherhood Of The Light' who afterwards ended up in Qumran out of harms way. The Brothers knew after his death what was coming. The Brothers knew that they would have to fight the forces of evil. As they would know of the seven hills, and what they stood for. Many would know what it would stand for in the future, together with the fact that the Jews had been trying to oust the Romans for such a long time. It is therefore not beyond the realms of possibility that they knew exactly the situation they were facing, or should I say, was facing them.They were of course slaughtered and hunted down to what the Romans thought was the last man. And it was to happen again and again as history unfolded, with the Knights Templars etc. But as usual, they were wrong, they didn't manage to get them all.

Now it might strike you as a little peculiar that Rome whilst fighting a major war with the Jews, should set aside so many men just to hunt down, kill and destroy these apparently harmless, and as they are often depicted, fanatical members of some obscure Brotherhood. Rome apparently did not consider them as any such thing. They knew the Brotherhood were about knowledge, and as Caesar wanted to be a god they might just upset his apple cart, and the apple carts of many of his ilk. Again the story of the struggle to own the hearts and minds of men, for one's own benefit and for the satisfaction of one's ego has not changed over the centuries.

The Brotherhood knew as we all know, that Jesus disappeared from general view for a long time. They knew where to, and to what purpose. He was with them. Being taught how to handle what he was, and what he had within him. As happened to the five before him, and to me and to many 'Caulbearers' over the centuries. This process is necessary for all 'Caulbearers', and especially for the 'High Caulbearers'. For 'High Caulbearers' the process is a lengthy one and thorough in its purpose. The obvious reasons being that there are only to be seven.With the passing of each one the situation gets closer to futility, and more and more desperate.

The other purpose was for his protection from Herod and from others who would have preferred Jesus dead. And they went to a great deal of trouble to render him so. Jesus had to be tough. If he wasn't he could not have survived at all. He would have been taught the things that we are all taught, and maybe even more so.

Things today as far as 'Caulbearers' are concerned are different, as so much more knowledge has been accumulated and we live in a very different World. As you read the Prophesy you will begin to look at him in a different light. A more positive light, where you can learn to hold him in even higher esteem. He was greater than religion. Greater even than the religions that use his name and claim to follow him, would want you to believe. His use to them is different than it was meant to be and certainly different than he would have wanted it to be. He was the son of man, himself a man. As are we all. 'Caulbearers' secondly, following a purpose to a greater or lesser degree, but still with purpose. That purpose is depicted by something that is unseen. Something we do not fully understand, or maybe we do not understand it at all. We only know that it is there.

The presence of this force is self-evident to everyone, and more so to us. To us it is the force of nature. The Old Order called it, 'The Goddess'. Because it is said, "From whose womb all things are born". Therefore the ancient ones thought of it in female terms. Today we are fairly sure that it is neither male nor female. It is not a god, as we understand gods. It is not anything that we can say to you, "This is what it is", because in truth we have no idea what it is, and neither has anyone else. Whatever it turns out to be exactly, we are sure that it is logical, reasonable and will make perfect sense. It will not be like anything from the chaotic World of man's imagination. We will discover it one day, but only through the application of knowledge and reason. Only by looking with a clear and open mind, without beliefs in the fantastic to cloud our reason and rob us of this wonder.

The proof of that thing of which I speak is around you every where, you can see it, you can touch it, so we know that it is there. Belief is not necessary. We do not understand why some people are born with a 'Veil', or 'Caul', or why the coming is always written in the stars. The proof of their existence is there. I am here. Jesus was here, so was Moses, the saviour of his people. Buddha, again bringing enlightenment to his people. Teaching them a better way. Marduk, the Astrologer and King from the thirteen cities. Odin a warrior and seeker of knowledge, the founder of the Brotherhood. Not forgetting the one we know so little about, the first to come. He, or she who is lost to us, who considered his or her own existence as so unimportant.

The Seven Signs are now complete, and we now await the ordinary 'Caulbearers' to present themselves, though there is nothing ordinary about a 'Caulbearer', in order that the purpose can be fulfilled. The same purpose, the saving of the species of man, mostly from stupidity, greed, arrogance, ignorance and extinction by his own design. And when the 'Caulbearers' come forward they can take their part and the purpose can be completed. Upon its completion the "ending of days" may be averted.

The Earth shall be in a terrible state by this time. It already is, from all that false belief. God will not provide. The ending of days will be painful, dirty, shameful, miserable, disgusting, pointless, useless, and degrading. Men will fight one another to take from each other by force the little there will be. Those of us who are prepared will have to fight these dogs, like dogs. For the way of the beast is all that they understand. Even now they do not understand. That is why they are as they are, and not you nor I, nor anything will alter their minds. They are bent on their own survival at all costs. Even at the cost of their own survival, for they will believe it will not happen to them. The baseness of the beast like his perversions are absolute. And man shall know no reason. Such will be the way of things. Many drugs and their casual use will be legalised, though taxed for profit. Excuses will be made, but they will only be excuses. This does not bother me in the least, as the type of person who takes drugs for any purpose other than medical is the type of person who has no place in the scheme of things, or in that paradise to come, anyway. They only take up space, as their minds do not work in a reasonable manner, though they will protest this, they always do. They obviously do not take life seriously, and life is a serious business. The future of the human race if built on such foundations will surely crumble and fall again. Thus wasting all the effort and pain of those of good mind and intent.

There are many pleasures to experience in life, normal, natural ones that do no harm to either your health, your life or lay burden upon your fellow man, or the society you live in. People will still try to 'find themselves'. They will only try, as they might not like what they see should they be successful. I consider "finding one's self" about the stupidest thing imaginable. You know where you are, and if you don't, I suggest you consult a map. If you wish to find yourself you must first lose yourself, and that is an impossibility in fact. It is what you are, and only what you are, that matters. These illusory pursuits such as 'finding one's self' help us to avoid our own reality and take us into a sort of 'no, no land', of confusion. We then are faced with the impossible task of making sense out of it all. And we don't want to know, so it is easier to invent some abstract load of cock and bull than face up to our own realties. Yet it is reality, cold as it is, which sustains and it doesn't confuse.

Jesus was a realist, he is not supposed to have been, but he was. He was realist enough to hang on the cross for three hours, knowing that if the Jewish hierarchy and the Romans thought him dead, he and his family and those who supported him would be safe. There is more than adequate proof of his doing just this. It is amazing what people see in the presence of a good hypnotist.

Very few people realise the importance of hypnotism in matters. There are those who say, they do not believe in it yet go to church every week, receiving a weekly dose of hypnosis. Just the same as you would do should you consult me, for some psychological problem or other. The reason for the seven day ritual is, that your subconscious mind clears itself every seven days and it goes back to base, and anything implanted in it will be wiped off the screen of your mind. It will do this until well set by a long period of exposure. Hypnosis is something that happens to you every day in life. Turn on your T.V., talk to yourself in your mind, think. It's all a form of hypnosis, and it works. It can be used for your benefit or the benefit of someone else. That is why the churches use it. It is simply brain washing. See how quick they are to accuse one another of it, especially some new 'cult'. A dirty word, or is it? Do you belong to a cult? "Most definitely not" I hear you say with conviction. Are you sure? The dictionary gives the meaning of the word cult as. 'A system of belief and worship. A system of devoted study'. Now do you belong to a cult? You really have to watch the word games. Ask yourself "Why?" when they start their word games. Why do they want you to look in a different direction? If so, "Why"? Why do they want you to go to church every seven days and pray every day? Easy, as long as you do this you are brainwashed, controlled. "Close your eyes" they say, "and let us pray". You are hypnotised, both by them and by yourself.

Self-hypnosis is great. It is the most singularly useful thing to men on the face of the Earth. It is natural anaesthetic. You do not need to feel pain. So why you ask, if it has been known since long before the time of Christ, why was it not used? As the pictures of all those poor devils being operated on for amputations, and all sorts of things flash through your mind. Seeing them writhe in agony, hearing their screams echoing down the years. Untold horrors that could have been avoided. The answer is simple. The churches did not want it, as it showed them up and spoiled their act. Remember the Christians when thrown to the lions? The Caesar was amazed at the way they behaved. Hypnosis was used. Everyone does not have the correct personality that will enable them to become a good hypnotist. Some will say anyone can become a Hypnotist. Well it is not true. You may have a little success, many will have none at all. So not just anyone can hypnotise.

Where would this leave the Priests? They are trained in the use of standard prayers and use a set pattern. They stand at a distance, like behind an altar or up in a pulpit, and they all say "Let us bow our heads in prayer" So you do as you have been taught and close your eyes etc., and bingo you're down loaded. Most of them know not what they do. Now there's caring honesty and all those great Christian values for you. Where was all that compassion for those in pain? None of this suffering was necessary. It is not necessary for you to suffer from asthma, depression, pain in childbirth, anxiety and a hundred other life destroying disabilities. But they choose to let you suffer, both in the past and now, just to protect the belief systems that have kept men slaves as surely as if they were manacled and chained, for two thousand years. And who started it? Well in fairness we do not know exactly. The ancient Jews certainly knew of it, you can see it work if you know what to look for. As they pray you see the candles, the monotonous rhythmical swaying and nodding. In Christian churches the flickering candles, the bell and incense. The flat monotone voices of the priests as they relate their stories. The Anglican Catholic Churches have different but still similar methods if you know what to listen for. The 'subliminals' in those stories, in those prayers make the point obvious. The stories spark the imagination. The imagination is the pathway to the subconscious mind. The subconscious mind reacts without reason, and you're bought and sold and you didn't even know that it was market day.

The Brotherhood Of Light are proud of me, they now say. They taught me and I learned well. It is all part of the profession of being a priest or a psychologist or even a salesman. Insurance companies have it down to a T, and they do not have your best interests at heart, no more than do your governments, or anyone else. It changes the image a bit, does it not? I teach the people that come to me to control their own minds. It never ceases to amaze me how many people only want to be able to control their own minds, in order to allow them to manipulate others more easily. Needless to say, these types go away just a bit short of the mark. The main fact about hypnosis is that no one can make you do anything you do not wish to do, but only if you are aware of what is happening at the time. And who would not like to either follow the wonderful ideals of Christianity, (or appear to follow them), so that you are thought a good guy. This of course leaves you a smooth road to screw your more gullible fellow man.Trust is built in advance. If you want to know who the real rats are in your area, go to a church and see who is always there, in the forefront, handing round the plate. Then avoid them.

It has always been a sad fact of my life and many others that I know, that if someone is going to do something really low and nasty to you, nine times out of ten it will be a drum beating devotee of one religion or another.

Our society is sick and to every thing there is a cause. The causes are many on the surface of things, but they all come down to just one major cause. Living our lives through belief as we are taught is the one factor of all the ills of our societies. We believe that our politicians will do their best for us. We are wrong. We believe that the religious leaders of our different 'cults' are all good men and always tell the truth. They do not. We believe that it will all come right in the end. But not this time. We believe that someone out there will come up with a cure all. There is nobody out there. We believe that God will always provide for his children. He will not because he is just a figment of imagination, a fantasy and does not exist. Few realise how daft belief can get and still be held as facts. For instance, Martin Luther said, "We know on the authority of Moses that longer ago than six thousand years the World did not exist. "One Dr John Lightfoot DD stated that, "Man was created on the 23rd of October four thousand and four years before Christ." He made this statement in the year 1859, the same year that Darwin published his work. Not so very long ago! Isn't belief a wonderful thing?

There is something out there, but it is not this God who was, and always has been like the Devil, purely invention. So you are out of luck again. We believe all sorts of things while we look away from reality. Reality is a cold thing, not always the way we would like it, but it is real. By looking at it hard it will help us to guide our lives in a more reasonable manner, and by so doing we will save ourselves. Man has everything in him to save himself. We must accept that to harm our World is to harm ourselves. You must drink the water you poison, and if you look at the present situation, most of the water on the face of the Earth is now fast becoming poisoned and will become undrinkable for both man and beast, in the very near future. Disease is at this present time being spread through your water supply. Your immune system constantly is being damaged by all the second or third hand antibiotics that you consume daily through your water, as well as through your food. No wonder we are all ill nearly all the time these days. Its getting to the point where you are nearly afraid to ask someone how they are, unless you have an hour or two to spare to listen to all the things that are wrong with them. They are not all neurotics. The constant colds in Britain and in Ireland that I know of, you just get over one and another starts.

The Order Of The Ancient Way as it is now called has always been against anything that damages the natural environment. That is not to say that it is against all forms of chemistry, or changes in the way of doing things. Just against that which causes damage. Because an idea is new doesn't mean it is harmful or should be discarded. Man must advance. There are so many things that cause damage to our World, many of them subtle, and often unnoticed till to late. Belief that there is a God who will provide and protect, keeping us always safe is one of them, because it leads to carelessness. Belief that the Earth will always replenish itself is another. The belief that man has dominion over the birds of the air the fishes of the sea and all that crawls upon the Earth is probably the most heinous of them all. This one makes men think they have the right to kill, maim and generally do as they like with the other beings that we share the planet with. I once complained to a man about beating his dog, unnecessarily and somewhat brutally. He said "It's my f****** dog and I will do as I like to it." Mind you he treated his wife in much the same way.

Because of the belief that the World will always replenish itself, man has used the resources without thought, except the thought of how much it will enrich him financially.

## THE SEA

When I was fishing for a living the sea used to literally team with mackerel. At that time my son Harry was about six, he is now thirty-one, so it is not so long ago in the great scheme of things. When you were out fishing, acres of them would make the sea seem to boil. You could hear them brushing against the hull of the boat. I used to use a trace with six hooks and feathers and every time you dropped a line in you always came up with six fish. Even Harry had two hooks and always managed to fill them. At this time the Russian Factory ships were working off the coast of Scotland, mainly on herring. The sad and bad thing was that they were using the herring for fertilisers. The wrong way around in my opinion. You usually eat the food before turning it into fertiliser. Later a ban was put on fishing herring, as they were nearly wiped out.

When I first went fishing we used long lines and drift nets. We always had good catches. Far better than they are having now and the size and quality of the fish was a lot better. The most important thing was that we did not drag the bottom, killing a thousand fish for every one we landed, therefore it was easy to see why men believed that nature would always replenish herself. There were people who knew better, but it was not in their interest to inform the rest of humanity. Not to say that any notice would have been taken of them if they did, but they might have showed willing. I wrote to a newspaper at the time, pointing out the fact that too many fish were being taken and to the average fisherman, the depletion was obvious, I was more or less branded a crank. I was also a crank, when I said that it was against good sense to land 'berried' lobsters. These are the females covered in eggs, while at the same time we could only land a lobster that was eight inches from the base of the head to the tail. A hen lobster can literally have thousands of eggs attached to her, ready for fertilisation, and it takes a minimum of ten years for her to grow to this standard of maturity, so it made no sense.

Preservation was, and still is governed, if it exists at all, by some faceless wonders who have absolutely no idea what they are talking about. Especially in the case of fisheries. Their only interests is to serve the political opinion which usually only has the vote count in mind, so all becomes expediency. The trawl net causes so much damage that it should have been banned years ago, though I must confess that I have used one myself. We used to use pots to catch prawns. The prawn lays her eggs in holes in the mud but with trawling for them the chains and trawl doors bury them. So again for every one caught there are thousands killed to no purpose. It is the same story with salmon, and all in the name of jobs and money.

In Ireland the government is cleaning out the salmon in the fisheries it owns and controls, like the 'Moy Fisheries'. Soon one of the greatest salmon rivers in Europe, the River Moy, will be just a memory. Yet much lip service is given, by the politicians, to this matter, but as long as there is profit they will only give lip service, and hope that no one notices. They say it is all about jobs. The jobs are forfeit anyway, and when there are no fish there will be no money. We also lose a valuable part of our ecology system, because as we carry on using destructive methods we shall not only kill all sorts of fish now, we will in fact kill our future's food supplies, that are and will be badly needed. Not just to maintain a balance in the maritime scheme of things, its effect will be felt right across the food chain.

The birds of the air are no different. Look what we have done to them. Look at the cruelty that is poured upon their heads from the belief that man has a right to do to them as he likes. Battery houses, feeding them on unnatural foods, making them produce eggs that are of very doubtful quality. Imagine not so long ago, you could not eat anything that was better for you than a raw egg. Now you dare not eat one. They are contaminated with all sorts of things and if they are not well cooked, they can kill you. Do you know, your oven ready chicken that you buy in your supermarkets is only twenty- eight days old? Apparently they are fed a hormone that makes them eat, and convert food so fast that they grow to three of four pounds weight in so short a time. It is immoral. Never mind all the other wrong things it is, that come to mind. And all for what? So you can have a cheap chicken, and some lower forms of life can make a lot of money. Someone should do it to them.

There is also the matter of jobs, and jobs mean political careers. This we must take seriously. Where would we all be if the political careers of our top politicians were to be placed in danger and they could not get any richer? How would the World survive without this quality of person at the helm of life. I nearly called them human beings, but you must forgive me. They are the same shape after all, but there sadly, the similarity ends. Belief is a many destructive thing, it makes people act in the most ridiculous of ways. They kill one another for it and in the name of it. They destroy all before them because they believe what the leaders of Religion tell them. They destroy their very lives because they believe in falsehoods. Men have always believed that belief is necessary to their existence. A kind of circle, and have thus managed to either deny facts or ignore them in the service of their belief.

The most powerful thing on the face of the Earth is the mind of man. There are more connections between the right and left hemispheres of the brain than there are telephone connections in the World. Each one carrying more information at any given moment, than all the telephones in the World. To command a man's ears is to access his mind. Access his mind and you own his whole being. One of the Popes once said, "Give me the mind of a child till he is seven and I will give you a Catholic for life". He was, and is right. Once the mind is accessed its owner is no longer in charge. This fact is exactly what gives belief it's strength. If a man knows something he will not fight over it, but should he believe he knows something, he will kill his own brother in the defence of it, even though that belief is ridiculous. Beyond common sense or reason. Even if it is wrong. He does not know, he only believes. It makes no sense. It does however make sense to the powers that be. "Vote for me and I will create jobs" What jobs? Jobs create themselves out of a need for the service, or of product. Jobs cannot be created. Your politicians say, "I believe this" and "I believe that". Listen to them. They don't know anything, they just believe. It also gives them a way out. They say "I really believed it to be true at the time". Rubbish! They should have known, but they didn't, or worse still they did know, and knew what they were saying was wrong, so they used belief as a get out. Nice honest chaps!My old Mother used to say "Never expect anything from a pig but a grunt." I don't know why I still live in hope of finding honesty in politics.

In the Old Order we have our theories, but we recognise them as only theories till they are proven. There are those who will say that we follow prophesies, therefore we believe. Only partly right. We follow the Old prophecies as they are, and in particular The Prophesy of Christ, or the last Prophesy, because it has been proved to be right so often. The Prophesy has never been known to be wrong in two thousand years. Perhaps a little out on the times once or twice, but right nevertheless. Taking this into consideration, it would be foolish not to hedge our bets in that direction. Every part of the Prophesy of Christ has come about, so far. So it is therefore reasonable to expect the rest of it will as well. He has proved himself right far too often to be ignored. As well as that, what he says makes sense in the light of what we know from our everyday experiences, and in watching, and taking note of the happenings all about us.I am not a gambling man, but if there were two horses in a race and I knew that one of them only had three legs, then I would certainly place my money on the one with four. Wouldn't you?

The reason that the Old Order has decided to come out into the light now is that, it is simply the time. It has been far too long known as the religion with no name, as it evolved in a time when men did not realise that it needed a name, as it was the way of things. They couldn't foresee any other ways of life ever becoming a reality.

To them the very idea of acting in an unreasonable manner was beyond comprehension. As far as they were concerned, there was only knowledge, reason, logic and common sense that you could use to run your life. They could not foresee all the belief systems catching on, they probably never even thought of such things. We in the Order still have the same attitude today. The Order Of The Ancient Way is not so much a religion as a way of life that we live religiously. We have no deities, no system of worship and no dogmas.

To be considered a religion, firstly you must have a recognisable dogma, such as you must believe in this, or in that. We have no belief systems. The title "Priest" means only teacher. We accept only proven knowledge and the only devotion we indulge in, is the devotion to that knowledge. Although there is no belief or faith involved, we recognise and are concerned with the spiritual needs of man. We object to the title 'Occult'. I pointed out the meaning of the word earlier, and we also know what that word has become to mean. Therefore we object to being lumped in with the lunatic fringe, or with those of doubtful sanity. We cannot deny that we are an 'occulted' order, from the point of view that we are of an ever-changing nature. As we learn and acquire knowledge, we change according the light of that knowledge. It makes sense to us. Learning and knowledge bring about growth. Growth brings about change, and so we change. It all seems logical and reasonable to me, but you make up your own mind. We are also constantly searching for more answers and proof of the validity of those answers. We don't always find them, but when we do, these answers may cause us to change and to then search for more answers.

It is often suggested that we indulge in devil worship, black magic and the like. This very false belief again like all belief is based on imagination not fact. It helps to turn people away from us, and very often against us. At its very best it makes us appear to be crackers, at worst totally evil.

But it is the ones that make up such stories, often knowing that they are wrong, who are the evil ones. They so like to do harm, these pious ones. They love to show off their power so much and inflict pain, that they have even gone to the point of holding trails for cats. You know, Moggies! Pussy cats! Accusing them of serving Satan, who does not exist. They even found them guilty. Whether to serve their own sick minds or influence the minds of others is debatable, but probably for both purposes. The cats were either sentenced to burn or to hang. Poor old pussy, who never did any more than be born black, or maybe it was because cats were once worshipped by the Pharaohs among others. The practice had to be stopped, and the competition with Christianity removed, in a manner not so likely to be forgotten. Like the cats, we have always been considered a great threat to organised religions who have even gone so far as to deny our existence. They usually attribute their own darker side to us, shouting "Evil". As they must know their own minds best, they attribute their own imaginings to us. But that's 'believers' for you. Reality, even their own, has been lost to them along with any thought of reason.

This is why we have until now remained secret and underground. Not I hasten to add because we are evil, but because we have to suffer the evils of the supposed Christian Churches and other religious denominations. We know what they do to pussycats. They have also done it to us. We had a big problem and that problem was that if someone was dying, and the priest was called. He would say his prayers and splash on the "Holy Water" or whatever they all do on such occasions. Should this not work, then it was assumed that the patient was meant to die and it was by the expressed will of God. The distraught family would sometimes call on the services of a wise one to try to prevent the demise of their relative. It was deemed OK if the patient died. It helped to assert proof of the power of the priest and the lack of power of the wise one. At least the Christian Church wasn't challenged in any way. If however the wise ones efforts proved fruitful and they often did, and the patient lived, the wise one had gone against the will of God, and that was heresy. For this you were usually burried, to prevent the spilling of blood, by the Anglican Church or the Church of Rome. They did this as to spill blood was considered by them to be a sin. You work it out.

The reason for the breaking of the silence now by the Order, or if you like the 'coming out', which is the popular term, is simply that we are now facing the ending of days', the time is right. We consider that the minds of men might be ready to accept reason, at long last.We hope that this is the case, although I myself remain very pessimistic and await that knock on the door, or that burning pain in my back. If I am wrong then what's the difference? We are all finished anyway.

Parts of the Order will remain secret for my protection and for vengeance if need be. You see, I am not a forgiving person like the last one to come. In fact he wasn't either. As he says, "The days of the forgiveness for man are over". Those who must remain secret will mainly stay that way for their own protection, and for the protection of the Order. Their mystery being part of their strength. The last hope is death. Until then we carry on regardless, as far as is practical. The World is dying beneath our feet, everybody knows it. But, what have you done about it lately?

You can literally blame false doctrine of one type or another whether political or religious. They are both the same you know, in concept and in make up. We provoke thought, not a good thing in the light of belief. It is with thought that we find out and learn. We accept that which is demonstrable, or at least reasonable, or logical. But only as a theory, until proved one way or the other. If it proves wrong, it's out. No matter how good it has been thought to be, or how much we would like to believe it. A theory is only a point from where you start to search. It is in fact the seed of thought of which the harvest is doubtful. We never turn against anyone because they do not agree with us, we don't always agree among ourselves. And we have never burned a Christian, though we would have been better thought of if we had. This is not only because we do not kill without good reason, but mainly because we have found and reasoned that the truth will always be true. No matter what you try to do to alter it or camouflage it or interpret it, the truth is the truth, and is as it is.

In the Old Order we have found it to be true that each and everything that crawls, swims, or flies is a beast, including man. We bleed and breed. We feed, live and die, as do all other beasts. We also fear, as do they. We feel pain, as do they. We see that inside every beast that lives upon the Earth, there is a varying degree of humanity. You can see it everywhere. Sadly you can see the lack of it everywhere too. This varying degree of humanity, either does or does not control the beasts that we are. The beast is just the base nature of man, and all other beasts. From this simple idea the devil was born. They had just invented a new God, the one and only, so he needed some opposition, just to lend a balance. The horns and the tail were put on the idea of the beast and 'Old Nick' was born. The bogey man. This base nature is part of us all, and is not a separate entity that you can blame for temptation or ill luck or whatever, and so avoid responsibility for your actions and blame it on someone or something else. The beast is you and it is your responsibility to control it. Humanity ranges from none at all, to more than is good for your well being. Somewhere in the middle is about right. Therefore I say to you, "In all things, show balance and beware of the beast". And so did 'Old Nick' become the bogey man for the new beliefs.

To be used to put the 'frighteners' on you all. And this new God was designed as the loving, kind and gentle one. Who together with the help of his arch enemy will burn you in hell should you disobey his priests and his commandments, which they will lay before you. Woe betide you should you transgress. God is the all seeing one who protects and feeds us all. Except of course in some places like the German labour camps, in Chile, Bosnia, Sudan or other 'hell holes'. But we are told the Lord moves in mysterious ways his wonders to perform. The evil that men do is only surpassed by the evil that men think, and the things they would do if they thought they could get away with them.

We are a practical people, and where knowledge is unavailable we use logic, reason, and common sense based on what we do know. If the workability of a subject is demonstrable, even though we may not understand it, we will accept it. Because by demonstration it proves itself to a point, and we do not, and at this time can not know all things. And we never will. So instead of weaving a belief around things we do not understand or know about definitely, instead of accepting belief as fact, we accept that we do not know, and then set out to find out. People often find the idea of our priesthood difficult to understand. You must remember that we were here first, and the idea of a priest being just a teacher was ours till other perpetrators of religion realised that it could be used in other more base ways, for even more base reasons.

In the Old Order anyone can become a Priest or Priestess. The duties of the Priesthood in the Old Order are not so very different from those of a priest in other religions, except that we do not go around praying, or handing out blessings, or in fact curses. We are not pious or righteous. The other major difference is that we are directly involved in the lives of our people in practical ways, such as in arranging bulk buying of foodstuffs and anything else they might need, thus saving them considerable money, while working to ensure the purity of the foods as far as possible. Hence we have a direct positive effect on the health of our people. This we consider of the ultimate importance given the state of the World we live in today. We play a part in the political lives of our people as well. When you enter the Order either as an associate member or a full member you must pledge your vote and cast that vote as directed. This is not quite as dictatorial as it sounds. What happens is, that each chapter will hold a meeting near the time of an election, and they will decide which candidate is doing his or her bit as that chapter sees it. Then they will vote for a particular person on that basis. What party he belongs to is of no importance to us, it is the person that counts. This gives us political leverage in matters that concern us. For example, at this time we are involved in getting asbestos water pipes that have been down for some forty years, replaced, because of the unusually high rate of deaths from cancer in the area. As usual the politicians have failed to notice, even though they were approached about six years ago. We have found, as have the Unions, that the block vote carries weight and so like them, we use it for the benefit of our members and hopefully for the society we live in. It means that you are no longer one vote, and therefore expendable. Any politician being unhelpful will find it most unprofitable should he or she not at least give it an honest go in our cause, whether that cause has anything to do with us directly or our fellow citizens on whose behalf we may be acting. We even have one or two politicians in the Order. So you see there are a few good ones. They remain obscure for obvious reasons.

If someone wishes to become a Priest or Priestess, they can rise through the ranks to exalted level. This however is a far as you can go, unless you are a 'Caulbearer'. This is designed to stop the rich or powerful from taking over the Order for their own base reasons. A king's or a street sweeper's child can be born with a 'Caul'. The 'Caul' is a mask of skin that is over the face at birth with two loops over the ears to keep in place. The Caul is a membrane, that is attached to the face of a child when it is born.

It is a full face mask and completely covers the face. It is held in place by two ear loops. These loops distinguish it from the 'lucky cap' which is placenta stuck to the head or face of a child, or both. Astrologers of the Old Religion which had no name and is now known as The Order Of the Ancient Way, were able to predict the exact time and place of the birth of a 'Caulbearer'. This is mainly why the 'Caul' is held in such high esteem and has been down the ages. More information of the 'Caul' may be obtained by contacting The Order Of the Ancient Way at the order website **www.orderoftheancientway.com**

It is so often mistaken for what is known as the lucky cap', which is placenta stuck to the head and is absolutely without and relevant meaning as far as we know. I saw a programme on T.V recently called, "Taggart" and they had a bit about people born with 'Cauls'. They showed these odd little things, supposed to be 'Cauls'. And as is usual for the acting or theatrical fraternity in these matters, they got it wrong. They were not 'Cauls', and were nothing like 'Cauls'. The real thing as you can see from the picture, is very distinctive and is also very rare. The way we use the 'Caul' in the Order has probably hampered our advancement for obvious reasons. The main obstacle being, that if the king's son can't have all his own way, then nobody is allowed to play the game. And if in the Old Order you are not a 'Caulbearer', you cannot rise above the level of Exalted Priest.

From High Priest upwards it is 'Caulbearers' only, as it is in the Guild of Tarot Masters, who just carried it on from the Rune Masters. The Brotherhood and The High Templars, are all under the same rule. The priesthood starts with the novice Priests, then the Priests and the Exalted Priests. The 'Exalted' can be chosen for the Upper Temple, but only for particularly good effort and rarely at that. The Upper Temple consists mainly of the sons and daughters of 'Caulbearers', again only those who have excelled themselves in some way. Then comes the Noviciate High Priesthood who are 'Caulbearers' at the bottom level. We all have to learn. They consist mainly of children up to eighteen. They may stay at that level as some have no wish to go further, as it is with all the Priesthood. This decision can be affected by family, or often business pressures, because none of us are paid, it is done purely on a voluntary basis. We all must eat, and pay our way. From Novice, the next step is to High Priest. The responsibility is heavier as you climb from there to Exalted High, to Grand High, to Exalted Grand High, To Great Grand High, To Exalted Great Grand High and so to Supreme High Priest, which is the top of the ladder. The Supreme High Priest is the only one who cannot be demoted or removed from office. He or she cannot refuse the position once chosen and will choose their successor when death is close. There is always an envelope somewhere, just in case.

Anyone can become a Priest or Priestess, male and female, black, white or in between, it makes no difference. What does make a difference is the way that you think. We have been know to turn down 'Caulbearers'. Although the 'Caul' has a very important place in the Order, the person must also be of suitable mind, with the right attitude and motive for wanting to be a Priest or Priestess in the first place. As Priests we are human, and so prone to human failures and weaknesses. We are not pious nor are we very righteous. We are mostly well meaning. Mostly, I think and hope, good. But the odd one slips past. When discovered they are dealt with immediately. We are all obliged to report any wrong doings of either Priest or of members of the laity, as wrong doings affect us all. Should a Priest or Priestess become greedy and start dipping into the till, and it has happened, we must know. It is no use protecting such a person, we simply can't afford it, financially, practically or indeed morally.

We are well aware that to command the ears of a man is the way to imprison his heart. You see demonstrations of it every day in the media. If it is not big business, it is big brother. We prefer men to feel with a free heart, and to think with a free mind. When a man or woman seeks to rise to the priesthood, on acceptance they pledge their lives to the Priest/Priestess who accepts them, and to the High Priesthood of the Order. All literally give their lives into the ownership of the Priesthood, all the way up to the Supreme High Priest. All priests are directly responsible for those below them and they in turn for those above. As well as being responsible for, you are also responsible to those above, and they in return can be brought to book by those below. All must serve to the best of their ability. Sometimes a Priest or Priestess will be paid for some service or other, such as assisting with a personal problem that would leave them out of pocket. We try to make sure that no one is out of of pocket. In fact we must because if we don't we will quickly run out. No one could afford it. We do not object to fair payment, but the emphasis is always on the word "fair". We accept that we do not live by bread alone, but instead by that other bread. The bread of life that feeds not the body but is so necessary as a nutrient to the inner, and whole being. The bread that overrides the beast. The very stuff of humanity, that which overrides the base nature of the beast and makes us human.

177

All those chosen are chosen solely on merit. Each has to prove worthiness. All members of the Priesthood give account at the Solstices by tradition. These days it is necessary more often and can be given by telephone, email etc. Technology has made a big difference in this matter, and for the good. Account may be given shortly before or shortly after Solstice, due to the numbers involved these days. But account may be requested or indeed demanded at any time, and attendance is compulsory, no excuses will be accepted. To be accepted into the priesthood is the highest honour there is. Our badge is of service, and our honour is the performance of that service to our members, our fellow man and to the World we live in as a whole. Our World has arrived at this sorry state directly because of the organised religions and their belief systems.

We have twelve laws as I have explained, each one self-explanatory. We have other unwritten rules. Take godparents for example. We do not have them. It is accepted that we are all responsible for all the children. Partly because they are vulnerable and helpless, but also because we live on in the blood, or if you like, our children are our genetic information going on into the future, giving us everlasting life. That too must be part of the picture. Living on into the future through our genetics is not only provable but very obvious to all. When a child is accepted into any Christian Religion, and is 'christened', the god parents make all sorts of promises and then in the majority of cases quickly forget them.

The things that are taken as mainly Christian, Muslim or Buddhist as badges of piousness and outward shows of goodness, are by us just taken for granted, and are part of our everyday lives. They are right or they are wrong and as we do not expect reward in an after life, or in this one, for our deeds, we do as we do solely because it is right, or we do not do so, because it is considered wrong. As far as we are concerned to do something with reward in mind is base and unworthy, and the perpetrator though doing good, cannot do good, should that good be done for the wrong reason. That reason being solely for the reward hoped for, not just for the sake of that which he does being right. In many cases if done only with reward in mind, be it for self satisfaction or an eternity in some hoped for paradise, better if it is not done at all. All these religions as part of their cult claim such things as charity, love, consideration, generosity etc. as their own. It would be beyond the concept of the average follower of The Way to act or think in any other manner.

# Equality

Our Order is not one of equality. Instead it is based on reason and common sense. To us men and women are different and long may it be so. The difference is obvious. We are made differently and we think differently and are therefore suited to different purposes, again mostly obvious. This to us does not mean that women are less than men, neither does it mean that men are less than women. It simply means that their capabilities are different and as it is wise for everyone to remain within their range of capability, again the reasons being obvious. We tend to do so as far as possible. If the man is ill or incapacitated in some way, it may be necessary for the woman in that partnership to stretch herself to fill the gap. One day the roles may well be reversed such as during pregnancy. In such times it is up the husband to take over from the wife to enable her to do the more important job of bearing her child and attaining the necessary rest etc. that she needs at that time. For instance it would not be advised that she should continue carrying bags of potatoes at such a time while her husband sits watching the T.V. and I have seen this happen.

Should her husband break a leg we would expect her to do the chores he would normally do. Hopefully it would not all happen at once, but if it did we would expect other members of The Order to rally round and help out. Women are simply not built nor are they mentally equipped to follow a man's role. Men are not built nor are they mentally equipped to follow a woman's role. Even though today everyone seems to be trying to reverse everything especially with the march of homosexuality gathering such momentum. Their propaganda seems to be taking over the minds of even the most heterosexual amongst us, to our everlasting detriment. If they repeat their rubbish long enough it will have an effect. Nature has given us all limitations, but she has also given us all assets. It is therefore reasonable for us to use our assets to our best advantage, for the advantage of others and the World we live in. While putting our minds to the wheel of our weaknesses or limitations, and turning them into strengths as far as possible, whether these weaknesses are real or imagined.

Aside from the man/woman thing it is obvious to anyone that we are all made differently, each from the other. Therefore it is reasonable to accept that we can only be ourselves. We simply cannot be anyone, or anything else. Putting ourselves beyond our real capabilities, psychologically or physically, is at best foolish and at worst destructive. In the Old Order we take care of each other, including each other's children. So that in the event of death or illness within a family the children have someone that they really know to take care of them. So that they will be spared the trauma of being placed among strangers, stuck in a Home or as so often happens, be separated from each other. The track record of the Christian Churches in this particular matter is bad to say the least, even into present times. As is becoming obvious, the religious homes in the past have been there only for the making of money, with little genuine concern for the well-being of the elderly or orphaned.

This also applies right across the board. We still take care of the old folks, and keep them at home if at all possible, in order to avoid the unnecessary stress caused, should they be placed among strangers, and strange surroundings. Particularly against their will, no matter how pleasant and humane their carers and surroundings may be. Some of the elderly can become impossible to care for at home, for one reason or another e.g. illness, and in such cases reason must prevail, no matter how hard it may be. A hospital situation may be the only course open. We look on this, as a last resort only. We always try to follow the natural laws of nature and natural things. Sometimes we get it wrong and sometimes we fail miserably, we of course do not advocate failure, but in failure there is profit because we learn, and therefore know better next time.

We have other peculiarities as some may see it. We only eat meat killed in a certain way. We accept that we are caught up in the food chain and therefore must eat. Part of that food chain is meat. We always eat our meat before we eat anything else on the plate, as it is bought at a high price, something has to die to provide it. We therefore see no reason except financial reasons, why the poor animal should be killed the way Christians and particularly Muslims do it. There is no need to be unnecessarily cruel.

We kill when we must, as quickly and painlessly as possible, taking into consideration the psychological pain of fear, as well. The beasts have the same feelings as we do, perhaps not the same reason, though this could be brought to question. They experience pain, and fear just the same, and most of it is totally unnecessary, so we do things differently. If anything should be left on the plate let it be vegetable not meat. We never burn food nor bury it to rot. It just might save the life of another creature. It can lead to that creature eating something else that might just kill you, should its natural predator have previously died of hunger. It is all a little simplified but I am sure that you can work it out from there. If you have waste food it is better to feed it to the wild things, it can do no harm, and is bound to do some good in the long run. And kill only as necessary and as painlessly as the killing will allow. The Christian commandment, which is a bastardisation of the old law says, "Thou shalt not kill". Our law says, "Kill not without good reason". It doesn't say, "Kill not men without good reason." The law is very plain. It doesn't require a degree in divinity to understand it. None of our laws do. The law says simply, "Kill not without good reason, not man, beast, green thing, that which flies or lives in water, even that which is harmful, all things have their purpose". If man had not been led to believe falsely, that he was born godlike, separate, and in control of the World and all therein, and upon and above it, imagine what a difference it would have made. We would not now be facing 'the ending of days', we would have cared and that would have made a difference, all the difference.

The position we now find ourselves in is so far out of any control, that it can be no longer hidden from even the most stupid of us. Nature could not live up to the beautiful and impossible dream that was invented by the organised religions, to bring humanity to them. Backed up by the power seekers and controllers, they believe that you will all forget about the problems facing us. In their conceit they forget that they too will perish, as they also are just mere members of the species. They will try to divert your attention. Don't let it happen for the sake of that species and its survival.

Life is a circle. You get out exactly what you put in, and it goes around and around. Life is neither an end nor is it a beginning to anything. Life is energy, and energy does not die. You cannot kill or destroy energy. You come from energy and to energy shall you return. Energy can be used, altered, but never killed or destroyed. It is a provable fact. You may have heard people talking of the ether that surrounds us. They mean the energy. Our World was born of energy, so the Old Ones said twenty thousand years ago, and so it was. It took energy for the big bang, the implosion of the black hole, which incidentally happens more often than you think. So there is a fair bet that there are other worlds out there, similar to ours. Hopefully, not in the same mess. Einstein proved the old theory about energy when he invented Quantum Physics. Thus the old theory became a fact. At the same time he also proved beyond doubt the non-existence of God. And as he did so he proved our old idea of the 'Godforce'. This very energy, that is the force of nature that makes up all things, seemingly with purpose. This energy was presumed female by the Old Ones in times gone by, as they said "From whose womb all things are born". This energy has been floating round since long before the World began, and so have you and I in one form or another. So reincarnation is more than a possibility. In what form, is up for grabs. It is still only a probability, not yet proven fact.People see ghosts, which is the manifestation of the energy of those departed. It is not those departed, just the energy. That is why they are always transparent. Some people are more susceptible than others to their presence and so appear to be able to not only see, but to communicate with them as well. Susceptibility also appears to depend on conditions and mental states. So have no fear. You have been round for more than five billion years in one form or another, so you will probably be back. In one form, or another.

Although we realise that the World runs on belief, and that without belief some would find it very difficult to cope with the trials and tribulations of

181

every day living. Belief acts as a screen that we erect to hide ourselves from whatever we fear or do not want to know about. It acts like blinkers. Still I would urge you all to think, to face reality. It is often very hard but in my experience it is best to know than 'believe' when so much hangs on the outcome of a decision, and the decision depends on the method of the thought. Your very existence stands or falls by and because of, the way you think. There is the certainty of knowledge, even if that knowledge is uncomfortable, or the uncertainty of wrong or misguided 'belief', even though it may give comfort. It is for you to choose.

We find it hard in the Old Order to get people to accept the way of knowledge and reason. To accept as organised religions teach, that you are made in the image of God, is nice, but not true. They teach you that you are superior, again it is not true, but nice and acceptable. We tell you are just beast, and no more important than any other beast. Which is true, and a biological fact, but not so nice, not so acceptable. So you can appreciate our problem. If we tell you as other followings tell you, how Godlike you are, we would have to drive you all away with a big stick. But as we tell you the way it really is, and in fact the way you really know it is, then you don't like us.

It is obvious that you are born and you take your place in the circle of life, the same as all beasts. You wear out and die, and return to the energy from whence you came. Most people find the concept of being Godlike, though it be only belief and known to be untrue, easier to accept than ours. Ours you can see easily, and know it to be true. Such is the madness of belief. People often say to us that we have a beautiful religion, they really like it. Then they say "But I need my God". They need a God who doesn't exist. Mostly they are aware of this. They are afraid to lose the dream, the fantasy, and accept the reality. You can alter fantasy, but fact like truth is solid, and remains constant. This attitude is why the World is in such a mess. Because of this unreality, this fiction. And then some wonder why I despair.

Some of you will no doubt know of the pentacle that we wear. "The sign of the devil", they say. Well it isn't. The devil doesn't exist either. But the propaganda has managed to get people to turn away from reality for two thousand years. You would be amazed should you look at the wheels of many cars, with their 'five spoke' arrangement. Then there's America's law enforcement badge like the famous Texas Rangers wear.

The Pentacle has always been reputed to have magical qualities for protection against evil. If you cut an apple in half across the direction of the core, you have a perfect pentacle. It is the same in many things, flowers for instance. There are those who believe the Pentacle to be evil itself. It is believed that it is used by witches, to cast spells of evil on their fellow man. And indeed many would be witches today believe it as well. They are all wrong, so typical of believers. It is all belief, based on more beliefs. In reality it represents the seven responsibilities of man only, and always has. (See insert) Memorise them and think of them every day. Reflect and become whole and worthy of your kind. Perhaps the Pentacle does contain magical properties. Perhaps it does protect against evil. Or perhaps its believed goodness or badness depends, as with so many things on the intent of the user. There are usually two sides to every coin, and the pentacle represents a coin.

The Pentacle is a very ancient symbol, shrouded in mystery. The Pentacle is also associated with Jesus himself, and through Mary Magdalene, his wife who had to flee to France after the Crucifixion, for her safety and for the safety of the child she was carrying. His child. There is a circle of hills, five in all with a hill in the middle. If you place the Pentacle over the hills there is one exactly on each point of the star and one in the centre. Should you then just draw a circle round them, you have a Pentacle. The Roman Church in particular denied this till recently. But it can now be seen clearly from space, by satellites. So it is just not mentioned anymore. But it will not go away. Most Christians would be horrified at the very thought of Jesus being a father, but there is a lot more about him that would horrify them, if only they were allowed to know. He too lived his life out in that area, after his crucifixion.

Like I have said so often, he was a very unusual and fantastic man to say the least. I will never understand why they could not just portray him as he really was. He was in fact even greater than the myth drawn around him. I feel that it was probably because he was so great, that no one would have believed them, and those who profess to follow him would themselves not look so hot, in the shadow of him. There have been a lot of books and stories written about this, and I and my fellow members of the Brotherhood are often amazed how close the authors have come to the real truth. Then 'belief' has got in their way, and they have 'blown it'. Probably just as well, as I don't think that most of the World will ever be ready for reality, to this extent.

All our laws are self-explanatory and were used as a blueprint for the Ten Commandments, and the laws and rules governing most religions. The laws of the Old Order read as follows.

1. Honour the seven responsibilities of man, as laid down. Alter not, interpret not, they are as they are.

2. No man shall kill without good reason. Not man, not beast, green thing, that which flies or lives within water, even that which is harmful. All things have their purpose.

3. Take not any thing that you do not put back. Should you cut down a tree, plant six. Lay nought to waste especially flesh as it is bought at a high price.

4. Take no thing that is not yours by right.

5. Protect that which sustains, against those who know no better.

6. Lay not man with man, or woman with woman. Such thing goes against the natural way of things. That which goes against the natural way of things is a danger to nature itself. Death shall visit those who break this law.

7. Harm no child.

8. Each is his, or her own being and may do with according to his or her own wish. Providing no harm shall befall any other living thing. Adultery is such a thing, and cannot be forgiven. Cast them out.

9. Eat only meat from the beasts which have been killed without fear or pain, so far as the killing of them has allowed. All pain of the spirit, and the flesh must be avoided.

10. All things that move upon the Earth are beasts. Honour them all as you would like to be honoured, and treat kindly.

11. Take care of forefathers, and respect and honour them. Feed them and house them as they did you when you could not care for yourself.

12. Honour your Priests, but should they offend seek judgement from a High Priest, and should a High Priest offend, seek out another High Priest and again seek judgement.

As you can see they are all self-explanatory. No law is given without reasons for that law.

The first law deals with the seven responsibilities, represented by the pentacle.

The second is to do with killing. It is part of the nature of the beast to kill and man being a beast kills, and sadly sometimes only for fun. Very often out of jealousy and hate. We therefore do not indulge in the baseness of blood sports in any shape or form. We will kill wild animals if they should either kill or threaten our domesticated animals or threaten our lives or livelihood in some way. We will kill where killing is the only option, say should a man break into someone else's home or threaten someone's family. We would see no wrong, if this person was killed by whoever he has threatened, or offended against. If the person was hungry or in need, he could ask. In such a society he would know the risk involved, so if he chose to take the risk, the fault would be considered his. As far as killing green things is concerned, there is the story of the pious man who cut down a row of trees so that he could see the wonder of his God in the sunset as he prayed. That winter a powerful storm came. He prayed. But the wind still blew his roof off. Better to have left the trees and see their beauty, which is equal to any sunset. If you want to see the sun set walk a ways, the exercise will do you good.

The third is putting back that which we take. If you cut down a tree plant six. It is said that if you plant six trees, the beasts will eat two. The storm that will come in the time of their growing will take two. Should you plant them, it is wise to plant them close for their protection against the winds. So as they grow they will be too close and you will have to cut one down in order to allow the remaining tree to grow to its full potential. So you are left with one. Now if the wind and the beasts happen to leave more than expected and they often do, then you and the trees are better off. So all is gain, and gain for all.

The fourth law is easy and cannot be misunderstood. You don't steal.

The fifth law is simple, but only on the surface. To protect all things that sustain covers a lot of ground. It comes down to what sustains? Well, literally everything. You may think that what goes on out in the rest of the World, is no concern of yours. What about ecology? What the Russians or the Chinese do may well have an effect on you, as does Chernobyl. All that concrete, without reinforcing, so now it breaks up. They say, "Mind your own business". What they really mean is, "Don't bother us, we don't give a damn". I don't mean the ordinary people. I mean the beasts who are in control, with apologies to even the lowliest of the beasts. Common sense tells us that all that happens upon the face of the Earth, and above the Earth and below the Earth is your business, and mine. It's everybody's business, so protect it with your very life. It is your life.

The sixth law is the 'tricky' one these days. Again think of the fifth. You will find when you get down to them, they are all interconnected. Homosexuality and paedophilia go closely hand in hand. One can easily lead to the other. Both seem to be the 'in' things at the moment. The lowest a man or a woman can get is the latter. To harm a child for sexual pleasure. Once you have got down there, there is really no place else to go. You are really only a sub species, and should be considered as just that. A sub species of the lowest sub species. We do not tolerate any forms of perversion. We have been known to accept certain individuals that are obviously suffering from a genetic deformity as far as sexuality is concerned. As with all others who are unfortunate enough to be born genetically malformed in some, or in any way, we will do everything to make them as happy, and a comfortable as we possibly can. Within the Order they will be treated with understanding, and valued for their contribution to us and to the rest of the World. But all the other types, who are just perverts, we will not tolerate.

Now in the Old Order because we kill 'not without good reason', though this is a very good reason, we try to do the best we can, so we make them an offer. Either slavery for life, with their 'meat and two veg.' cut off, or death. They can choose. We see no reason to bear the cost of their maintenance, and prison is no answer to this thing. It is just as well for them at this time that we do not have sufficient control in any country to enforce these laws of ours. Homosexual lobby groups are trying to make the whole thing look as if they are doing the natural thing, and the rest of us are a 'bit queer'. Sadly many people go along with them, as it is deemed the 'Christian' thing to do, to live and let live, regardless. They try to be nice when it makes no sense at all. Where homosexuality is concerned it is more, let them live their way without consideration for the rest of the World. And the rest of the World can die. It cannot be justified. Perversion is perversion, and it is absolute. They have a way of making people feel guilty of being normal and they play on that guilt. This tactic is as dirty as their perversion. I have however promised to change this law as has been requested, and demanded under threat by some groups. I have promised and will again verify that promise, that I will change that law when, and only when, a man gives birth to a healthy baby by natural means and without medical help, and not until then. I am well aware that this law upsets a large number of people, but I make no change and no apology. Neither for myself, nor for the Order. Those who are offended must either see homosexual perversion for exactly what it is, or stay offended.

The seventh law is tied to the last laws very strongly. A child is it's parent's genetic information going forward into the future, their everlasting life. From this the law draws strength. It also draws strength from the fact that a child is helpless, and in that innocence is so easily tricked and hurt, the hurt lasting all it's life. As I have said before, the worst thing anyone can do is, harm a child. Christ is recorded as saying, "Suffer little children to come onto me". He did not mean for sexual purposes, or gratification. When we say harm no child, we do not mean chastisement. As a father I am more than aware that sometimes a hot bottom is the only answer when little Johnny pushes his luck, just to see how far he can go. It is sometimes necessary for his own good to stop him, before the World does it for you, with less kindness, and no love at all.

The eighth law concerns adultery. In modern times it happens a lot. We condemn it because of the hurt it can cause to a spouse emotionally, but mostly because of disease. With Aids so prevalent, and these new strains of Syphilis, Gonorrhoea and Herpes all totally immune to antibiotics thus rendering them incurable. You don't have the right to dose your spouse with something nasty, so that you can have further sexual experience, for whatever reason, for feeding your ego or anything else. If you no longer love your spouse or if you are not happy with your spouse, then split up and go your separate ways, but don't do this. The pain generated is not worth it and the risk in our time is so great.

The ninth law is also self-explanatory, dealing with the way we kill animals in order to eat. There is no need to kill animals the way that they are killed in slaughter-houses today. They are herded into pens, usually beaten with sticks, or prodded with electric prods, which cause considerable pain. I have felt like prodding some of the Directors of one or two slaughter-houses I have seen in the past to see how they like it. Their excuse is that they are only dumb animals. I don't mean the Directors, but this too may be right. In modern thinking, profits must be made or jobs will be lost. They do not think what else may be lost. Handling the poor creatures like this is the most efficient way. The poor beasts are herded together in a pen or pens. They can hear their fellows making sounds of pain, as they are being killed and they can smell the blood. They are

187

terrified. It is all carried out like a kind of torture for them. Imagine if it was you. They feel and fear as we do. Their lives might not be as our lives are, but their lives are just as precious to them as yours and mine are to us. They are then dragged into the killing room, or driven in by the infliction of a great deal of pain. A so-called 'humane killer' is used to stun them. It is a very good and efficient tool if used right, but so often it is not. As often as not the operator will miss. They then have their throats cut and bleed to death. The line must be kept going so they do not have another go, there is no time. Time is money. I have heard it all. As I have said they have their throats cut, very often while quite conscious. If they were to cut the carotid artery, the blood pressure to the brain would drop immediately and they would then be rendered unconscious, but they don't. The butchers concerned are usually very hardened to the task, and seem to have no feelings at all left in them, probably due to familiarity with death. Breeding contempt for both death and for the beast that is about to die.

Chickens are killed mainly by machine. They hang on a conveyor belt and are supposed to be stunned by electric shock as they go along. Very often due to struggling, it misses, and they then can end up in the boiling water baths, still alive and very conscious. Scalded to death. I was once told to mind my own business. What did I know? He said "Its their own bloody fault, they should hold still". I wonder would he hold still, under similar circumstances? Chickens are reared under the most inhumane circumstances and slaughtered under even worse, at the ripe old age of twenty-eight days. Veal is heartbreaking to say the least. It should, and would be banned in any right thinking society. Our attitude to the way we deal with out fellow creatures shows exactly what we really are. Certainly not Godlike, at least not the usual view of God, all loving and kind.

We kill only one animal at a time, only when necessary, and seldom in the same place. The reason for contamination in meat is mainly because of the slaughter houses where killing goes on all the time. Blood is ever present, giving a perfect medium for bacteria. If as we do, you kill in the fields, the beast has no idea that he is going to be killed, and he never does if it is done with a little thought. Animals these days are used to being in trailers. To the animal it's just going somewhere like so many times before. He comes into the yard or field, just like so many times before, the little trap door opens like so many times before. He has no need to fear. There's nothing strange or different, so he has no fear. There's a bang that he doesn't even hear, and it is all over. Without fear, or pain of any kind. It's a bit messier for the butcher, as the animal has not been starved and thirsted for twenty-four hours, so the stomach is full. It's a bit more difficult as it has to be hoisted quickly in order to be bled correctly, but that is our problem. So what sort of a human being would pass the problem on to the beasts and make them suffer because it would cause him trouble or effort? After all the animal loses his life in order that we may have food and live. He or she deserves better be they fowl, fish or beast. Then there are the sporting types. Buy a shotgun and join the so-called nobility. Off we go. Isn't it fun, with a bang, bang here and a bang, bang there? How can anybody who calls him or herself human, never mind 'noble', possibly consider hunting as 'fun'. It is unnecessary cruelty just for the fun of it. It simply does not compute. It makes no sense.

How can dealing out pain to another creature possibly be fun, unless you are a very sick individual indeed? I go hunting. I have hunted for food, and took no pleasure in it. I never saw it as either fun or pleasure. I did however and still do take pride in my ability in the skills of hunting. Even now I will sometimes shoot a fox or two when they decide to kill my chickens or ducks, but I never see it as a game. I am sure that the creature that is hunted, usually by some 'plonker' who can't shoot anyway, doesn't think it fun. Especially if lying wounded, and dying in agony, because the 'Hooray Henry' who shot it didn't do it properly and didn't take the trouble to make sure whether he had really missed. Probably because he is more used to missing than hitting. I once remember a chap coming to Scotland to shoot deer. He said it was something he always wanted to do. He had all the gear and had spent a fortune just because he had always wanted to shoot a deer. Couldn't he shoot him with a camera? Deer and birds can be shot over and over again with a camera, and there's no pain involved. This chap thought that he was sane and I was mad. He was partly right. I was mad, hopping mad. My opinion on what he had said and in his purpose did not go down well. But neither did it deter him. He was just another pig at the trough of life, believing all while knowing nothing and caring even less.

The tenth law is an extension of the ninth and to my way of thinking, only reasonable. And if followed out, your natural instincts will prove you to be human. And if followed at least from shame, it will help the situation, and shows some hope.

The eleventh speaks of your forefathers, where you came from. Like it or not you are half your father and half your mother. You are their genetic information going forward into the future, their everlasting life, for real. You owe each other a lot, and this debt must be carried on in the interests of those genetics, and the future of the human race.

The last law is to do with your Priests, or teachers. The title 'Priest' has always meant 'teacher' to us. As I have said before we are not holy, nor are we pious. We are the passers on of knowledge, the settlers of argument, the witnesses to contracts, such as in marriage, the watchers, to make sure that all is as well as possible. The guardians of your morality and spirituality, and advisors on both. We are your friends, your confidants, your anchors in the storm of life.

We sometimes get it wrong, but mostly I hasten to say, we get it right more often. That's why people put up with us in the first place. Sadly the odd one gets through the net and turns out to be a 'bad apple'. Should you come across such a Priest or Priestess, don't blame the whole barrel and do nothing, as this will only serve to ensure the continuance of bad practice. This will become even more true as time goes by. Right across the whole of society. It is considered that, he who stands by and does nothing is just as guilty as he who does an evil act. Tell another Priest or Priestess, get it brought to light, and we will deal with it. This is the only way that we can ensure that such things do not go on. The 'lay man' is as important as any Priest in the Old Order. We must all serve our purpose to the best of our ability. Mistakes are allowed, deliberate wrong doing is not. Each of us is entitled to the honour we earn, but only to the honour we earn. And should not be honoured beyond that. The Order Of The Ancient Way is for the benefit of it's people and for the benefit of the Earth that sustains us all. It is a way of life that has little to do with wealth or status. A certain amount is forced upon us by the society we live in, and we must survive.

Survival in the future will be extremely difficult because the World will go mad as the seven planets line up in 2006. The closer they come together the worse it will get, and as they draw apart the influence will decrease. By then much damage will be done all round. Fear in men, together with arrogance and stupidity will do the rest. Most of what will happen, you already know about and don't need me to tell you once again. The problem is that you do not see, neither do you hear. As I have said you will not dig your well till your behind is on fire, therefore you do not deserve to survive. The World will do better if your genetics are no more. Your genetics have an influence on your thinking, and this kind of thinking is not only destructive to you, it is also destructive to the very World you live in. So better for the World if such genetics are no more. If I am to ask you, "Do you think in a reasonable manner?" You would answer "Yes". If I ask a man in a mental hospital if he thinks in a reasonable manner, he too will answer "Yes", for he believes in fact that he does. It is invariably the rest of the World that is wrong.

You may say on reading this that I am mad. If I am, then I don't know that I am. But I do know that all that I speak to you of is real. It is provable or it makes a certain sense. Unlike the chaps who have genetically altered soya beans so that they can stand being sprayed with weed killers, while ignoring the fact that the weed killer stays in the beans. In their reason, they then put soya meal into seventy per cent of products that you buy on your supermarket shelves, and so you are consuming weed killers as you eat. I grant only in small doses, and they say they 'BELIEVE' it to be safe. But again they only 'believe'. Ask them and they will assure you that they have reasonable minds. What do you think? I think that they are mad. In fact I would go so far as to say "criminally insane".

This book is something that you will have to make your own minds up about. Is it real? Is it nonsense? Is it true? All I ask of you is to think. To open your eyes and see. To allow realisation of what is happening to enter your minds. If you have no interest in the Old Order then that's fine, but think. Use Reason, Knowledge, Logic, and Common Sense. This I ask of you for your sake, and also a little for mine, as by asking you I can then go my way, my duty done. To join the Lords who have gone before me, and all those who have tried, and paid dearly for the trying. As they have all said "Go you in peace, even unto death"

For myself I hold nothing against you, if it is done for right reason. I hold all else against you that is done for any other excuse. As Jesus himself has also said. "None of us likes to be interpreted in the service of base use, or indeed in any use. The truth is as it is, and we were and are, as we are". Let you who have ears hear me and you who have eyes read what I say, and you who have good minds reason as you read. The rest of you are of no concern to any of us. Should you think that what is written is false, then that's up to you. Should you think that, that which is written is without substance, then so be it. Should you think that I am not the seventh, as they say that I am, then so be it. None of these things matter. What does matter is that you think and reason. Look about you at your World. See what is happening every day then do something about it. You may say to yourself, "I am only one and can make no difference". You are wrong, because if seventy thousand people in the World, individually realise that they can make a difference, then that difference will be made.

The Seven Signs have been. Our Seven Seals are now open for you. No more will come. I have much more to say should there be a point. If there is no point it will remain unsaid. All there is for me to do now, is wait.